ENTREPRENEUR LIKE A MOTHER

ENTREPRENEUR LIKE A MOTHER

BUILD A COMPANY THAT BUYS YOU
FREEDOM
NOT OWNS YOUR LIFE

BETH MAZZA & VICTORIA SIVRAIS

WILEY

Published by John Wiley & Sons, Inc., Hoboken, New Jersey.

For general information on our other products and services or for technical support, please contact our Customer Care Department within the United States at (800) 762-2974, outside the United States at (317) 572-3993 or fax (317) 572-4002.

Wiley also publishes its books in a variety of electronic formats. Some content that appears in print may not be available in electronic formats. For more information about Wiley products, visit our web site at www.wiley.com.

Library of Congress Cataloging-in-Publication Data is Available:

ISBN 9781394448876 (Cloth)
ISBN 9781394448890 (ePDF)
ISBN 9781394448883 (ePub)

Cover Design: bookcoverworld.com
Cover Photography: © Colleen Chrzanowski, October 2025
SKY10163471_072426

*To my dad, who got me out of every scrape imaginable,
and Fish, Ava, Soph and Sam, who gave me
the best job on the planet.*

—Beth

*For Bill, the backbone—my unwavering champion;
my kids—the heartbeat—Ali, Billy, Kate, Vivi, and Evelyn;
and my mom—the shield, who trusted my path and
defended it fiercely.*

—Victoria

Contents

Introduction

An Empire Built Between Carpools and Calls

When was the last time you saw a pregnant woman pitching to VCs? How about a mom pumping breast milk between investor calls? Never? That's because the start-up mythology was written by the type of man who thinks *work-life balance* means choosing between golf with the corporate board and tennis with college pals.

The entrepreneurial world needs a reality check. While Silicon Valley celebrates another hoodie-wearing founder who "disrupted" an industry from his parent's garage, millions of women are quietly building empires between school pickups and bedtime stories. It's time to shatter the myth that successful entrepreneurship requires choosing between ambition and motherhood.

Here's a story that isn't likely to show up on your social media feed. It is a glimpse into the lives of mothers of multiple kids—Beth and Victoria—who also happen to be seven-figure entrepreneurs. We are two middle fingers to the patriarchy disguised as soccer moms. Our reality is far from the stylized images of vest-wearing tech bros or Chanel-clad women in power suits, ruling supreme in their perfect start-up worlds.

Picture this: the two of us in a conference room, surrounded by a staff of 40, some in-person and some Zooming in from multiple office locations. We're powering through client requests, sales prospects, and yet another update on when our internal training system will (finally) be completed. Our beloved office manager interrupts the meeting multiple times with crises. First, the school nurse calls to say a kid with period cramps needs to be picked up. Next up, the CEO of a large retail company is considering a hostile takeover of their biggest competitor and wants our thoughts on how investors might react. The third, a call from a nanny reminds Victoria that it's her day to be the mystery reader back at Lines Elementary School (in the suburbs!) and she needs to get in the car, STAT. And last (at least for that staff meeting), another senior executive from a Fortune 500 company wants our advice on how to communicate a top executive's abrupt departure and is asking if one of us can hop on a board call in the next 30 minutes to discuss.

Mind you, it's 8:30 a.m.

And as we both remember it, this was, at best, only a mildly unhinged morning for us at Clermont Partners, our most recent professional services business. Just another morning building a multi-seven-figure business while raising nine kids between us. The constant ping-ponging between boardroom emergencies and mom duties wasn't some heroic balancing act we'd mastered; it was survival mode disguised as success. Sure, we'd collapse into bed most nights clutching a wine glass like a life preserver, wondering if we were completely insane. But here's the thing. This beautiful disaster was exactly the kind of entrepreneurship we wanted: messy, chaotic, and unapologetically ours.

That morning we just described? It was also the day we realized we'd cracked the code to a version of entrepreneurship the old boys' network overlooks. Instead of failing at entrepreneurship because we couldn't separate our mom lives from our business lives, we were succeeding because we refused to. That realization became the foundation for everything we're about to teach you.

Welcome to *Entrepreneur Like a Mother*—a set of Power Moves for building a business without sacrificing your sanity or your family. These aren't cookie-cutter strategies because there is no one-size-fits-all formula for mom entrepreneurs. Whether you're launching a start-up with a baby strapped to your chest, scaling during school hours, or creating your empire after bedtime, success comes in countless forms. The venture capital gatekeepers want you to follow their playbook because it's the only one they understand. But we've watched fearless women build multimillion-dollar businesses in ways that would make Silicon Valley's head spin—and we're here to show you how to find your own path to financial freedom.

Our Power Moves are designed around a fundamental principle: picking the right business idea matters more than following your passion. This approach will guide you toward a scalable model that doesn't demand huge up-front capital—a crucial distinction because large initial investments always (and we mean always) create do-or-die scenarios with impossibly short timelines for success. Rather than setting you up for that kind of skull-splitting pressure, we've crafted this book to help you focus on what actually works—building profitability quickly and systematically while surrounding yourself with the support you need to sustain long-term growth.

This road map is the entrepreneurial equivalent of a strategic cheat sheet for female founders. As moms, we need a steady, methodical approach to building a profitable business, one that allows us to take breaks when necessary without sacrificing the upward trajectory of our businesses. So that's what we're presenting here. We promise you will have enough flexibility to create some balance in your life and that the choice of how much will be in your hands, not in the hands of the finance frat boys holding the purse strings.

And here's the thing that separates this book from every other entrepreneurial guide cluttering your bookshelf: we've actually done this shit. Not once, but twice. Over 20 years, we've built and sold two seven-figure businesses while raising our families—and we've got the battle scars and bank statements to prove it. These Power Moves aren't theoretical frameworks dreamed up in some MBA classroom; they're forged from real decisions made in real boardrooms while dealing with real mom crises.

The game is rigged, and we're tired of pretending it isn't. While male founders fail upward with golden parachutes, we're expected to be grateful for the chance to prove ourselves—again and again and again. This book isn't about playing their game better; it's about changing the rules entirely. And the two of us are ready to step in and rewrite those rules ourselves. Because we've made the mistakes, learned the lessons, and figured out exactly how to Entrepreneur Like a Mother all the way to financial freedom. We've refined our system, so you can skip straight to the good stuff.

Ready to discover why the traditional entrepreneurial playbook is complete garbage for moms like us? Then let's do this.

PART

I

Burn the Either/Or Playbook: Claim Both CEO and MOM

CHAPTER

1

You Aren't Supermom, and No One Cares If the Elf Forgot to Move

We've just settled into our seats for a 6 a.m. flight when it hits us—the elf. It's still in the spot we left it two days ago. We can't make a call during takeoff. The kids are waking up right as we're wheels up, running in to tell their oblivious dads how the elf forgot about them. There's no last-minute save, no way to fix it. We spend the entire flight spiraling, letting this one forgotten task confirm what we've secretly feared all along: we're failing at the job that matters most.

Sound familiar? The Elf on the Shelf becomes every working mom's recurring anxiety dream. Each November, we pray our kids have somehow forgotten this godforsaken toy. They never do. By Thanksgiving morning, all they can talk about is the elf.

We stay on top of it for a few days, maybe a week—moving it religiously, staging elaborate scenes if we're feeling ambitious. Then one morning, we woke up in a panic. We forgot. So we tell our kids the elf "decided" to stay put. They buy it. We don't. One more thing we couldn't pull off, one more way our kids are missing out because their mom works. The guilt floods in.

That spiral? It's by design. The classic entrepreneurship playbook doesn't include a chapter on mom guilt: that overwhelming, all-consuming wave that crashes over you without warning and leaves you feeling like you're failing at everything. Instead, it assumes you can compartmentalize, shutting the door on the rest of your life while you build your business. But that doesn't work when you're a mom. You can't live in your parents' basement for two years perfecting your product. You can't pull all-nighters fueled by pizza and Red Bull. You have school pickups and pediatrician appointments and at least three emotional meltdowns per kid per week. That tired playbook assumes you have nothing else demanding your time, energy, or heart. But you do. And pretending otherwise means you'll fail at both.

For most of us, mom guilt is always in the background as a low-level buzz in our heads. But it becomes downright deafening in the mind of a would-be entrepreneur mom standing on the edge of a launch, second-guessing if she should leap. One emotional sucker punch and suddenly she convinces herself that now just isn't the right time. Never mind that she's already done the work. If this is you, the capable-but-torn would-be founder, you know the agony of resigning yourself to putting a launch on pause. But you also remember that vacillating is part of the process. You've got a brilliant idea, a solid plan, a real path to revenue. You decide you're ready after all. Let's go. And then you hear it: the wail from the other room. Your toddler's latest attempt to shove a square peg into a round hole just flopped, and the meltdown that follows breaks your heart. That voice creeps in: *Who am I kidding? I can't run a business and miss being here for my kid.* So you shove your plan into that cluttered drawer you swore you'd clean out before giving birth to your first and return to that massive pile of laundry—at least finishing it gives you some fleeting sense of control. If you've put your business dreams on hold or walked away entirely, you're in very good company. Ninety-two percent of women dream of becoming their own bosses,[1] yet only 11 percent actually take the plunge.[2] Participation by female entrepreneurs isn't just a nice-to-have—it's as much as a $2.3 trillion global gross domestic product (GDP) missed opportunity.[3]

> *Participation by female entrepreneurs isn't just a nice-to-have—it's as much as a $2.3 trillion GDP missed opportunity.*

Those of us who do take the plunge, as expected, suffer emotionally. Studies find that 94 percent of mothers report feeling parenting-related guilt at least once a day,[4] and 68 percent tell researchers they feel it multiple times a day.[5] (And that's *all* mothers, not just entrepreneurs.) Seriously, let that sink in. Part of this guilt is purely biological. Women typically have higher baseline levels of oxytocin than men and release even more during key bonding experiences like childbirth and breastfeeding. This hormone deepens our caregiving instincts and makes us more attuned emotionally to our kids. It's why we feel especially responsible when they lose their seat at the cool lunch table or fall off their skateboard and need a Band-Aid.

But it's not just biological. It's structural, too. Despite working full-time, women still carry the bulk of domestic labor, handling 76 percent of unpaid care work globally.[6] We sit at work distracted by the mountain of dishes waiting at home, the ice skating liability form we forgot to sign (again), or the fact that our kid just showed up to school with a Lunchable—for the third time this week. Together, these forces conspire to make us masters of the "it's not the right time" excuse.

It feels like a cruel joke of the universe that aspiring female entrepreneurs build their empires smack in the middle of their prime childrearing years. The average woman with an advanced degree has her first child at 30,[7] and the average age of a start-up founder is 36.[8] Odds are some entrepreneurs will be just starting their business in the middle of pregnancy, postpartum, or the everyday chaos of raising kids.

We're "jump first, look later" kind of girls, so we didn't feel this crippling mindset killer before we launched. We just went for it. The real trepidation, anxiety, and overwhelm hit us after we started Clermont Partners, our second professional services firm. And then it hit us like a freight train. We were completely unprepared for the mental gymnastics of doing double duty as founders and mothers, and we made some spectacularly messy mistakes—both at home and at work. The more our business took off, the more sensitive we became to those oh-so-casual comments from family and friends about our kids' recent antics at school or how we could "keep up with such an insane travel schedule." Hyper aware of the sacrifices of being away from our families so much, we pushed ourselves even harder. It all had to be worth it, right? We beat ourselves up (hard) for lost clients and missed opportunities. We didn't sleep—unless you count the accidental naps we took in workout clothes, pretending we were about to exercise. And, unhealthy habits crept in that would take us years to undo.

But still, we persisted. We looked at mom guilt as a hurdle, not a deal-breaker. And we know that deep down, you're doing the same. You know that parenting pitfalls can be powered through or you wouldn't still be reading. (If you were looking for a permission slip to tap out, sorry, not sorry, you're in the wrong book.)

Powering through is a two-part strategy. Your first and most important job is to shut down that nagging inner voice that keeps hissing, *You can't do this*, and to muffle those sneaky little whispers insisting, *If you try to build a business, your kids will start calling the babysitter mom*. We are telling you from personal experience—they won't. They'll remember the time you showed up as room mom and your table pulled off a surprise win in the marshmallow engineering contest. Or when you threw them a blowout birthday party complete with a DJ and photo booth—the one their friends still talk about in college. They will be more independent, more resilient, and more adept at dealing with unexpected situations. Your kids are way tougher than you think, and so are you.

And so are we, though we learned that lesson through hard experience. We woke up each day, caught between two identities. Behind door number one: world domination. But behind door number two? *Oh crap, did I forget to make Chex mix for the First Day of Spring party?* Which version of ourselves would rule the day? We were always bracing for the next "important call" that would pull us out of a meeting, only to find out it was one of our kids in the school office, begging us to drop off the iPad they left at home. Or the doctor's office, wondering why we missed our kid's well-check appointment—again.

The paradox we wrestled with was this: we knew building our business was the right move for us and our families. We were never going to be the moms who thrived (or did our kids much good) by being with them 24/7. And yet, every time we saw stay-at-home moms absolutely crushing it, we had the same internal tug-of-war: *I wish I could do that*. . .. That push-pull haunted us daily, until we finally realized the problem wasn't our choice. It was our perspective. One that needed to change.

You have to learn to look at parenting as a decades-long journey. Big picture wins, not minute-by-minute panic. Kids do everything in their power to make this hard. They have a sixth sense for our guilt triggers and know how to weaponize them. Victoria's youngest quickly mastered the art of crying on demand when things weren't going her way, and she almost always did it when Mom was on an important video call. And her oldest learned to stick a knife in hard with a little twist at the end when work got especially busy for mom. Victoria once asked her if it was okay to skip her basketball game that day for work. Her response, "Yes, that is okay; I actually prefer it."

Yes, Victoria has learned always to have a stock of Ring Pops nearby to bribe Evelyn and to shake it off (kind of) when Ali made these biting remarks. But our big learning was to rewire our brains around one essential truth: the parent-child relationship unfolds over years, not single moments. We learned to let our kids cry, yell, and stage their mini rebellions, because that's their prerogative. But we didn't spiral into guilt, convincing ourselves they were acting out because we weren't always there at every critical moment they needed us. Instead, we made peace with the fact that sometimes our kids would be furious with us—or even yell, "I wish you weren't my mom!"—and that didn't mean we were failing. It just meant we were parenting.

We also learned that hyperfocusing on what other moms are doing, and wishing we were doing it just as well, only fuels mom guilt. So we dialed down the comparison game with the stay-at-home moms who always looked freshly blow dried and cutely dressed. We looked the other way as they marched their kids off to yet another enrichment activity designed to ensure their children outpaced ours in cello, test scores, and probably their future career advancement.

Beth still vividly remembers the guilt from the Great Kindergarten "Lunch Bunch" debacle. Back then, kindergarten was only half a day, so some moms formed informal rotating lunch groups. One mom would take a handful of kids for lunch and an activity, giving the other moms a glorious day off once a month. Beth, being a working mom, had no clue these existed. She only noticed when every Tuesday, her son, Sam, was the only kid standing alone at pickup while the rest excitedly paired off for their lunch dates. Now, was Sam heartbroken? Traumatized? Left with deep-seated emotional scars? Nope. He was unbothered. He had plenty of friends, regular playdates, and a healthy level of self-confidence. Plus, once Beth found out what was going on, she arranged something even better for Sam. On those fateful Tuesdays, he got to go on ridiculously over-the-top adventures with his Aunt Linda. (Think Enchanted Castle and Chuck E. Cheese levels of indulgence.) While her guilt remains as of the writing of this book, Sam *still* couldn't care less. Moral of the story: comparison is pointless, mom guilt is often wasted energy, and your kid is probably doing way better than your inner critic gives you credit for.

The second step, and it is just as crucial, is activating your mom radar to recognize when your kids really do need you. Even on the busiest days, there's always a way to carve out some one-on-one time when you're present (not just nodding while mentally drafting an email).

After a long travel day, Beth would crawl into bed with her kids, letting them stay up a little later than usual to spill the day's biggest drama, victories, or heartbreaks. Those late-night chats often revealed whether they just needed to vent or if something bigger was bubbling under the surface. And every once in a while, she'd unilaterally declare the next day an impromptu "mental health holiday" for everyone. (Try pulling that move in your corporate gig.)

We learned that our kids remembered a few uninterrupted minutes—no phone, no distractions, just them, talking about their day. Stop beating yourself up that you can't set clear boundaries between work and motherhood. (What a load of crap that is.) Some days, you crush it as a CEO; other days, you are a supermom. And then there are those days when everything is a chaotic mess, and you're just trying to survive until bedtime. Some days, your kids need you to be fully present, and other days, they barely remember you exist. It's all just part of the ride.

Releasing mom guilt and getting all Zen about the long game of parenting isn't a mindset you master once and move on from. It's daily work. Relentless, invisible, internal work. And on the days it hits hardest, these are the strategies we turn to for staying grounded, or at least sane:

- **Keep a "mom wins" folder on your phone—filled with notes, goofy selfies, and snapshots of those fun, love-filled moments with your kids.** Even if it's just a five-minute dance party in the kitchen or an unexpected pickup from basketball, complete with a favorite treat. And, if your kids have phones, send them a pic with a "Can't wait till next time!" text. Make sure your ride-or-die best friend or work wife gets in on the action when you are running on fumes. We celebrate our wins with each other almost daily, just so we have a little memory bank when one of us needs a pick-me-up down the road. Victoria likes to remind Beth how her kids have become her hype club, while Beth recently made Victoria tear up by texting, "I just love your and Ali's relationship."
- **Proactively plan your time to make sure you're getting those must-have moments with your kids.** Victoria swears by a Sunday night schedule check used to scout openings for quality kid time. If the calendar is looking tight, she calls for help: a friend to pick up one twin while she has some solo time with the other; Grandma on deck with the big kids, so she can focus on the little ones; even a babysitter for an hour, so she can play a few mean games of chess with Billy.

- **Become a pro at shutting down negative thoughts.** The next time they creep in, ask yourself, *Would I judge another mom for this?* You already know the answer: of course not. So why on Earth would you do it to yourself? Give yourself the same grace you'd offer your best mom friend, talking her off the ledge in a heartbeat.
- **Finally, get regular with your mom tribe—the ones who get it.** Swap stories, vent, and laugh together to normalize your feelings and reduce the sense of isolation we get as crazy busy moms who can't coffee klatch during midday playdates. If leaving the house feels like a mission, join an online community or phone a friend. During the most stressful days of getting Clermont Partners up and running, Beth would schedule a Zoom call with her out-of-state bestie. Thirty minutes of laughing, maybe a little crying, and boom—she was back in mompreneur mode, ready to take on the week.

It's never going to be flawless, and your odds of banishing mom guilt for good are about the same as the two of us going a full day without texting. The real goal isn't perfection; it's power. You can't let mom guilt call the shots. Now, to really reclaim the driver's seat, you need to write a *new* story to tell yourself once you have mom guilt on the ropes.

Toss the Supermom Script; Create Your Own Plot Twist

Every time someone called Victoria "Supermom" during the Clermont days, she cringed. Even when it came from well-meaning friends, it never sat right. Because the truth is, we've never effortlessly juggled the endless roles that title implies. Our houses never looked perfect, we most definitely didn't show up for every meeting on time and well-prepared, and we are still the moms speeding into soccer practice forgetting the Capri Suns and Goldfish we signed up to bring.

We can almost guarantee that part of your negative self-talk is rooted in the "Supermom" myth: the belief that a "good" mother should do it all—flawlessly, effortlessly, and without ever breaking a sweat. This dangerous narrative loops in our heads, whispering that if we're thriving at work, we must be failing our kids. The only fix is to hustle harder in every direction. It's a no-win setup. A dream killer.

The myth started out innocently enough. Feminism in the '60s and '70s opened new doors for women professionally. The problem is that society never adjusted expectations at home. Instead of redistributing the domestic load, we just piled a second full-time job onto women's backs. Doing both became the de facto new standard for working mothers without any meaningful structural support, such as paid leave, affordable childcare, or flexible work options. And there were zero expectations that men would step up. Even now, men get gold stars for doing the bare minimum, like packing a lunch or showing up to a parent-teacher conference. (Yes, many do much more.)

What if we stopped letting other people define our story? Stopped buying into media narratives that paint every successful female CEO as either childless or conveniently silent about her kids? Tuned out the social feeds that split women into two neat lanes—moms over here, founders over there? And let go of the male-dominated "best in business" lists that pretend leadership looks only one way?

Instead, we can flip the script. We can tell ourselves, and actually believe, we can do the important things well. Not every day, but most days. And that's more than enough. Enough to build a thriving business and still have your kids light up when you walk through the door. Picture it—you come home, tired but proud, knowing you crushed it at work, and the reason you did it is sitting at the kitchen table, doing homework, waiting for you.

We know what you're thinking: *How the hell am I supposed to pull that off?* You don't undo years of telling yourself the same story overnight. But here's the truth: it's not a light switch. It's a process. One shift, one decision, one rewritten story at a time.

And that process starts right here.

Jot down the first story your brain served up when you woke up today—unedited, unpolished, exactly as it came to you. That story probably changes as often as your moods. One day it will be a really tough self-critique. Other days it might reflect moments of triumph, utter frustration, or low energy where you just think, *I'm okay. . .but nothing special.* The point is, your inner monologue is a moving target, and one rough (or great) morning shouldn't define the whole picture. Try capturing it every day for a week; you might be surprised at the patterns that emerge.

We did this before launching Clermont Partners, and it forced us to confront the stories we'd been telling ourselves for years.

Victoria's inner monologue echoed what so many soon-to-be and new moms wrestle with: uncertainty, pressure, and that ever-present voice asking if they're doing the right thing. She had two small kids at home, Ali and Billy, and everywhere she turned, someone was telling her she should be home—really home—with them, not "letting a nanny raise them." So, when the opportunity to build something of her own came up, it's no surprise her mind spiraled with the doubts so many working moms know all too well: *How can I possibly juggle launching a business while growing my family? And how on Earth can I support them on the unpredictable income of an entrepreneur?*

Beth's narrative was similar, just with older kids and a fancier job title. After selling her first firm, she landed a high-level role at the company that acquired it. On paper, it looked like a dream. Behind the scenes, it was a corporate circus. Her days were a blur of bureaucratic meetings, endless layers of approval, and less and less of the hands-on client work she actually loved. Ironically, she had *less* time with her kids than when she was running her own business.

She kept an apartment in New York near HQ, juggled quarterly exec meetings in random cities (never Chicago), and spent too many Sunday nights on calls that began with "Here's what we really need from you this week." She missed her kids. She missed the flexibility and ownership of her entrepreneurial life. But the business that later became Clermont was going to mean more scale, more employees, more travel, and higher-pressure gigs. Was this just a continuation of her corporate stress but with a less reliable paycheck?

We both knew that those fears—which drowned out any positive "we can do this" narrative—weren't going anywhere unless we faced them head-on. Left unchecked, they'd mess with our heads and keep us from dreaming big. Worse, they'd rob us of the excitement and possibility that comes with building something of our own. We had to find another voice. One louder, bolder, and rooted in the confidence we truly had in our potential. One that could outshout the doubt and remind us why we started in the first place.

Beth had to rewrite her internal narrative, one that didn't just say she could do it again but that she could do it bigger and still stay true to her values as a mom. She dusted off her résumé to help her remember who she really was. Not just the woman who'd built and sold a successful business but the one who powered through night law school while climbing the corporate ladder, got published more than once, and aced a notoriously brutal corporate finance exam. She just needed a reminder that she was already a master juggler and multitasker at heart.

Beth also knew from experience that building a business didn't mean abandoning her role as a mom. When her oldest son was adopted, she carved out time to help him settle in, even bringing him to work because she couldn't bear to leave him. She routinely left the office early to be with him, no apologies given. When IVF entered the picture with her daughters, she made space for that too, learning to give herself hormone shots on the road while managing the emotional roller coaster of running a business and struggling to get pregnant. She'd already proven she could do both: build something big and still show up for the people who mattered most. There was no reason to believe she couldn't do it again.

Victoria's old narrative centered on doubts that she could be the present mother she wanted to be for her growing family. To cultivate a new internal voice, she leaned on Beth, who was about a decade ahead in the parenting and badass-boss-mom department. After a few honest chats, Beth convinced her that, yes, she could juggle both motherhood and entrepreneurship—but only if she was the one calling the shots, not answering to some corporate manager who played by the HR rules. She also realized that to make it work, she'd need to do a few things differently. First up—support. It became clear Victoria needed a full-time nanny and a husband willing to truly coparent their young kids. So she and Bill had a series of honest conversations about sharing the load. (He was fully on board, as always.)

Next, she and Beth had a series of real, no-BS talks about how to juggle kids while showing up for each other and the business. They pinkie swore on two things: (a) kids would always be part of the strategy conversation, and (b) they'd have each other's backs when kid pinch points arose. No exceptions. We set real boundaries. We committed to taking the 4:45 p.m. train home to be with our kids and getting back online after bedtime. We limited weekend work (when it was possible). Before taking on any high-maintenance client, we'd have an honest conversation about whether we had the capacity to deliver what they needed. And we would ensure that both of us staffed our largest clients, so one could step in if the other needed to be out. We weren't trying to be superwomen; we didn't want to be. But we could be strategic, creative, and proactive about identifying pressure points before they broke.

Those boundaries gave us something powerful, the confidence to believe that we could be present moms and kick-ass founders at the same time.

By now, it's obvious that rewriting your inner narrative isn't some quick weekend project. And honestly, it shouldn't be. From experience, we know this work is tough, but it's foundational. It shapes how you wake up, how you move through your day, and, ultimately, how you show up for your business. In fact, we'd argue it's the make-or-break factor in failures to launch.

Now it's your turn. The trick is finding the tool that works for you. Maybe it's visualization, a personal fact-finding mission, or a no-nonsense talk with the people shaping your narrative. But don't panic if those don't quite do the trick. Here are a few other tools that might help you rewrite your story:

- **Ask yourself, *What would actually change my mind?*** This little inner debate can shine a light on what's really holding you back and, as a bonus, might turn into a to-do list of things to tackle. For extra impact, try a little role-playing with a friend. Ask them to play you, listen to the fears they're mirroring back at you, and try to convince them to change their mind. Hearing your own excuses spoken out loud might just be the wake-up call you didn't know you needed to kick-start the rewrite.

- **Tell yourself the story you wish were true.** Time to dream a little. Imagine you're talking to your future self, the one who's already nailed both personal and financial success. Walk her through exactly how you got there and don't skimp on the details. While we're not fans of the whole "fake it till you make it" thing, storytelling helps you visualize the path forward, making it feel real before you've arrived. Victoria believes this is what convinced her to jump off the corporate ladder. She pictured weekends at a home in Northern Michigan, surrounded by friends and family. She imagined unforgettable trips with her kids and the ability to care for her aging mom exactly the way she wanted to. And despite the naysayers, she held onto one quiet, unwavering belief: she could.
- **Choose a mantra that drowns out the old script and anchors you in your new one.** Your affirmation can be as simple as "I am capable and strong" or "I trust myself to make good decisions." The key is consistency. Repeating it regularly helps rewire your brain, reminding you of how far you've come and pushing you forward. Let your mantra be your personal hype song, a reminder that you're on the right path. Better yet, share it with your bestie (or work wife) so she can text it to you when you're knee-deep in the latest business mess.

Our mantras are pretty on-brand. Beth always carries a bit of a chip on her shoulder for motivation, so hers is "Go right ahead and doubt me; I am still going to make it happen." Victoria, on the other hand, is perpetually geared up for battle (and, of course, victory!) with "balls to the wall!"

Find your own tool that works best for you. But make sure to cut yourself some slack. Rewrite your story with the same kindness and encouragement you'd give to someone else. You wouldn't tell a friend, "That'll never happen," or "You're doomed to fail," right? You'd tell them to dream big and remind them you believe in them. So why not extend yourself the same grace? Self-compassion means recognizing that you're human and that imperfection is part of the deal.

Finally, remember that turning down the volume on mom guilt and writing yourself a stronger narrative isn't a magic wand. Some days, no strategy will save you, and you'll find yourself white-knuckling through the grind. For those days, find a friend—the kind who won't judge you for showing up in yoga pants and yesterday's mascara—and make a pact to work through these together. At the very least, pull up your story and run through each step once a week by yourself. Beth repeats her internal narrative out loud a few times, just to make sure it doesn't sound like she is bullshitting herself. Victoria runs through her mental highlight reel of mom wins—usually while sprinting to carpool, so she doesn't feel as guilty about being 10 minutes late (while nodding at the other moms who were 10 minutes early).

Ditch the harsh judgment, quiet the inner critic, and start building an inner monologue that actually has your back.

Gut Check

Have I Rewritten My Story?

- ☐ When I look back at the "misses"—the Elf not moving, the missed Lunch Bunch, the meltdown in the school office—how did my kids actually react? *(Were they devastated. . .or was it mostly me carrying the emotional weight? If devastated, did this last longer than an hour?)*
- ☐ What are three recent "mom wins" I want to remember—big or small? *(Think: your kid being the bigger person in a playground drama, cooking dinner in the kitchen while kids are at the table entertaining themselves, an unexpected hug from your teenage daughter.)*
- ☐ What boundaries could I set—like Beth and Victoria's 4:45 p.m. train rule—that would give me breathing room as both a mom and a founder? *(Even small boundaries count, like "no emails during bedtime" or "Fridays off limits for guilt spirals.")*
- ☐ If I rewrote my inner story this week, what would the headline be? *(Try: "Capable mom juggles life and still crushes goals." Or, "Working mom ekes out another successful week and her kids still want to hang out with her over the weekend.")*
- ☐ What's a simple mantra I could try this week to drown out the noise of mom guilt? *(Try "I am doing more than I thought I could today." Or, "My kids are turning out to be empathetic and resilient little human beings." How about, "My son knows what a strong woman looks like.")*

CHAPTER

2

Moms, Media, and the Boys Club

So you've wrestled your mom guilt into submission. Or at least stopped letting it paralyze you. Congratulations. Now brace yourself for the real fight: the relentless gaslighting that tells you women like you don't get to do this.

Society has peddled a false narrative to women about entrepreneurship since day one. From childhood, we're fed the toxic narrative that successful founders must sacrifice everything on the altar of business success. And it's very rare, if not impossible, to be a kick-ass entrepreneur *and* a mom. There simply isn't the time. We're tacitly told it's better to pick one. Choose entrepreneurship and expect to be childless, and possibly alone, or embrace motherhood and resign yourself to middle management mediocrity.

This either/or mentality is complete bullshit, but it's so deeply embedded in our culture that even our fictional role models reflect this impossible choice. Sure, Lorelai Gilmore bought an inn by herself, ate all of Sookie's cookies she wanted, and maintained an enviable relationship with her daughter, Rory, on *Gilmore Girls*. (Okay, until she didn't—but then she did again.) But let's be honest, that's fantasy television. In the real world, pop culture serves up female entrepreneurs who are either completely unlikable or total train wrecks we're supposed to learn from.

Take Olivia Pope in *Scandal*. She made bank and looked incredible doing it, but her life was a cautionary tale of what happens when ambition consumes everything else. Jules Ostin from *The Intern* builds a successful fashion start-up from her kitchen, but the entire movie revolves around whether she can "have it all" without her marriage falling apart. And let's not forget Murphy Brown, the sharp-tongued investigative journalist, who was television's ultimate career woman—until she had a baby. Pre-motherhood Murphy was fearless, snarling, and "one of the boys" who shattered glass ceilings without apology. But after giving birth to Avery, the show couldn't figure out how to maintain her edge alongside motherhood. The woman who once grilled presidents became a typical sitcom mom who lost her bite, proving the entertainment industry's belief that motherhood inevitably softens women and makes them less formidable in business.

Even when we move beyond fictional cautionary tales to celebrate real-world female entrepreneurs, we still can't seem to focus on their business brilliance. Martha Stewart became the first female billionaire and somehow befriended both Snoop Dogg and Justin Bieber, yet women want to emulate her kitchen skills, not her business empire. Yes, we worship entrepreneurs like Oprah and Kim Kardashian but get so caught up in their personal brands that we forget they're two of the sharpest billionaires on the planet.

Here's where it gets infuriating. We dissect every corner of successful women's personal lives like forensic investigators. We love them until we don't, ready to turn on them for a snarky comment or when scandal touches their inner circle. God forbid their kids make headlines—then we question everything about their priorities and parenting choices. Now contrast that with how we treat male entrepreneurs, and the double standard becomes blindingly obvious. The Tony Robbins sexual misconduct scandal? Ancient history. No one aspires to be Abby Lee Miller of *Dance Moms* fame, but everyone wants to be Jordan Belfort (a.k.a. The Wolf of Wall Street). Both went to prison for fraud, yet he commands $100,000 per speech, while she struggles to revive her reality TV career. We didn't know a thing about Jeff Bezos's personal life until he divorced amazeballs philanthropist Mackenzie Scott and married Lauren Sanchez. And, as for Google founders Larry Page and Sergey Brin? Can you name their spouses? Probably not, because nobody gives a damn about male founders' family lives.

We'll admit we're guilty of this ourselves. Despite literally writing the book on female entrepreneurship and motherhood, when a brilliant woman who worked with us for years had a baby, our first thought was "What's she going to do now that she's a mom?"

This bias hits women entrepreneurs hardest when they try to scale and helps explain the staggering funding gap between female- and male-led ventures. When male entrepreneurs pitch investors, it's all about scale and how much cash they need to raise to hit the market. It's human nature to cut to the chase with the guys—asking if they've got the right product, the guts to square off with the big players, and whether their contacts will pay off. But when a woman takes the same leap, we can't help asking ourselves, *How will she balance this with family?* Or, *Do you think her mom can help out like ours did?* The unspoken assumption? That a woman's personal life—her role as a mother, wife, or caretaker—will somehow hold her back in business. But for some reason, a man's personal life doesn't raise the same concerns, even though more and more men are taking paternity leave, leaving early to coach Little League, and chaperoning school field trips just like the moms.

So how the hell did we end up here? And more importantly, how do we break free from this limiting narrative that's keeping millions of brilliant women on the sidelines?

Business Media (and Beyond) Has a Man-Crush on Entrepreneurs

The answer starts with understanding how deeply this bias runs through every system that shapes entrepreneurial success, beginning with who gets to tell their story in the first place. Men in business receive more media coverage than women. A *lot* more. And this has real consequences for women who want to become entrepreneurs.

Here's just how stark the disparity is: female CEOs snag a mere 5 percent of mentions and quotes in news articles, and articles featuring female CEOs are shared 42 percent less often than those spotlighting their male counterparts.[1] Even magazines dedicated to start-ups, like *Entrepreneur*, practically roll out the red carpet for male entrepreneurs, featuring them nearly three times more often than their female counterparts.

So, what's driving this massive imbalance? Is this the result of some secret club of male business reporters? Nope. The number of male and female business reporters is practically 50-50.[2] Instead, this is likely another classic case of "follow the money." Since fundraising often drives the bulk of initial media coverage and female-led start-ups get less than 2 percent of this capital pool,[3] we're already behind the eight ball. Media tends to cover businesses that already have coverage. So women stay invisible.

The implications extend far beyond just media mentions. Recognition in the media often opens the door to the big leagues: awards, accolades, and general fanfare (including funding opportunities, since investors love to pile on once a respected publication or organization has already validated the business). Predictably, these doors remain firmly closed for most women. *Time*'s "Person of the Year" has featured a solo woman only six times in its 98-year run,[4] while just four women have earned EY's World Entrepreneur of the Year award in 25 years.[5] And don't get us started on the Inc. 5000 list—it's still a boys' club, with only 10 percent of companies led by women in 2023.[6] Whether it's because most women-owned businesses fall under the $2 million mark or because we don't always have the time—or the swagger—to chase these awards, the result is the same: we're underrepresented.

When women entrepreneurs do manage to grab some headlines, they often face subtle media bias. Headlines can take a patronizing turn, focusing on their domestic roles instead of their business savvy, while male entrepreneurs are showered with powerful, business-centric language. Some of our favorites include "Four Ways to Maximize Family Time as an Entrepreneur,"[7] "From Deals to Diapers: Mompreneurs Can Handle It All,"[8] or "Founders and Motherhood: Advice on Balancing Leadership and Childcare."[9] Conversely, headlines for our male counterparts sound like they're straight out of a *Top Gun* movie: "The Rise of the Modern Entrepreneur: How Men Are Redefining Success in 2025,"[10] "Who Do Young Entrepreneurs Look Up To? Elon Musk,"[11] or "I'm a Billionaire Entrepreneur at 34—This Is My Easy Secret to Success."[12]

This bias isn't just annoying. It has real consequences: research shows that 70 percent of female respondents believe gender stereotypes negatively impact their entrepreneurial spirit, and unsurprisingly given that background, 61 percent believe these stereotypes impact their business growth.[13] The inequity has gotten so bad that the National Women's Business Council recently published a special report begging reporters to cover more female entrepreneurs, arguing that "more women will launch, grow, and/or scale their businesses if we saw more successful women-owned and women-led companies spotlighted in the media."[14]

It also goes beyond just business media. In a world where entrepreneurship gets peddled as Willy Wonka's golden ticket to financial freedom, there's one toxic message that has infected nearly every content platform—books, podcasts, social media feeds—we consume: men are naturally better entrepreneurs. This stereotype has become so deeply embedded in start-up culture that it's practically gospel. But here's what's truly messed up: even as self-proclaimed business content addicts, we've caught ourselves buying into this garbage at the worst possible moments, usually right when we're about to bet on ourselves.

Take a stroll through your favorite bookstore or browse Amazon, and you'll see the same damn story repeated over and over: "Solo Dude Fearlessly Builds Obscenely Huge Business Empire." Elon Musk, Jeff Bezos, and Warren Buffett have been exhaustively chronicled in more than 50 biographies over the past two decades. Definitive guides to fast scaling and innovating a business start-up continue to be penned by male Silicon Valley legends like Peter Thiel, documenting their rise to the top of the tech stack. Meanwhile *Lean In*, the only legitimately female-focused business blockbuster book, was written nearly 20 years ago and was largely focused on how we, as women, need to change our behavior to fit in a male-dominated business world!

Open up Spotify—or wherever you get your podcasts—and the pattern continues. Men lead the top 20 by largely interviewing other successful men about how they made their first million. They turn to female CEO guests only when the focus moves to retail and fashion. Internet entrepreneurs Sam Paar and Shaan Puri's blockbuster podcast, *My First Million*, has never featured more than one female guest in any of its seven seasons. Guy Raz's fantastic *How I Built This* doesn't fare much better: two-thirds of his interviews are with men.

Everywhere you look, there are close-ups of male entrepreneurs in tight-fitting shirts touting their "can't miss" strategies for making money. Gary Vee, an iconic Instagram entrepreneur with more than 10 million followers, delivers daily business advice in a T-shirt, baseball cap, and morning stubble. Alex Hormozi is mostly pictured with his pipes in full view, pitching start-up truisms to his three million followers. Real billionaires, like *Shark Tank's* Mark Cuban, Daymond John, and Kevin O'Leary, reach millions of followers daily, while constantly being tapped by the media as "the" experts in tech and retail start-ups.

The few women with heavy followings? They were celebrities first and business owners second. Kylie Jenner and Hailey Bieber—both impressive businesswomen in their own right—have more than 800 million followers between them, but we suspect that this is less about their business prowess and more about whom they're dating and what they're wearing. Ex-Spice Girl Victoria Beckham (who makes the best eyeliner we know of) and Oprah Winfrey (and all of her Favorite Things we buy) have nearly 60 million followers between them. But here's where it gets depressing—the list of female founders with large followings falls precipitously after that. We're talking about a cliff drop that would make your stomach lurch. You don't believe us? Look it up yourself. Sara Blakely—the genius behind Spanx—has less than one million followers. Whitney Wolfe Herd—founder and CEO of Bumble—has 285,000. Shockingly, Melanie Perkins—cofounder and CEO of Canva—does not even have 50,000 followers. At the time of this writing, few businesswomen we could find have more than a few million followers, with most numbering only in the thousands at best. Want more proof? Even iconic shark and real estate billionaire Barbara Corcoran has half the followers of fellow shark Mark Cuban. Same show, same expertise, half the audience—because apparently having boobs makes you less quotable in the business world.

Here's what happens when you're constantly bombarded with the message that entrepreneurship is a boys' club: you start believing it, even when you know better.

The Result: A Spiral into Self-Doubt

Living day after day in this echo chamber can't help but have a real impact on women with start-up dreams. It can either ignite a woman's entrepreneurial fire, like it did with us, or douse it with a bucket of cold water, like it does with most women. When women see business ownership glamorized as an attainable goal, we are likely to dream big and aim high. But with the media constantly serving up a steady diet of male-dominated main courses, women are left wondering if we should just stick to the sidelines.

To this day, it astonishes us that this media coverage didn't make us run screaming the other way. Hell, we weren't even smart enough to tune it out while we were grinding away on our business plan. If anything, listening to this endless parade of male success stories helped us build a chip on our shoulder the size of Texas, and that chip became our secret weapon. Balanced in equal doses by the support we had from people we loved (including Victoria's husband, our brothers, and a handful of other really great men in our lives) and a healthy dose of what we now recognize as complete delusion, that anger fueled our fire. We were absolutely sure we would be successful—in spite of being women and mothers—because we were pissed off just enough to prove everyone wrong.

But before we go any further down this rabbit hole of righteous anger, you're probably wondering, *Who are these women, and what makes them think they can rewrite the rules of entrepreneurship?* Fair questions—and ones that deserve real answers, not some polished LinkedIn bio fluff. Our story isn't the typical Silicon Valley fairy tale you've been force-fed, but it's exactly the kind of chaotic, mistake-riddled journey that proves there are countless ways to build entrepreneurial success. Here's how two corporate climbers became business partners, ride-or-die friends, and living proof that moms make kick-ass founders.

Beth and Victoria: The Anthology

The Before Work Wife (BWW) Era

Long before our "work wife" era, the two of us were living eerily parallel lives—just one decade apart. We both grew up in families of entrepreneurs and immigrants, which meant showing up to school in last decade's finest fashions and reluctantly unwrapping homemade sandwiches while begging for lunch money to spend on inferior cafeteria food. Our moms were loving, no-nonsense, and basically invincible—so naturally, we assumed we were too. Our dads were tough as nails and constantly dished out business advice to us, not having gotten the memo that women shouldn't become entrepreneurs. And our six combined older brothers? Well, they were and still are all brilliant, loving, and highly entertaining. They protected us, teased us like it was a competitive sport, and treated any boy within a 10-foot radius like a security threat. Every day was a crash course in holding our own—an early preview of the skills we'd later need while navigating an almost entirely male client base.

Beth's dad truly broke the mold, mostly because he had no choice. His construction career ended almost as soon as it began, after her grandfather, a mason who built her childhood home with his own hands, saw just how hopeless he was with basic power tools. At that point, Beth's grandmother gave him some firm advice: go to law school. And he did.

But when he graduated, the big-name firms weren't exactly rolling out the red carpet. As an Italian immigrant in the post-*Godfather* era, he found himself up against a wall of stereotypes. Apparently, hiring someone with a vowel-heavy last name came with too many mob jokes. So, he did what entrepreneurs do. He started his own law firm. And with whatever was left over, he began quietly investing in troubled assets on the side.

Victoria's dad was a serial entrepreneur, having learned from his Greek father, who owned everything from movie theaters to car washes to restaurants. Her dad literally wrote the book on investing in a credit crisis. (Though we guarantee you haven't read his page turner, *The Coming Credit Collapse*, just know that Victoria isn't the first author in the family.) He also ran a highly successful investment firm for more than five decades. Some of Victoria's earliest memories of her dad feature him sitting behind a massive mahogany desk, cigar in hand, burning the midnight oil as he cranked out economic reports and investment research. He was building an empire for his family and determined to make sure his kids wanted for nothing while also making very sure they inherited his work ethic, whether they liked it or not.

So naturally, with fathers who'd built empires and brothers who'd taught us to fight for every inch, we both waltzed into corporate America assuming we'd be judged purely on merit. Nobody had warned us that being a woman would automatically put us at a disadvantage.

Beth's first post-college position in the early 1990s was with a Fortune 500's finance and accounting training program. When she stepped into the corporate world, as a bright-eyed 21-year-old, she had no idea implicit gender bias even was a thing. But she learned fast. While Beth's male counterparts were immediately handed substantial financial roles, she found herself on the sidelines—working with smaller clients, on less important projects, and with more promises of opportunity than actual follow-through. She noticed a few more things about the corporate world that troubled her. First, there was a stark gender disparity in work-life balance and career progression. The women, Beth included, were consistently overworked, stressed, and often sacrificed weekends to stay competitive. In contrast, her male colleagues appeared more at ease in their roles and advanced more rapidly. Second, company culture tacitly condoned inappropriate male behavior. A partner at the firm once targeted her with some questionable sexual overtures, and both HR and Beth's own father (who was right) told her to simply stay away from him. Ahhh, the '90s.

Beth didn't bother dwelling on the reasons behind the challenges women faced. Instead, she just doubled down on how to beat the odds. She convinced herself that people were smarter than her (and the Ivy League guys she was up against didn't stop her from thinking any differently). But no one worked harder than her. When she took the plunge with a partner and started Ashton Partners, her first firm, in 1999, she was blissfully unaware that she was breaking the mold as a female founder *and* a mom.

As a mompreneur, Beth lived in a constant state of controlled chaos, hyperventilating through her days and staring at the ceiling through sleepless nights. Despite the growing success of Ashton Partners, she was locked in an epic battle with impostor syndrome that wouldn't let up. The more the business thrived, the more intense these feelings of inadequacy became. She literally couldn't turn off her brain. When she heard a competitor had snagged a deal she'd pitched and lost, Beth would go into full-on stalker mode, cold calling their clients until somehow, she managed to steal one of theirs. In her mind, if her firm didn't win *two* clients for every one lost, the business was doomed, and Beth would be branded a failure. And that philosophy worked—her first business hit one million, then two, then three. . .and honestly, after that, it all became a bit of a blur.

Meanwhile, in a completely different headspace, Victoria was discovering how mind-numbingly boring the corporate world could be—a realization that would ultimately lead her down a very different path to entrepreneurship. Fresh out of Indiana University, she swapped finance for computer programming, joining a Fortune 50 company with 10,000 other employees. Those first few years post-college, her life was a scene out of the movie *Office Space*, including a colleague who looked just like Milton. She would quickly finish a week's worth of work in about an hour and then fill the rest of the week playing online euchre and counting down the hours until she could get home (or to happy hour) and hang with friends.

Victoria may have been the wunderkind in a group of corporate lifers, but she wasn't challenged. She had this nagging feeling that something more was out there, and so she contemplated law school. (Her innate stubbornness and persuasive skills would've made her an excellent litigator.) But the thought of taking on $300,000 in debt just to "retire" once she found her Prince Charming and had a few kids didn't seem like a solid life plan. Entrepreneurship wasn't exactly on her radar, at least not this early in her career. In her mind, she was destined to be a stay-at-home mom, and she was just keeping herself busy until that dream materialized.

Bored out of her skull, she decided to find another job, stumbling upon Ashton Partners, a small but fast-growing investor relations firm founded by—well, you know—Beth. The job she snagged there required a perfect blend of her skills: business acumen with a little sprinkle of finance and a whole lot of the consulting skills she'd honed in between rounds of euchre. She figured this role would give her a change of scenery and the opportunity to meet some new people. It was perfect for a few more years treading water in corporate America.

How I Met My Work Wife

By the time we met, Beth was already the ultimate badass mompreneur who was well on her way to building her first multimillion-dollar business. She was a force to be reckoned with in the field of investor relations. Everyone knew her, and she had this amazing ability to just command the room—be it a boardroom or a copy room.

And she was kicking butt as a mom, too. Beth made raising a family and building a business look like a walk in the park. When obstacles got in the way, she barreled through them like a freight train, both personally and professionally. When she had difficulty getting pregnant naturally, she went to Vietnam, adopting her first child, a son named Sam. Then she plunged head-first into the thrilling world of IVF to give birth to three daughters next. Expanding her family became an extreme sport, and she was definitely going for the gold with four kids. Motherhood has always been a thread in our relationship—Beth already had her first two kids and was eight months pregnant with twins by the time Victoria joined Ashton.

In those early years, Victoria still bought into the myth that as women, we get to pick one or the other, motherhood or a career. But being a driven, ambitious, type A woman, she wanted to make a name for herself with the time she had left in the workforce. That turned out to be even easier than she'd anticipated. It became obvious pretty quickly that Victoria was pretty good at this "keep yourself busy job" she'd stumbled upon. For the first time, she was doing work she was passionate about. But even more intriguing? Beth opened her eyes to a whole new path—one where being a female entrepreneur and a mom wasn't an either/or choice.

Suddenly, Victoria's entire perspective shifted. She didn't just want to move up in the organization, she wanted to own the place. Victoria was in Beth's ear trying to work on the best clients, be a consigliere for executives at multibillion-dollar companies, and grow into a leader at Ashton. While she was just arrogant enough to believe she could get there, she was also humble enough to know she needed to put in the hard work. Before long, Victoria became Beth's right hand, with Beth delegating responsibilities for some of the firm's largest clients.

A few years after Victoria joined Ashton, Beth and her partner sold the firm to a much larger consulting powerhouse. Initially, Victoria thrived, climbing the ranks to become the youngest managing director in the new firm's history. Beth, meanwhile, became one of its few female senior executives. Everything was great—until it wasn't. As the merged firm grew into its own entity and leadership showed its true colors, its cutthroat, "kill or be killed" culture was a total mismatch for both of us. Nearly all the senior leadership team was male, and while they were very welcoming to junior women on the team, the few female MDs weren't made to feel as comfortable.

No one talked about kids, and there were zero pictures of kids anywhere except the CEO's office. Aside from Victoria, we can remember only one woman being pregnant during our entire time there. The root of the problem was some men at the firm simply didn't know any ambitious women who were also moms. Victoria was told more than once, both while pregnant and after returning from maternity leave, that she needed to "reevaluate" her priorities between work and family. And then there was her personal favorite: being told she looked like a linebacker when she came back from leave, because she had yet to shed the 60 pounds she'd gained while baking a human. To maintain her executive leadership position, Beth was expected to be in New York four days a week, when she wasn't crisscrossing the country for two-hour management meetings that could have been two-minute phone calls. The CEO's concession for her being forced to be away from her four young kids every week? "We'll get you an apartment . . . ."

When the idea was floated to break out of the mold of corporate life, Victoria didn't hesitate. Her answer was "Hell, yes." Now, did she have any idea what she was getting into? Not a chance. But she knew that staying on the corporate hamster wheel would snuff out her soul. It didn't hurt that her husband, Bill, was always right behind her—steady, relentless, and ready to give that extra shove whenever doubt tried to creep in. As for Beth, she already knew the grass was greener on the other side. And that the garden leave her contract required was worth it to get the hell out of this world. With unwavering faith in each other and a shared vision, we began crafting our plans for our own company. And in January 2015, we took the leap and left our roles at the big consulting firm (and the fat paychecks they came with) to start Clermont Partners. In truth, Victoria jumped first, alongside two other partners, while Beth waited out her garden leave. We'd prepared for the inevitable legal battle, knowing the firm would throw everything it had at us to stop us from taking a few of the firm's clients.

Clermont Partners at launch was an investor relations firm catering to large public companies who were looking to elevate their investment narrative to Wall Street. When we sold it, it was a leading investor relations *and* environmental, social, and governance (ESG) communications firm, one of the first to market in ESG communications, catering to even larger public companies.

Looking back at this wild transition, Victoria still can't quite figure out why she was so confident in quitting her big-paying gig for a start-up. Maybe it was her own arrogance or naivete?

Or knowing that Beth had done it before? Or the fact that we made a great team? Maybe all of the above? During our first year in business, with Beth sidelined by that pesky garden leave, Victoria had to go it alone. Predictably, Clermont Partners (and Beth personally) got sued by our former employer. Not as predictably, they went for the jugular. They hired a sharp-tongued New York lawyer—complete with a flashy silk pocket square—to intimidate us into abandoning our launch plans. Oh, and did we mention Victoria was pregnant with twins at the time? She was deposed on the Friday before she gave birth to Kate and Vivi the following Monday. In the end, we kept the clients but lost a whole lot of start-up capital to the hefty legal defense bills and ultimate settlement.

Pretty quickly after Beth came back from her garden leave in 2016, we realized that the two other initial founding partners didn't share our vision for Clermont. So we decided to buy them out and build this business together, just two moms and founders. During those years of building our business and raising our families—Victoria with five little ones and Beth with her four kids in those perilous middle and high school years—we often fell victim to impostor syndrome. We felt like all the voices around us were saying, "You can't do it all," "You must hate being away from the kids," "You can't continue to grow the business with all those pressures you have to be home."

To compensate, Beth, once again, went back to her chaotic pace. At her best, Beth was a frenetic and fun-filled mom, whisking her kids out of school for spontaneous adventures whenever she had a free afternoon. At her worst, she was a short-tempered parent who looked at her phone as much as a screenager. Beth's kids quickly figured out that once she answered her business cell, they should go silent—those calls could stretch all the way through a carpool ride. They warned their friends to do the same.

Victoria found herself overworking and under-parenting one day, then underworking and over-parenting the next. She burned the candle at both ends, even fielding a client call from the delivery room moments after giving birth. Guilt was her constant companion. When she left work to be with her kids, Victoria felt like she was letting the business down. When she focused on work, she felt like she was letting her family down. And yes, success helped quiet some of those voices—but it also amplified others. The more we achieved, the more that toxic media narrative we'd been consuming for years tried to convince us we were frauds. We'd land a huge new client, and then one of us would race to bail a kid out from the principal's office, immediately triggering that familiar spiral of self-doubt: *Maybe the business bros were right. Maybe we really can't do both*. Or we would finally take a much-needed vacation, only to return to a shit-show at work that took us days to untangle. Each "mom moment" felt like evidence that we were failing at the impossible balancing act society told us we shouldn't even attempt.

But here's what all those vest-wearing bros and their cheerleaders in the media got wrong: our "mom moments" weren't bugs in our entrepreneurial system—they were features. The same skills that helped us navigate the principal's office emergencies made us better at handling client crises. The multitasking that came from managing our collective gaggle of nine kids translated directly into running multiple business units. Our ability to make quick decisions while someone was literally tugging on our sleeve? That became our superpower in high-pressure negotiations.

Our "mom moments" weren't bugs in our entrepreneurial system—they were features.

So, there is a happy ending—obviously. Our kids have watched not one but two badass female entrepreneurs grow seven-figure businesses and cash in on them, big time. They've seen that the either/or choice society presents to women is complete crap. Our relationships with our kids couldn't be better, despite the guilt that they'll never remember us as the Pinterest-perfect mothers we were trying to be. And as for us? We're living proof that the entrepreneurial success stories missing from those business magazines and podcasts are happening every day, in conference rooms and at kitchen tables across the country. Right now, we're living out our vision to help other women see that motherhood can be an entrepreneur's greatest strength.

Why Investors Won't Show Us the Money

So yes, we've proven the mom entrepreneur myth wrong, but let's not pretend the system makes it easy. The media might overlook us, but the real gatekeepers are the ones holding the purse strings. Let's talk about why getting funding as a woman is still the ultimate uphill battle.

Today, there are millions of female entrepreneurs worldwide, spanning every industry, country, and continent. From chatting with some of them, it's clear we all share the same "illness." We don't want to work for anyone else, we're convinced our business idea is the next big thing, and once we're on a path, we're not turning back. But here's the kicker: most of us end up pivoting our business models to better fit our lives. And we, and our businesses, are all the better for it. Collectively, we have learned to live with the systemic obstacles the financial industry has put up to keep us relegated to underfunded start-ups and/or scraping money together to scale.

Less than 2 percent of all venture capital and only 16 percent of total distributed dollars for small business loans go to female founders.

The facts aren't pretty. Start-up funding for women-led ideas is as elusive as either of us fitting into a size 0 any time soon. Less than 2 percent of all venture capital (VC) funding[15] and only 16 percent of total distributed dollars for small business loans go to female founders.[16] Moreover, only 15 percent of women-owned businesses have ever scored a private business loan and—wait for it—their average loan size is 50 percent smaller than that of male-owned firms.[17] Our favorite and oft-repeated line from venture capital friends is, "If we got better ideas from women-owned businesses, we'd fund them." It's a twist on the same bullshit line you hear from every male-dominated C-suite in the corporate world, namely, that they would elevate more females if they had the right skill set. The truly scary part? They actually believe it. They don't seem to notice the systemic discrimination and patriarchy women have to navigate just to get in the door with a potential funding source—even when they're pitching a business that's already running and (surprise!) profitable. Let's not forget that the networking circles to even meet the VCs funding start-ups historically started with drinks, golf outings, and multiday boondoggles most mompreneurs don't have the time for.

The numbers speak for themselves. Moreover, the staggering disparity in funding for female founders has remained stubbornly stagnant for the past decade, despite the number of female entrepreneurs growing at an impressive clip. The good news (yes, we're stretching here) is twofold. First, if a woman is a cofounder (with a man, of course), they received nearly 40 percent of VC capital in 2025 (double that of 2024). And VC firms with at least one female partner are 2.3 times more likely to invest in female founders.[18] Well, at least that's something.

The story is pretty similar when it comes to government-issued Small Business Administration loans. In 2022, 25 percent of women had their loan applications denied, compared to just

19 percent of men.[19] Fast-forward to 2023, of the nearly $28 billion in SBA 7(a) loans that were approved, majority female-owned businesses accounted for only 28 percent.[20] It seems like we're always waiting on the sidelines to get put into the game.

So instead of securing funding from traditional sources, women have had to get creative: borrowing from personal savings and making heartfelt pleas to friends and family to get started. Seventy-four percent of us are forced to rely on this strategy.[21] This means we are often starting our businesses with an uphill battle against better-funded competitors who haven't had to scrape together every penny. (We also think this makes us craftier and better business owners if and when we beat the odds, but more on this later.)

Someday this will change, but there are only a few glimmers of hope on the horizon right now. The more women that get involved in the investment and loan process, the more likely we are to secure earlier-stage funding. But don't expect some grand, disruptive moment where the floodgates open and the "girl money tree" magically appears in our front yards. We're bracing for slow and steady progress—two steps forward, one step back.

This is exactly why millions of talented women decide to skip the entrepreneurial gauntlet altogether and stick with corporate careers. Stable income, clear advancement paths, and no need to grovel to investors who don't think you're a safe bet. On paper, it sounds like the smart choice. But the reality is far more complicated.

CHAPTER

3

Picking the Path That Works for You (and Your Family)

Corporate America promises women a clear path and work-life balance, but the reality is far messier. Our network is full of brilliant women who've aced the corporate game—launching products, managing crises, closing deals, all while juggling motherhood. They're successful but perpetually torn between climbing higher and controlling their own schedules. When we ask why they don't leave, the answer is always "flexibility." (Never mind that they're breathlessly telling us this while racing across town after work, late for their daughter's lacrosse game.)

Companies have admittedly done a brilliant job creating policies that seemingly make it easier for working parents to thrive. Flexible hours, unlimited paid time off, expanded paid parental leave—these perks are aimed at offering the essential "air cover" moms need to escape to home base when real life demands their attention. On paper, these policies sound like a dream, and for some parents, they are.

Early in our careers, we got to take advantage of these flexible working hours too. But as our careers progressed and we became the go-to people for all strategies, deliverables, and asks related to the next big business opportunity or major client deliverable, things changed. Those once-reassuring policies started to feel more like abstract concepts than tangible lifelines. After Beth's first company, Ashton Partners, was acquired, we went full throttle into corporate mode. We had big clients—including the number-one beverage company in the world. They were paying our sky-high hourly consulting rates, so it wasn't really acceptable to tell that CEO we couldn't make his 4 p.m. strategy session because we had to run home to relieve the nanny. And we couldn't tell our big boss—the CEO of the company that acquired us—that we couldn't travel this week, even though our team was behind on hitting this quarter's double-digit growth target and our sales guy had just landed two make-or-break meetings (New York on Tuesday, San Francisco on Wednesday), because our kid was reading the Pledge of Allegiance at the school assembly. Despite the "flexible" facade of corporate life, the truth is the higher we were on the ladder, the more chained to our desks we found ourselves.

As our families grew and we were forced to take advantage of that flexibility a bit more, it started to strain relationships with our colleagues at the firm. And understandably so. The first few times they had our back, but after a while, regularly tapping into these "generous" policies began to feel like we were freeloading on their goodwill. Ironically, we found it happening more often than not with other women, whether or not they had families of their own. The "if I can figure it out, so can you" mentality spread like toxic waste. So, in the end, rather than ask for help, we ended up doing most of our own heavy lifting by ourselves, working insane hours and growing more frustrated by the minute.

Hybrid work policies should have been the great equalizer, right? Working from home some of the time could help us better balance the needs of our families with the demands of our high-octane jobs. But in reality, all it really did was change the *when* of our work, not the *how much*. We still found ourselves pulling late nights and sprinting to meet deadlines, only to feel like we had to drag ourselves into the office the next morning to show face to our junior staff and prove to our big bosses that we were really working. Like us, the average worker still spends three and a half days a week in the office.[1] So, despite the promise of working virtually all the time, the office was always close by, lurking, ready to remind us who's really in charge.

When we talk to our would-be founder friends and mention the glaring gaps in the corporate world's supposed "flexibility" for working moms, their next best argument for staying corporate is the risk of trading guaranteed income for the far-off dream of future wealth. They are right. Managing our finances with the lack of guaranteed income felt like a full-time job, one that came with a side of constant anxiety. It lurked in our subconscious every single day, all day, from the moment we woke up to the moment we finally managed to sleep (after stressing about it some more). Putting groceries (and even our kids' tuition) on our credit cards became a normal occurrence during the ramp-up phase of Clermont.

Here's the thing: many corporate jobs come with just as much financial instability, but we've just been trained to see it differently.

Most companies turn over at least 18 percent of employees annually.[2] Some employees voluntarily jump ship, seeking greener pastures and fatter paychecks, but many don't. They do everything "right," following the corporate playbook to the letter, i.e., conservative jobs, patient ladder-climbing, maxing out

401(k)s, and buying discounted company stock with the precision of a financial surgeon. And then? They get laid off. Not because they underperformed but because corporate chess moves—mergers, acquisitions, market shifts—care nothing for individual dedication. It's like preparing for a marathon, only to have someone move the finish line just as you're about to cross.

The painful truth? Corporate "stability" is increasingly becoming an oxymoron, much like "airline cuisine" or "government efficiency." Your steady job might be steady right up until it isn't.

Don't get us wrong; if you love your job, love the paycheck, and feel like you are exactly where you want to be, the entrepreneurial life isn't for you. But if not, or even if you have a nagging feeling it might not be the right choice, don't let the myths of corporate flexibility and job stability keep you frozen in place. It is worth taking a closer look at the options. The short-term pain you might need to endure for that sweet long-term financial freedom we're all striving for just might be worth it. Remember, Victoria didn't always think she was going to be an entrepreneur like Beth did, but she *did* know she wanted to build a nest egg for her growing family. And accepted that she'd have to take a potentially outsized business risk to make that possible. Thankfully, her often blind confidence allowed her to take the plunge.

There are ways to soften the financial blow of launching a start-up, like preplanning (for months, or years)—making sure you've saved enough to cover contingencies and then adding another three months on top of that for good measure—or, if you can swing it, starting with a side hustle to build up some savings and getting a feel for what the financial realities of entrepreneurship will really look like.

In our case, we chose the combo platter when we launched Clermont. A side dish of preplanning with a main course of delayed gratification. We didn't try to keep up with our friends, because frankly, we couldn't. Not with the limited salaries we were pulling and the constant reinvestments in the business.

We were the last to upgrade to shiny new cars or buy big, beautiful dream houses. (We still are; Beth has a metallic forest-green Subaru to prove it.) We stayed in our less-than-glamorous city apartments long after others had moved into their suburban McMansions. And we didn't start saving for our kids' college tuition until those kids were already in kindergarten. (Or later, ahem, Victoria.)

Here's one financial truth we have to own: we had partners who contributed financially. It would have been tougher to do without them. Beth's ex-husband was also building his own business, so money was tight, but he covered things like health insurance. Victoria's husband was climbing the corporate ladder, and while they couldn't be a one-salary household, Bill brought in a steady paycheck that helped keep the lights on. We know that for moms flying solo, the pressure is multiplied tenfold and that it will impact the risks you take in your business and how much time it takes to scale. Don't worry, the Power Moves in this book are made for you too.

Looking back, all those trade-offs and delayed dreams were worth it for the chance to build something of our own. But if you are still on the fence about staying put, at least consider that corporate America still isn't playing fair. The deck is stacked, and women are the ones left holding the short end. We're shortchanged on pay and flexible working hours. Our absences from the office mean we can be sidelined for important projects and big promotions. And we are mostly expected to grin and bear it, all while pretending the system isn't broken.

Why Women Still Have to Break the Rules to Win

Forget the emotional side of our argument—as persuasive as it may be. Let's talk cold, hard facts. Women are underpaid, under-promoted, and often left to navigate the executive ranks as lone wolves. It's been the same grim script for the last several decades, and much of the corporate world still isn't exactly rolling out the red carpet to talented women.

We know because we lived it for years before we launched Clermont and bore witness to it even afterward. Over the course of a decade, we sold two firms to two highly respected consulting giants. At both, women made up a small percentage of the senior executive ranks, both boards were male dominated, and most internal meetings were more "boys' club" than we'd like to admit (both in head count and in who was hogging all the oxygen in the room).

Keep in mind that second sale happened in the last few years. The numbers don't lie. The hard truths haven't changed in 50 years, and spoiler alert, they probably won't change in your lifetime.

Depressing Stat #1

If you stick to the corporate route, odds are you will not make more than your male counterparts in your lifetime.

The gender pay gap will not die. In 2023, women working full-time year-round earned 82.7 cents for every dollar a man made, meaning a wage gap of 17 percent.[3] And that's actually *worse* than the 84.0 cents women made in 2022 (a 16 percent gap).[4] But wait, it gets better or, should we say, worse? When you include everyone with earnings—full-time, part-time, and those who work only part of the year—women were paid just 74.8 cents for every dollar a man earned, a gap of 25 percent. That's down from 78.3 cents in 2022 (a 22 percent gap).[5] And for moms, the situation is even grimmer. In 2022, mothers earned on average 63 cents for every dollar fathers made.[6] (Side note: Beth's co-CEO in the corporate world made 100 percent more than she did. You read that right: 100 percent.)

Depressing Stat #2

Your chances of leading in the executive suite suck.

Even if you make it to the executive suite, your chances of becoming an in-charge "she-EO" are pretty slim. The pace of progress for women in C-suites at public companies remains embarrassingly slow. Fun (or not so fun) fact: we represented only *two* female CEOs in eight years at Clermont and a whole lot more guys named Bob, Brian, Bruce, etc. (you get the picture).

Today, women hold on average 14 percent of C-suite (CEO, COO, CFO) positions in S&P 500 companies, and just 11 percent have seized the top role.[7] According to Lean In research, at the current rate, it will take 22 years for white women to reach parity with white men and more than twice as long for women of color. It will take 48 years (yes, 2072) for *all* women in senior leadership to reflect their share of the US population.[8] Are you really willing to wait that long?

Depressing Stat #3

Even when women reach the top, they're significantly less satisfied.

The emotional state of women in corporate America isn't exactly glowing. While female executives often boast impressive professional achievements, they also universally confess to an ongoing battle with work-life balance. And if these powerhouse women happen to be mothers? It only becomes (a little) easier when their kids are in college or beyond. During the Clermont years, we once represented a female CEO who decided to have a baby, and we knew investor reaction was likely to be shock, surprise, and concern—not for her, for their investment. To prepare for the media onslaught, we had to arrange an exclusive interview with the *Wall Street Journal* to announce the pregnancy, along with a comprehensive communications and crisis plan for every possible scenario, from birth to beyond. It may sound like overkill, but this was a fast-growing company amid a high-stakes, high-reward expansion. The largest institutional investors were all male, and this was something they simply hadn't experienced before.

They had no idea if they should be worried about focus or job continuity, and after speaking with many of them one-on-one, it became clear they needed to be reassured so they wouldn't panic and sell the stock. The kicker? She took just a two-week maternity leave—spent mostly on Zoom calls—and was back in the saddle, on a plane, and ready to roll when her baby was only 15 days old. Talk about commitment.

We found being a senior-level mom in the corporate world was a master class in loneliness. (Thank goodness we had each other to commiserate with.) The dads would glance politely at our latest cute kid pics, but the men without kids? Well, they seemed to mentally check out when we'd launch into what we thought was a hilarious story—like the one where our tough-as-nails son got body-checked off the ice by number 19, who turned out to be a girl and as cute as a button.

And we weren't the only ones feeling this way. A McKinsey study found that women's low job satisfaction often stems from the pressure of being the "only" one in the room. And those pressures come in all sorts of delightful flavors: 44 percent of women feel heightened pressure to perform, 33 percent are always "on guard," 25 percent feel like they're under a microscope, and 20 percent report feeling left out.[9] There are too many instances to count where we found ourselves out at a bar too late, just trying to act the part, rubbing elbows with the boys' club of the large consulting firms. And while we watched them throw back beers, we sat looking at our watches, hoping our husbands got the kids to bed on time with little resistance (especially since we knew we would be the ones dragging them out of bed the next morning for school). It's crazy this "only woman" trend continues in the year 2025. This isn't middle school, and women aren't new kids trying to figure out where to sit in the cafeteria. We absolutely deserve—and can do—way better than this. So here we are, caught in a system designed to keep us out. Corporate America built a glass ceiling and then sold it to us as security. The media doesn't care much about us, investors won't fund us, and society keeps insisting we choose between building businesses and raising families. But here's what they're all missing: we're doing it anyway.

Every day, millions of women are launching businesses from kitchen tables, closing deals from minivans, and proving that the traditional playbook was never the only way. It was just the only story anyone bothered to tell. The funding gap is real. The bias is real. The exhaustion is real. But so is our determination.

What we need is a way to have the emotional and financial benefits of entrepreneurship without taking on the potentially crippling financial risk that so many founders face. What if a different framework for female entrepreneurship existed—one that's challenging, sure, but actually attainable for women who crave balance or moms who want more quality time with their kids? And what if, by embracing this new way of thinking, you could secure the kind of economic stability for your family that often feels unattainable in the corporate world?

You can. And we'll show you how.

Here's How We Did It

We started out just like most of you—in the trenches of Fortune 500 companies. We stormed the corporate world like it was on fire, taking no prisoners along the way. We climbed the ladder at lightning speed, shouldered every responsibility thrown at us, and became the "youngest-ever" holders of senior titles at our firms.

Our corporate jobs weren't terrible; sometimes they were downright great. Yes, we got irritated being the only women in the room and tired of the locker room–type atmosphere that popped up often. But it wasn't the gender dynamics or the frat house vibes that really drove us to the edge. No, it was that we had killer ideas (at least, that's how we saw it), but no one was listening. We pitched well-thought-out strategies for expanding service offerings, introducing emerging business lines, and reshaping account management to balance profitability (which our bosses loved) with client longevity (which—shocker—also impacts profitability). What did we get in return? Polite nods and a lot of "maybe next year." It felt like the life was being sucked out of every idea, courtesy of corporate bias.

Having come from a family of entrepreneurs, we knew the only obvious answer was to start our own thing. We launched

Clermont in a tiny, subleased space at Victoria's brothers' firm. We borrowed money from family and Victoria's 401(k). (Note to all: This is a terrible business-funding route. Do as we say, not as we do.) We leveraged our good idea into a multimillion-dollar business. We fell in love with our staff, thrived on the daily challenges, celebrated the wins, and licked our wounds more often than we would like to admit.

Throughout this tumultuous journey, we somehow built and maintained a blissful family life (okay, not blissful, but pretty damn good). Having kids and our own business was never an either/or for us. We were always going to do both, let every bit of research and advice we ever received be damned.

And it paid off. Our families have given us a source of perspective when the world looks crazy, a reason to get out of our own heads and think about other people, and nonstop entertainment. We think about them, stress over them, and are generally way too involved in their lives. They are our biggest cheerleaders, which is readily apparent from the number of times daily they text us, "Mom, you need more hobbies." They became accustomed to missed Girl Scout outings, late showings at important hockey and volleyball games, and never quite making it to every carpool commitment. But they also loved how often we would happily call the principal's office with "sick" kids on a slow, snowy morning, play hooky, and spend the day as a family in our PJs.

Trying to be successful moms and business owners at the same time was a slog. Throughout the roller coaster of our thirties and forties, we were desperate for insights into how other successful female entrepreneurs managed to balance it all and scale their businesses more quickly. We marveled at how their business models differed from ours, and their lives seemed more exciting. The business media and start-up worlds were saturated with the voices and victories of men, while women like us were left searching for scraps of advice that actually applied to our reality. We felt relegated to the cheap seats, hustling behind the scenes and trying to find creative ways to scale our business without the luxury of venture capital or a built-in old boys' network. We still thank the stars for a bank loan officer willing to take a small bet on us, because in a world that rarely bets on women, sometimes all you need is one person willing to say yes.

It wasn't until we sold our second business that we finally realized there is one critical step that moms who want to be entrepreneurs and build financial freedom for their families need to take. All the people who say, "I can't believe you can have kids and still do this" don't know the secret. We have to find the models that work best for us as moms and never stray from them—no matter how much money gets thrown our way or what craziness pops up in our personal lives.

To hone in on which models those might be, we've got a tool for you. With a truly fabulous name, if we do say so ourselves.

The Mompreneur Mayhem Matrix, a.k.a. the Triple M

The key to Entrepreneuring Like a Mother is choosing the right business model. You have to build something that will earn you the financial reward you want, but it also has to align with the time, energy, and mental bandwidth you have to give. Our Mompreneur Mayhem Matrix, or Triple M, is going to help you choose right. It was loosely inspired by the fancy consulting firm Gartner and its eponymous Magic Quadrant, which we've adapted to fit our needs. While Gartner uses its graph to evaluate and compare technology vendors in a specific market, we've repurposed ours to help moms evaluate the personal and financial trade-offs in each business model. Picture it as a little bit more personal insight and a lot less business benchmarking.

Mompreneur Mayhem Matrix

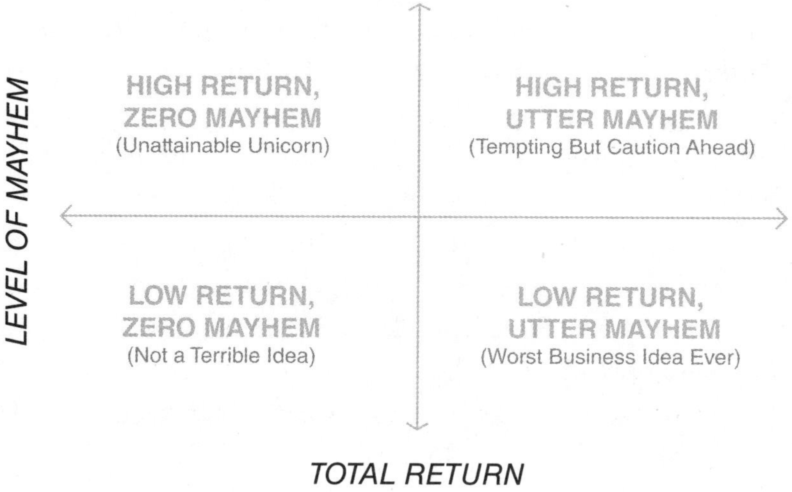

In a nutshell, the highest return model is likely to bring the most disruption to your life as a mom. It probably requires raising significant capital, facing a tight timeline to success, and yielding considerable control over your business. And rightfully so, given the money your investors are bucking up and the risks they are taking. Of course, this path offers a lot less flexibility to pursue the "mom" part of "mompreneur," but there is potential for significant upside. Many women who've taken this route (e.g., Whitney Wolfe Herd of Bumble and Emily Weiss of Glossier) have built billion-dollar valuations.

The other quadrants reflect the direct relationship between return and mayhem. Lowering the potential dollar return on your business should be accompanied by a commensurate reduction in the disruption to your family life. The real value of the Triple M lies in its ability to clearly highlight what you should steer clear of: the bottom right—low return and utter mayhem. You're working 24/7, but your bank account isn't growing. This is the trap you fall into when you've chosen an overly competitive business, one with a tiny market or massive scaling costs, and you've tried to bootstrap it solo.

The best way to avoid ending up there is to ensure you don't start there. More on this later, but take, for example, someone who starts a service-based business, undercharges for her time, and tries to do everything herself instead of building a team of experts. She ends up burning the midnight oil, not earning what she's worth, and often forgets to bill for the work she's already done. Start the business with the right model from the get-go, and you won't find yourself stuck on the hamster wheel, wondering how all your time (and money) disappeared.

So, just how do you use this tool to get clear-eyed about your ideal business model *before* diving in?

Using the Triple M to Find the Right Business Model for You

To ensure your chosen business model has the greatest chance of trending toward the top right, some genuine soul-searching is in order. Being honest with yourself during this process is key, this is a judgment-free zone. The risk if you pursue a business model that doesn't match your tolerance for chaos is you'll either miss your return targets or watch your family life spiral into mayhem.

Every woman has a unique situation with its own complexities, and what worked for us may not be (in fact, likely is not) the right fit for you. Consider these three essential steps to ensure the path you choose reflects the realities of your personal situation and maximizes your chances of happiness and financial freedom.

Step 1: Take a brutally honest look at your goals to figure out how much time you can realistically commit to working each day and how much money you need to earn.

Plenty of factors should influence your decision and your business plan, but for the love of all things profitable, focus on hitting the seven-figure mark. Two simple reasons. First, it's absolutely achievable; we promise. Second, hitting that milestone will change your picture. Big time.

Those of you having a mini anxiety attack right now, don't worry—the rest of this book is going to help you get there. It will lay out a methodical, step-by-step plan that will help you launch your business successfully in a year, not a week. There's no magic bullet, no matter how many Instagram "empowerment" posts you see from boss babes supposedly making $50,000 a month while working during their kids' one-hour naptime. This book is like eating Jennifer Aniston's *Friends* salad every day for a year and then one day waking up to find most of the clothes in your closet now hang loose on you.

Step 2: Take a cold, hard look at your finances.

If borrowing money or securing investors is a must, you need to face the facts. Beth borrowed money from her dad and brother to cover start-up costs. Victoria used her retirement savings and a small loan to fund the modest salary she needed. Once you know the funding requirements and the returns your investors (or even family, who may want a repayment schedule) expect, you'll really get a sense of the risks you're taking on.

Warning: This is a big step that many entrepreneurs overlook. When we say "cold, hard look," we mean the same feeling you get after bingeing all weekend with college besties in town and then waking up Monday to step on the scale. You have to face the financial hit you're about to take, accept it, and then move up or out. For us, giving up a year or two of financial freedom and stability for a lifetime of opportunity was a risk we were willing to take. But we also cop to the fact that if everything went tits up, we had a lot of family and friends to rely on in a pinch.

Step 3: Decide (no, get ready to tattoo it somewhere on your body) what personal priorities are absolutely nonnegotiable.

After years of professional face-planting and personal near-disasters, we discovered that some life priorities aren't just suggestions—they're emotional emergency brakes. Victoria learned that skipping date nights with her husband was a recipe for a huge fight that always took an emotional toll on her. Beth learned that keeping social connections with her big fat Italian cousin network wasn't a scheduling choice; it was the secret sauce to staying sane when her world had gone professionally bonkers.

The brutal truth? If you don't deliberately fence off certain personal territories—weekly family time, romantic connection, or whatever keeps your inner compass from spinning—you'll wake up one day wondering who hijacked your life and replaced it with an endless loop of spreadsheets and stress. Treat your non-negotiables like a kindergarten mom eyeing the field trip sign-up sheet. Go after them fiercely and unapologetically.

For most moms, the tattooed non-negotiables start and end with childcare. Most of us simply don't have the flexibility for a 24/7 business model without reliable childcare options. (And let's be real; those don't exist unless you're Angelina Jolie with two nannies per kid.) We need flexible arrangements, no sick days, and the stamina to juggle the nonstop shuttling to the endless activities we overschedule our kids with.

But that's still not enough. We also need a few ride-or-die friends who can step in when things unravel quickly to take on a carpool, pick up a sick kid at school midday, or make a late-night Target run for the red poster board your child forgot to mention they've needed for weeks. We both talk about our "villages" that got us through the craziest times (and are still getting Victoria through it). Without them, we will be the first to admit we couldn't have done it.

Don't despair if you're currently piecing together childcare and your system is far from perfect. Just make sure to take this into account when making your final plot point on the matrix. Remember that these non-negotiables are the things that will cause you brain-crushing levels of stress if they are ignored. And studies have shown that chronic stress can impair decision-making, creativity, and productivity—basically, the trifecta of start-up success.

Three Common Business Models (and Their Triple M Quadrants)

Now that you've filled out your Triple M and have a sense of potential chaos-cashflow trade-offs, let's walk through the business models that align with each. This is where you need to be realistic about your personal bandwidth, resources, and flexibility. If your personal life won't support it, don't choose a business model that depends on you being able to drop everything at a moment's notice. (Or get a work wife like we did who finds you babysitters and medicine and pinch hits on client calls when you are in-flight to another client's board meeting across the country.) If you've got a special needs kid or are a single mom, don't choose a business model that will level out someday but at first requires *all* of your time and attention. Take off the rose-colored glasses and get to work.

Here are a few potential business models that shake out of the Triple M to get you started:

Business model #1: Launch full throttle, ease up, rinse, and repeat. This is for queens who have a need for speed. They come out of the gate hard to get a product out, take a step back to see how the market reacts, and then dive back in with even more intensity. Now, you probably can't do this unless you're independently wealthy or able to raise six figures or more from the get-go. But if you nail it, this strategy could deliver the biggest return. It's ideal for fast-growing tech, retail, or healthcare/pharma/ wellness ideas that don't need a well-known brand name to capture market share—they need an unbeatable, hard-to-replicate product that can scale. And then scale again. The only difference between this strategy and pure pandemonium is that the founders are specifically making investment and competitive decisions to slow down the rollout (and grow a bit slower) to keep their sanity. Your business idea needs to be good. And we mean really good. If so, you have a potential goldmine on your hands.

Mompreneur Mayhem Matrix

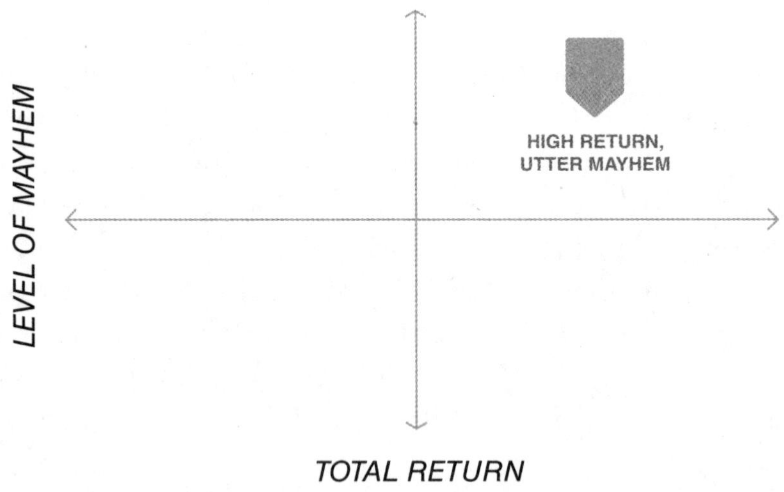

EXAMPLES: Bumble, Canva, Rent the Runway

Business model #2: Hot shot to slow burn. This is how we did it. We're not going to lie, the beginning was a total bitch. But once we had a bit of brand recognition and some economies of scale, we weren't coasting, but we weren't drowning either. This approach works for businesses like ours (consulting/client service), where the cost to develop the product or service isn't overly high, and you can add offerings little by little. You constantly reinvest cash flow to improve the product and build your brand, allowing you to charge higher and higher prices for your offering. Hot tip: If you're up against heavy competition or need a highly innovative product to stand out, this slightly slower approach is *not* for you.

Mompreneur Mayhem Matrix

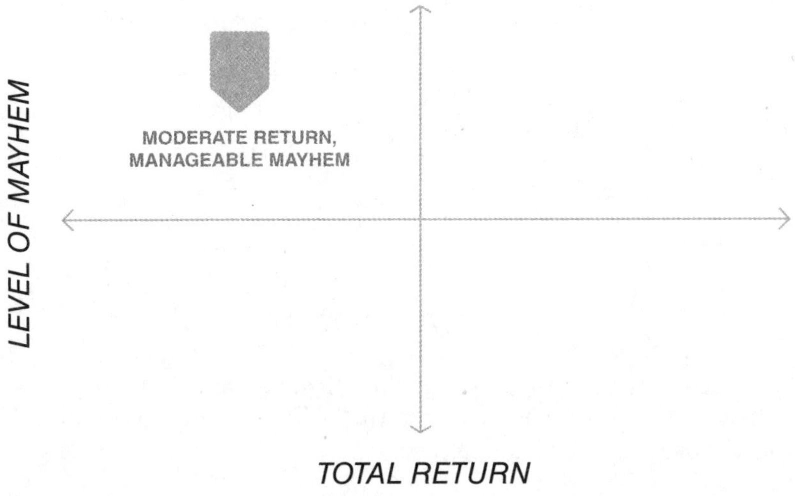

EXAMPLES: retail shops, specialty PR and marketing firms, healthcare and wellness services, catering

Business model #3: Slow and steady wins the race. This approach always seems the most attractive, and for some businesses, it really is. We felt it wasn't the right fit for us because of the highly competitive nature of our business. If your business has a large universe of potential customers, low-priced products or services, and can grow gradually without requiring heavy investment to keep pace, this model should work for you. It allows a founder to throttle up or down depending on her personal circumstances.

Mompreneur Mayhem Matrix

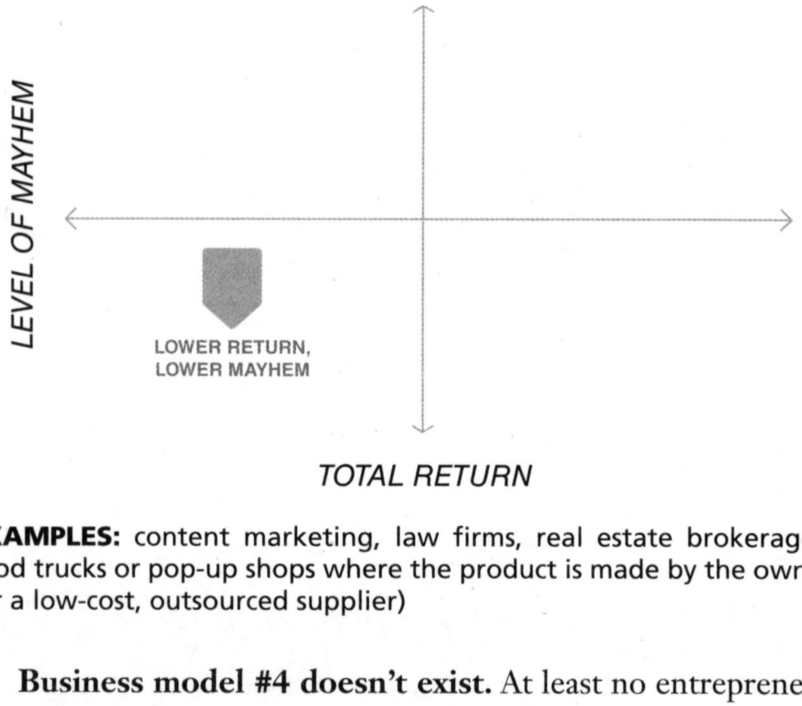

EXAMPLES: content marketing, law firms, real estate brokerages, food trucks or pop-up shops where the product is made by the owner (or a low-cost, outsourced supplier)

Business model #4 doesn't exist. At least no entrepreneur we know wants little return and a lot of personal craziness.

Crafting a business model that fuels your success while allowing you to be the mom you aspire to be is no small feat. But we promise it is doable with the right early choices. We know that if we had a different business idea that worked only if we went into overdrive, we would have gone that route and paid a serious personal price for it. So, yes, we got lucky. But you're smarter than we were. Take some time to think through your options. Not only will they shape your business's success, but they'll also influence your emotional balance and well-being for the foreseeable future. Once you've nailed your business model, brace yourself for the inevitable ups and downs.

■ ■ ■

Gut Check

Am I Ready to Take the Leap?

- ☐ Is there an idea, skill set, or passion I've quietly wondered if I could turn into something more? *(Maybe something I've shelved for now or something others have encouraged me to explore?)*
- ☐ How much predictability—financially, emotionally, and logistically—do I need right now to feel grounded? *(Is it having a consistent paycheck every two weeks? Knowing what my childcare situation looks like month to month? Or simply having one glorious free space on my calendar?)*
- ☐ What kind of flexibility do I currently have, and does it still work for the season of motherhood I'm in? *(Do I constantly feel like I am missing out on day-to-day activities or being home with my kids when they need me?)*
- ☐ Have any recent changes in my life—like becoming a parent, kids growing older, or shifts in my partner's work—created space to try something different? *(Are there transitions happening that might allow, or force, new routines or opportunities?)*

PART

II

The Power Moves: From Idea to Scalable Business

Over the past 20 years, as we built businesses and raised families, we made plenty of mistakes. But through the chaos and hard-won lessons, we established our rule book: five Power Moves you can learn, master, and put on repeat to reach your financial freedom goals. These Power Moves aren't theory. They were built, tested, and refined (and refined again) across our three businesses and countless pivots.

Power Move #1: Prioritize the Right Idea over Your Passion Project
Power Move #2: Build Yourself a Kitchen Cabinet
Power Move #3: Make the Money Moves That Matter
Power Move #4: Start Before You Are Ready
Power Move #5: Respect the Pivot

It's time to start building and scaling with the five Power Moves. And while they might feel like a lot now, by the time you hit the final chapter you'll know them like your oldest kid's Starbucks order.

CHAPTER

4

Power Move #1: Prioritize the Right Idea over Your Passion Project

Isn't the dreaming phase of being an aspiring entrepreneur electric? Everything feels possible, the ideas are flowing, and success feels so close you can almost taste the Veuve. You sketch out a preliminary business plan, line up a little bit of funding, and start to get the launch butterflies. Sorry to burst your bubble, but before you start toasting, there's a reality check you can't skip: you have to make sure your idea is built for scale, not just a glorified hobby with a business card. Passion is great for Instagram captions, but it won't keep the lights on or put braces on your kid's teeth. You've got to prove your concept can pull in real, seven-figure money, not just warm fuzzies and a few loyal fans.

Here's the tough love. Nearly one-third of the women we work with ultimately don't reach their financial freedom goals because they botched the revenue equation right out of the gate. Their business idea was basically DOA because they couldn't attract enough customers at a price that made sense, and they ran out of capital before they even got started. (Capital in this equation means all the cash you scrape together—from savings, loans, or sales—to get your business off the ground.) Don't let passion blind you to the cold, hard truth. If your idea can't scale, it's not a business; it's a side hustle at best.

These "fall short" stories tend to fall into one of two categories.

The first: the customers just aren't there—or at least aren't easy to reach—in the market being targeted. Think about a healthy mama who wanted to open a vegan restaurant in a small Midwestern town where the population is less than 75,000, the median age is 57, and hunting-and-fishing superstore Cabela's is a major tourist attraction. We had no doubt she would attract a small and devoted following, but enough to make a profit? Probably not.

The second: the cash needed to reel in customers is way beyond what most mom entrepreneurs can scrape together. Think about the yoga-loving mom who wanted to launch a boutique gym for expectant mothers in a town packed with health clubs and YMCA prenatal classes. We knew she could create the warmest, most inviting studio with the best instructors in town. However, we figured it would take months to build a customer base and likely require luring them in with introductory rates. She had the passion and the vision but not the bankroll to wait out the slow build. When we crunched the numbers in both cases, the reality was hard to ignore. Building meaningful revenue from either business would be an uphill climb. We're not saying they couldn't make money or that a bit of luck and a faster-growing following than expected wouldn't change the game. But the odds weren't in their favor, and neither had enough capital to sustain the business for the months (or years) it might take for customers to catch on.

This isn't a mistake only rookie entrepreneurs make. At Clermont, we had a very large and very well-funded client who discovered that their business fever dream was just a very expensive hobby. This client had a bold vision: an affordable, ultra-sustainable electric vehicle (EV) with solar panels integrated into the vehicle's body. Why was this so cool? Because instead of taxing the electrical grid like every other EV out there, this one could soak up the sun and get a small mileage range each day delivered straight from Mother Nature. For a growing base of eco-conscious consumers, this was the dream: a guilt-free, sun-powered ride at a price they could afford. But the reality? Right as this particular EV company was raising money to get to market, interest in EVs was going through a temporary swoon. Competitors were flooding the market just as the first wave of risk-taking EV buyers were getting tapped out. The next generation of buyers was far more hesitant—either priced out of the expensive early models or spooked by the lack of widespread charging infrastructure. They chose to sit on the sidelines, waiting for more affordable options and a better-built charging network. We still remember that bright-eyed founder, telling his story passionately to potential investors, certain they would share his vision. He just needed a year or two worth of capital to get through this rough spot until customers were back in an EV car–buying mood. Instead, the company ended up trading for pennies and burning through its cash reserves.

The moral of this story is simple: passion might spark your entrepreneurial journey, but revenue is what keeps the damn thing moving. A compelling business idea has to begin and end with a clear, can't-miss market opportunity, backed by solid growth data and a customer base that's relatively easy to reach. These two factors, more than competition or even funding, dramatically increase the odds of building a sustainable business.

Ultimately, one number can tell you everything you need to know: total addressable market (TAM). In simple terms, it's the total demand for your product or service if every potential customer who could possibly buy it actually did. Think of it as the biggest possible revenue pie. If your business could reach every ideal customer with zero limits, no competition, no budget constraints, and no barriers, TAM is what your total revenue could be. With few exceptions, your business TAM needs to be big and getting bigger to have a growing business.

To size up your TAM, you really need to dig into who exactly your buyer is. What's fueling any growth in demand from that buyer? And is your big idea grounded in market reality, or are you just riding the high of your own excitement? This Power Move isn't about fancy spreadsheets or wishful thinking. It's about grabbing your idea by the collar and shaking out every last "what if." Let's walk through this together and find out whether you are building a passion project or a legit business with the muscle to make you real money.

Power Move #1: Prioritize the Right Idea over Your Passion Project

1. **Narrow the niche; nail the need.** Before we start crunching the numbers, you need to identify your target customer base. Think of it as creating your brand's biggest fan. Who are they? What keeps them up at night? And how does your product or service swoop in to save the day?
2. **Cast a wide net when taking stock of your business TAM.** To define a TAM, you are going to need to do a lot of research and some math. You're looking for a number that's big enough to warrant all the hard work you'll be doing over the next weeks and months to bring your vision to life.
3. **Think three clicks ahead of the algorithm.** TAM isn't a static number; it's more like a weather system. It shifts constantly, depending on financial markets, consumer preferences, and new products and services introduced into the marketplace.
4. **Gut check your big idea and face feedback fearlessly.** Now for the fun part—pitching your big idea and market opportunity to your smartest friends and contacts. Think of it as a friendly firing squad: encouraging but not afraid to poke holes.
5. **Put your TAM to the test with investors.** You've spent months pitching your business idea over dinner and during long carpools. Now it's time to see if investors agree. While you won't be asking for money just yet, you will be validating that your idea can make you money.

Enough theory. Let's roll up our sleeves and get to the real work. Before you can convince anyone (including yourself) that your idea is more than just a passion project, you need to get crystal clear on who your customer is and what keeps them up at night. Only then can you dust off your inner spreadsheet nerd, crack open Excel, and figure out if you have a real shot at building a business that's as profitable as it is exciting.

Step 1: Narrow the Niche; Nail the Need

The first step in Power Move #1 starts with confirming that your idea is backed by a market opportunity big enough to match your financial dreams. First, start with the core value proposition (CVP) of your idea—whether it's a brand-new product or service or just a slicker, better version of something that already exists. The sharper the CVP, the faster your ideal customer recognizes "This is for me."

To hone in on your CVP, you have to answer a few questions. Does your idea solve a real, hair-pulling problem? Is it crystal clear who desperately needs that problem solved—and can they afford your solution? If they buy it, will they see a real, tangible benefit? Most importantly, what's that benefit worth to them? If you can't answer these, your idea might need a little more fine-tuning before it's ready to take off.

Don't worry if your idea does not revolutionize an industry like Waymo did for ridesharing or the Apple Watch did for lifestyle wearables. Plenty of people have made millions by leapfrogging a competitor who got a little too fat and happy. Sometimes all it takes is a simple tweak the market has been waiting for—one that breaks you quickly into a competitor's marketplace. Take Warby Parker. Their glasses weren't radically different from what you'd find at your local eye doctor. But trying them on from home? That was the game changer. No awkward sales pitch, no month-long wait for an optometrist appointment, just pure convenience and style delivered to your door. Or consider Bumble's strategic move against Tinder. The swipe-style interface was nearly identical but with one bold twist: only women could start the conversation. That small change struck a chord, and pretty quickly, Bumble began carving out a serious slice of Tinder's market share.

Narrowing the Niche, Practical Example

PRODUCT	TARGET AUDIENCE	VALUE PROPOSITION	COMPETITIVE ADVANTAGE
Workout App	**Vague** "Anyone who loves working out" ↓ **Focused** "Working moms with thirty minutes to get fit"	**Unclear** "Help you realize your fitness dreams" ↓ **Sharp** "Increase strength and endurance by 10 percent in one month"	**Undefined** "Get a great workout" ↓ **Defined** "Specifically created for overall body fitness in less time"
Organic Snack Food for Kids	**Vague** "Kids ages 3–13" ↓ **Focused** "Kids being picked up from school and running to after-school sports"	**Unclear** "Tastes good and is healthy" ↓ **Sharp** "Gives kids the protein and vitamin C they need to get through until dinner"	**Undefined** "Healthy" ↓ **Defined** "No preservatives or added sugars"

The key is being able to explain—clearly and instantly—why a customer would choose your product over someone else's. If it takes a long paragraph or a pitch deck to get there, you haven't nailed it yet. Go back to the drawing board. With enough research, contemplation, and insight, you should be able to cook up a CVP using this formula:

> We help ____________ achieve ____________
> *target audience* *specific result*
> by ______________
> *unique differentiation*

If you can complete this formula, you've figured out your value proposition. Now it's time to get inside your customer's head.

We are big fans of crafting a buyer persona: a fictional but eerily realistic person who would be totally jazzed about your product or service. Think of it as creating your brand's biggest fan. Who are they? What keeps them up at night? And how does your product or service swoop in like a superhero to fix their problem? We highly recommend giving them a name and backstory and even imagining what's in their online shopping cart. Trust us, once you start getting inside their head, it's borderline addictive.

At Clermont, we had to channel CEO/CFO types as well as the companies they ran. So we cooked up a buyer persona named "Robert" to represent the stereotypical WASP-y CEO. Robert had the right pedigree, the right connections, and a closet full of perfectly tailored suits. His company was growing but not nearly fast enough for his liking, and he had a lineup of bold strategies aimed at kickstarting growth. He loved big and brilliant ideas, as long as they were his. We quickly learned that our recommendations needed to be framed as if they were Robert's idea first. Then he was all in, and we could move swiftly into scoping out services and getting our contract signed. If not, he'd politely listen, nod thoughtfully, and hire another firm.

Then there was "Bruce," the no-nonsense Midwestern CFO. Bruce loved a good challenge—his default mode was devil's advocate. He knew he had to reignite growth at his company, but his instincts were wired for slow and steady wins the race. Bruce was all about the data. You could push back, but you had to be ready to prove your point with a chart or graph. He didn't flinch at being wrong and had zero patience for yes men (or women). Our style—firm, thoughtful, and just combative enough to pique his interest—tended to land well. He respected sharp thinking and clear rationale, which made him our ideal kind of client.

And then, there was "Mateo," our non-buyer persona. This persona represents the customers you *don't* want to target because they're a waste of your time and energy. In our case, Mateo had worked his way up the ranks, skipping the Ivy League/McKinsey-Bain track, and always seemed a little uneasy about his perceived lack of the "right" credentials. He used an endless string of buzzwords when talking about the company's soon-to-be-introduced growth strategy, like "narrow our field of vision" and "think outside of the box." He always knew the right places to vacation and the most appropriate brands to wear, and without fail, there was a Rolex on his wrist. Always. He wasn't looking for fresh thinking, instead he wanted a stamp of approval from the biggest, most established names in the business. No matter how good our pitch was, the small size of our firm lost him every time.

Defining these personas was game-changing for us and for Clermont. It helped us understand exactly who we were selling to, what motivated them, and how to tailor our messaging to win them over. Just as importantly, it helped us spot the clients we were never going to win, saving us from wasting time chasing ghosts. These personas aren't just some made-up characters; they're the real people sitting in the room, silently deciding whether you walk away with a deal or an unanswered follow-up email. When it comes to sizing your market, these personas keep you honest, making sure your calculations focus on the folks who are ready to buy, not just window shoppers. Sometimes, all it takes to kick-start your buyer-persona brainstorming is a quiet room, a cold brew, and a little daydreaming. If that doesn't do the trick, AI can help. Here's an example of a query we used:

> "Create a detailed buyer persona for a consulting firm aimed at helping public companies market their stock to institutional investors. Include demographics of the CEO or CFO, goals, challenges, buying behaviors, preferred content formats, and ideal marketing channels.
> Focus on small and midsize public companies where no single family or institution holds a controlling stake."

That AI-generated query led to a key insight: our strongest potential client was the leader of a company that had once been a fast-moving darling of Wall Street but had since returned to Earth with a still-respectable, though slowing, growth rate. He was looking for real answers. (And yes, it was a "he" in nearly every case.) The more data and original thinking we could bring to his company's problem, the more appealing we became to him, especially if we backed it up with real experience solving similar challenges, which we did. That profile matched exactly our past client base and confirmed that "Robert" and "Bruce" were the right buyers to target.

Cheat Sheet

Our AI query had several components that you can re-create for your own persona-building exercise:

> Create a detailed buyer persona for ______________
> *your business type*
>
> aimed at helping __________________________
> *type of company/person you're targeting*
>
> to ________________. Include demographics,
> *goal of that company/person*
>
> goals, challenges, buying behaviors, preferred content formats, and ideal marketing channels.
>
> Focus on ___________________________________.
> *additional details or traits that should be ignored/omitted*

Now, many of you will have more retail-oriented businesses than ours. All the better (and easier) to find real-life potential customers and start sleuthing. Interview some people whom you see as potential buyers, casually eavesdrop—er, observe—their conversations in LinkedIn or Facebook groups, or follow them on social media to see what they rave about (and what makes them want to throw their laptops out the window). Scroll their feeds. Look at what they're posting, what they're commenting on, and even the personal moments they choose to share. It all tells a story. Take in the kid and dog pics, the vacation snaps, and the enthusiastic posts about their latest obsession. Your goal is to get inside their heads until you can see them clearly: what they love, what they struggle with, and, most importantly, what would make them hit "buy" without a second thought. You've nailed your buyer persona; now the real fun begins. It is time to play detective and find out if your ideal customer is ready to open their wallet for you. Think age, location, income, and spending habits—the bread and butter of any good investigation. Some industries practically hand you a cheat sheet packed with consumer spending data, but if yours doesn't, don't panic; there are still plenty of reliable sources out there.

We've rounded up a few of our favorites to get you started:

Buyer Persona Research

Market Research Reports (Paid and Free)

- **Mintel/Statista** is a treasure trove of in-depth reports on consumer trends across most industries. The data may be a year or two old, but it's a solid starting point for figuring out how your buyer purchases, what they're buying, and how much they're spending.
- **IBISWorld** has good data on size of industry and drivers of growth. This is more global in scope, but with some digging, you can find regional insights on the potential pot of buyers for your product or service.
- **Nielsen** offers micro-insights tracking consumer purchase behavior and retail trends, though it leans heavily on content-based businesses, including video, digital, and radio.

Social Media and Online Communities

- **Facebook and Reddit groups** are goldmines for discovering the real questions your buyers are asking and for identifying other products or services they may have tried.
- **Instagram and TikTok trends** show real-time consumer data under industry-relevant hashtags (e.g., #doglovers #healthymoms, #veganbabes).

- **Amazon best sellers and reviews** give a bird's-eye view of top-selling products and reviews to help you understand consumer preferences straight from the verified buyers of competitive products and services.

US Consumer Statistics

- **Pew Research Center** has surprisingly rich data on retail and digital spending habits by demographic and type of buyer.
- **US Census Bureau** shows economic and demographic data across every group and industry in the United States. It's somewhat outdated but incredibly broad in scope.

Industry and Trade Associations

- **Food industry** resources include SNAC International, the Specialty Food Association, and SPINS Data, which all publish trend and demographic reports.
- **Retail industry** resources include the National Retail Federation for powerhouse insights and Nielsen IQ for more real-time data.
- **Tech industry** resources include CB Insights (cbinsights.com) for market growth and App Annie (now data.ai) for download and trend info. Also check out any public reports from Gartner, IDC, Forrester, and Everest.

If your business sells anything that women buy—and let's be real, that's pretty much everything since women make 85 percent of all household purchase[1]—then you need to read *Why She Buys* by Bridget Brennan. This book is pure marketing gold, diving deep into the psychology and behavior of female consumers, serving up real-world insights and marketing magic on how to reach, engage, and actually sell to women. Brennan doesn't give you fluffy advice; she delivers hard data and actionable strategies, especially for home goods, groceries, and personal care—three industries that could supercharge your TAM calculations if you know how to play them right.

Admittedly, the data rabbit hole is bottomless. At some point, you'll have to make a call and trust your gut on which criteria matter most, because it all depends on your product, your service, and how much caffeine you've had today. Just beware: go too broad, and you'll miss the mark completely. Go too narrow, and your target audience might be just your mom. (Well, maybe your moms. *Our* moms are tough cookies with high standards and tight wallets.)

Step 2: Cast a Wide Net When Taking Stock of Your Business TAM

We were first introduced to TAM in the investment world, where every overcaffeinated, overly confident analyst leads with, "So, how big is your TAM? Is it trending up and to the right?" If your answer wasn't "Huge and yes," the conversation was over before your latte got cold. The truth is investors rarely write checks for businesses targeting a shrinking, or even a low-growth, market. And you shouldn't either. A shrinking TAM is like trying to run a marathon in quicksand: you might be the fastest, but you're still going nowhere.

Defining your TAM involves some serious research, a good amount of math, and a bit of strategic guesswork. But, don't worry, there's a clear formula to follow. Some of you will fly through this exercise with a business idea that checks all the boxes. Others might need to tweak, test, and try again before landing on that seven-figure winner. Take all the time you need here. This is one number you don't want to get wrong because there is no easy fix for it once you've launched your business.

The goal here is to use all your research to estimate a ballpark number of potential buyers in your market. This back-of-the-envelope calculation should include not just buyers of competing products but also buyers of complementary products assuming switching costs are low. That usually means the price is affordable and the product is easy to access or try.

Now, armed with your buyer persona and market research to back it up, it's time to figure out just how much buying power your customers have in their collective wallets. Sharpen those pencils, because it's math time. We recommend approaching this calculation from two angles to get a more realistic and defensible estimate. Relying on more than one input can provide a sanity check and give you a little more confidence that your TAM is in the right ballpark.

Approaches to Calculating Your TAM

TOP-DOWN APPROACH:

Start with the total market size; then narrow it down by filtering out segments that aren't a fit for your product or service.

BOTTOM-UP APPROACH:

Start with the number of potential customers that could realistically buy your product; then multiply that by your price point.

The top-down approach is famously hit-or-miss, and it can vary wildly depending on the source of your data, but it's a start. You may need to explore multiple subsegments of the market to determine your TAM. Back in the "olden days"—as Victoria's daughter calls them (you know, when flip phones ruled our pockets and "streaming" meant waiting for a DVD to arrive)—banks used to hire entire armies of freshly minted MBA grads to tackle this type of market research. They analyzed industry reports, consumed reams of data from big consulting firms, paid for studies from research firms like Gartner, and even pored over census data. Now, AI can act as a pretty decent stand-in for the overachieving intern you can't afford, but fair warning, when it comes to research, it's still relatively early days for AI. Sometimes it makes things up, cites sources that don't exist, or confidently delivers half-truths. Use it but double-check your work.

Most importantly, be sure to fine-tune your AI prompts. Skip the vague "How big is my TAM?" and instead ask for the answer to include specific datasets like these:

- Historical trends in your market segment to shed light on emerging trends in use cases or buying patterns
- Market sentiment, including customer reviews and social media chatter
- Location-based data to estimate regional or demographic submarkets
- Competitive landscape information that includes competitors' market share, pricing strategies, and customer acquisition methods

We hit an inflection point at Clermont a few years into the business that required us to take a hard look at our TAM. We had to face the truth that our core business, investor relations, wasn't growing, and we needed one that would. Our bread and butter was servicing public companies, but with M&A on the rise and securities regulations getting more onerous, fewer companies were entering the public markets; i.e., our customer pie was shrinking. That meant tougher competition for a dwindling potential pool of clients, pricing pressure and a much slower growth trajectory than we'd originally anticipated. Since we didn't have the capital to grow by acquiring and absorbing another firm, we were left trying to find a new business segment with better potential for explosive growth.

Enter our environmental, social, and governance (ESG) advisory practice. Ultimately, this would be Clermont's growth engine (and valuation driver down the road), but it was an entirely new service, so there was basically zero industry research on market size. And obviously, we didn't have much intel on competitors either. So, to build our top-down TAM estimate, we used a market proxy—a business with similar growth patterns and revenue fundamentals to the one we were creating. It wasn't a perfect match, but it was a place to start.

Our proxies were other consulting firms that sold financial communications, investor relations, and strategy to the C-suites of IPOs and public companies. We were familiar with the industry, and fortunately, there was just enough financial data available to work with. While these privately-owned firms didn't publish much about their revenues, we reverse-engineered what we could, thanks to some heavy-duty Internet sleuthing. Using revenue-per-employee estimates, we guesstimated the size and growth rates of the top 100 or so firms. That back-of-the-envelope math pointed to a $500 million industry. When we layered in trend data—like millennial investors' growing obsession with ESG—it gave us the confidence that we were heading in the right direction.

The bottom-up method skips the big, industry-wide numbers and goes straight to the source, your potential customers. Remember those buyer personas you created? Now it is time to take your best guess at how many potential buyers are out there, including both direct and low-switch-cost complementary customers. Now, let's go one step further. Take a realistic stab at what each of those potential buyers might spend on your offering over the course of a year. Is it a $25/month subscription?

A $500 quarterly package? Maybe $100,000 in brilliant consulting? This is where you start translating theoretical market size into actual revenue potential.

The good news is that all that research you did earlier comes in handy here since consumer spending data is buried in most of those sources.

And if your numbers don't quite line up, you've got two options: (1) trust your gut (it's gotten you this far), or (2) play it safe and take the average. Once you have both the number of customers and the average revenue you could make per customer, just multiply them together, and *voilà*, you've got yourself a bottom-up TAM estimate.

At Clermont, our clients were US-based, small- to mid-cap public companies, and we estimated they would retain us for an average of $9,000 per month. So, if we were running this exercise today, as of year-end 2024, there were roughly 2,500 small- and mid-cap public companies in the entire United States. Multiply that by $108,000 in annual revenue per client, and you land at $270 million for Clermont's bottom-up TAM estimate.

Once you've crunched the numbers using both the top-down and bottom-up approaches, you can safely assume (okay, fingers crossed) that your actual TAM is somewhere between these two numbers. If the number is below $100 million, start again. That won't be a big enough TAM to merit the blood, sweat, and tears you are about to pour into it. On the flip side, if your TAM is $30 billion or more, it's time to narrow things down. Sure, that number sounds impressive, but it's unrealistic. This brings us to what we lovingly call the "1 Percent Rule," and yes, you'll hear us say it more than once. It's simple. Assume you can capture just 1 percent of the total market you're targeting. If that 1 percent adds up to at least $1 million in annual revenue, you're potentially onto a scalable business idea. But if

1 percent of your market is only $300,000 or $500,000? You'll have a hard time crossing the seven-figure mark, even if everything goes right.

The whole point of this Power Move is to focus on exactly whom you are going to sell to, not the ones you hope to land after you've given your blockbuster TED Talk and landed a feature in *Fast Company*. If the aspirational clients show up later, great! You've got a bigger business. But for now, count only the ones already using a similar product or cobbling together a crappy workaround. That's your real market.

Once you've nailed down your magic number, go ahead and give yourself a well-deserved pat on the back for all that hard work. If you've followed this road map, you should now have a solid TAM to work with. But don't get too comfortable; this is just the beginning. TAM shifts constantly, depending on financial markets, consumer preferences, and the introduction of new products and services into the marketplace. That's why you need to recalculate and reevaluate your TAM regularly. Think of it as checking the forecast before you plan your next big move. Stay curious, keep your numbers current, and you'll always be ready for whatever the market throws your way.

Step 3: Think Three Clicks Ahead of the Algorithm

Now that you have your TAM, it's time to dive deep into the forces that will make that market boom, bust, or stay steady as she goes. Channel your inner economist, sociologist, and crystal ball to uncover the most important global trends shaping your space and figure out whether they'll be tailwinds pushing you forward or headwinds slowing you down. You can't just pick your target market, launch, and cross your fingers hoping demand stays steady.

It's critical to keep abreast of patterns and trends that may influence your customers, suppliers, or the market at large. Your TAM could be the perfect size right now, but if it's going to plateau or shrink, scaling your business will be an uphill battle.

When the trends are working in your favor and your potential customer base is expanding, your TAM blows up, and so do your chances of winning big. Pretty obvious, right? The bigger your playing field and the faster it's growing, the more revenue you can scoop up. And if your market is on fire, you get a little extra wiggle room for the inevitable rookie mistakes and curveballs. You'll make mistakes either way. But a booming market gives you time to recover.

Ignoring market trends is like trying to hit a moving target with your eyes closed. You might get lucky, but you're more likely to miss big opportunities or get blindsided by new competitors. Researching trends that impact your TAM and buyers gives you the power to spot shifts in demand, anticipate new needs, and make smarter decisions about where to invest your time and money. Staying ahead of the curve means you'll be ready to pivot before your business gets left behind.

Here are a few resources that can give you deeper and more reliable insights into the trends that may impact your TAM:

- **Public company materials (investor days, earnings reports, annual reports, etc.):** All US public companies (and, on a more limited basis, international companies) are required to report their financial and operational results to investors periodically. In addition, they will present their investment story at conferences on a smaller scale, and at investor days on a larger scale. These public company reports are a gold mine of future-facing intel, including quantitative forecasts, industry trends, and the forces driving (or dragging down) their business. The best part is that the US Securities and

Exchange Commission (a.k.a. the SEC, a federal agency responsible for regulating the securities markets and protecting investors in the United States) pretty much forces them to make all this info public on their investor relations website. Think of it as a backstage pass to inside scoop on industry trends and dynamics and your competitors' innermost secrets.

- **Competitors' websites:** This one's a bit sneakier and every bit as crucial. Take a good look at your best-performing competitors and follow the money. What types of skills are they hiring for? What new products or services are they launching? How are they tweaking their marketing strategies? Established players have instincts you might not have honed yet, so paying attention to what they're paying attention to is a good way to get up to speed fast on relevant trends.
- **Sell-side reports:** Unless you've got a friend at an investment bank or are cozy with a Wall Street insider, these reports are about as rare as finding your dress size at a sample sale. But if you manage to get your hands on one (we won't judge how), it's like hiring 10 genius MBA grads for free. A sell-side report is Wall Street's version of a cheat sheet. Analysts at banks and brokerages dish out the real scoop on companies, breaking down financials, industry mojo, and growth potential, then slap on a "buy," "hold," or "sell" stamp to help big investors decide where to put their money. These reports—especially initiation ones—serve up a market or industry overview, break down the competitive landscape, and often name the winners and losers, with all the juicy reasons why. One hack: if you are a retail trader and using any of the online platforms like Morningstar, you often can get limited access to these types of reports or at least summaries of them.

Another great way to get a real handle on trends that could move an industry forward or hold it back is through focus groups. Talk to potential customers or, better yet, to people who know your customers well. When we were exploring ESG, we couldn't go directly to customers because the market was too new and there weren't enough of them. But we could approach people who had a front-row seat, including experts who understood the looming SEC regulations that were going to tell public companies—our future clients—how they had to communicate their ESG policies.

We zeroed in on the sharp minds in Washington, the ones who knew when the rules might pass and which mandatory disclosures were likely to make the cut. We started with well-connected, DC-based journalists who had an inside track on the upcoming regulation, poring over everything they wrote and tweeted and chatting them up whenever we could. Beltway lawyers who worked closely with lawmakers were experts at reading the regulatory tea leaves. Heavily caffeinated and on a first-name basis with every nearby Starbucks barista, we grabbed time with any willing to talk. Within a few quarters, the projections started to align. Different sources—reporters, lawyers, analysts—were all pointing in the same direction, often using the same language. That kind of consensus, especially early on, was hard to ignore.

Now, you might not have the luxury of chatting with these types to gather that kind of deep-dive research, but don't worry. Depending on your product or service, you've probably got a network to tap into. Just look at Sara Blakely for inspiration. She needed something to wear under white slacks that would smooth things over without showing off those dreaded visible panty lines (while she was selling fax machines door-to-door as her day job).

Enter Spanx. Blakely cut off the feet of a pair of control-top pantyhose, and all of a sudden, she had the slimming effect she wanted, without the dreaded roll-up.

But she still had to prove that women would wear her invention, and pay for it. So, she figured it out the old-fashioned way: old-school hustle and a whole lot of trial and error. She talked to every woman willing to chat, bringing her prototype to social events like a walking focus group, collecting feedback and tweaking as she went. She sent samples to a few Hollywood insiders for their feedback and ensured that everyday women also got their hands on her prototype. She also hit retail stores, striking up conversations with shoppers to see what they were buying and, more importantly, what they wished they could buy. The verdict was clear: comfortable shapewear was in high demand, and her product worked.

Now it's your turn. Make sure to keep your list of hot-button trends tight. Ditch anything that won't move the needle and try hard to separate the real market disruptors from the noise. Focus on the most promising trends: if the trend could shift your industry's TAM by 10 percent or more, it makes your hot list. If not, shelve it.

If you are having a tough time with this exercise, we suggest trying the business version of Miranda's pros-and-cons list she made about Steve in the original *Sex and the City*. Weigh the size of your headwinds and tailwinds lists to figure out if these trends support you or will stop you in your tracks. Can your TAM survive the toughest negative trends? If not, we're sorry, but you'll need to start from scratch. But if the outlook's mostly solid and the headwinds are more annoying than fatal, congrats, you're on to Step 4.

Step 4: Gut Check Your Big Idea and Face Feedback Fearlessly

Now for the fun (and slightly nerve wracking) part—pitching your big idea and market opportunity to your smartest friends and contacts. Think of it as a friendly firing squad: encouraging but not afraid to poke holes. Your job now is to listen, not defend. The goal isn't just validation; it's the kind of tough-love feedback that sharpens your thinking and strengthens your business. A little discomfort now is a whole lot better than a full faceplant later. What does this practice pitching look like in real time? Start with a quick, clear summary of your idea: Who's your target customer, what's the problem you're solving, and how does your solution stand out? Keep it short and sweet, no jargon, no fluff. Then, open the floor for questions and brace yourself for feedback. Listen more than you talk and resist the urge to defend every detail. If someone says, "That's already been done," ask them what's missing from the current options. If they say, "I wouldn't pay for that," ask what would change their mind. This isn't about getting pats on the back, it's about stress-testing your idea before you bet your life savings on it. The goal is to walk away with a list of blind spots, objections, and maybe even a few new ideas you never saw coming.

That's the *what*. Now on to the *who*. Talk to people who can focus on the quality of your idea rather than its immediate investability. Think industry peers, business-savvy folks, and the person in your friend group who always has it all together. Start with friends—or friends of friends—who work in your industry (or something close to it). These are the people who get your future business and can quickly sniff out whether your take on the problem (or solution) passes the smell test.

If you are currently working in your industry of choice, these could be people you've interviewed with, people you've interviewed yourself, people you've met at industry networking events, or even recent industry escapees who still have fresh insights. Push past that cringey feeling of asking for favors from people, including some you barely know. Wouldn't you help someone if you could? (If you wouldn't, well, karma might just come knocking.)

Here's our tried-and-true approach to Step 4:

- **Stalk (professionally, of course).** Do a deep dive on LinkedIn to find future competitors, adjacent companies, suppliers, and consultants in the space.
- **Map your network.** Make a list of your first- and second-level connections at those companies.

When you are mapping your network, for your first-level connections, send a simple DM. We bet three out of four will get back to you. Ping the ones who don't reply one more time and then move on.

Congrats on [recent news]! Could I have 15 minutes of your time in the next few weeks to pick your brain on a business topic? I'll work around your schedule, and I'd love to buy you coffee or lunch if you've got the time.

For second-level contacts, if you've got a solid mutual connection, ask them to make the introduction for you. For second-levels that lack a strong tie, send a no-nonsense InMail. Expect half of them to respond, and if not, give them one follow-up nudge and then let it go.

> *We're connected through [XX], and I'd really appreciate 15 minutes of your time to discuss a venture I'm considering in your industry. Hoping you can point me in the right direction on a few things.*

Once you hit 10–12 conversations, you've probably gathered some really great intel. Some of the people you speak with will be in the "it can't be done" camp. That's fine. They may be so entrenched in industry norms that they forget disruption is possible. Don't look to them for encouragement or validation. Instead, use them strategically; get their input to double-check your read on the market and confirm that your business idea addresses a real need. Then? Tune the rest out.

Step 5: Put Your TAM to the Test with Investors

You've spent months pitching your business idea over dinners and during long carpools, and by now, your family's either all-in or they've mastered the art of the convincing nod. It feels like a sure thing with blockbuster growth potential and a fast track to breaking that seven-figure ceiling. Now it's time to see if investors agree. While you won't be asking for money just yet, you will be validating that your idea can make you money and that's just as valuable at this point as the dollars you will ultimately secure.

As you enter this step, bear in mind that you are talking to people who fund businesses for a living: VCs, private equity folks, and wealthy angels. These folks treat TAM as the ultimate gatekeeper. Nail the TAM, and they'll lean in for the rest of the pitch. Miss the mark, and you'll get escorted out of the meeting as fast as your 9-year-old was 86ed from school for pulling the fire alarm during the school assembly. View these opportunities as quick-hits, 15-minute intel sessions aimed at getting them to read your investment teaser. If they love it or if they already invest in your space and are curious about new entrants, you'll get more time than that. Either way, it's your first real shot at pressure-testing your market opportunity to determine whether it's a gold mine or just a shiny distraction. Don't worry about reading the room—investors have notoriously bad poker faces. They will blurt their answer out with some serious sass. They have heard a million of these pitches before and have a Spidey-sense for when a TAM story is a real winner.

Here's a good cheat sheet for navigating these chats:

- Kick off the discussion with the size of the TAM you calculated. Only now will they be interested enough to put down their iPhones.
- Then explain the industry, very simply: who the buyers are, what solution they're seeking, and who is incompletely (or ineptly) filling the solution today.
- Summarize any top-line trends positively growing the TAM.
- Tackle head-on the trends that might negatively impact the TAM and why you don't think they are important.
- Finish with an answer to "What if there was a product or service that [directly addressed the solution] that was [better/cheaper/easier to access] and had a higher return on investment (ROI)?"

Their reactions to your TAM-plus-solution pitch are gold. You'll want to capture every bit of insight, good or bad. If, after your spiel, the investor can confidently fire back a snappy elevator pitch on why your business has a market, congrats—you're on to something. If not, listen to the pushback, fix what's weak, and show up next time ready to shut down the same objections before they're even asked.

How do you find investors willing to hear you out? Start with your friends, family, and alumni network of course. Once you've tapped out there, here are a few ideas for reaching beyond your immediate network:

- **Attend networking and pitch events.** Get in front of investors at start-up events, pitching competitions, and industry conferences. Even if you're not pitching, you can still network or snag a follow-up call.
- **Join accelerators or incubators.** These programs help you refine your business model while putting you in front of investors who are actively scouting for promising start-ups. They usually have pitch competitions and/or "meet and greets" with investors who will hear you out for a few minutes.
- **Leverage your network.** Reach out to fellow founders and entrepreneurs who may be willing to call in a favor to get you a few minutes with an investor to simply evaluate your idea. It's a low-stakes ask for your contact, and investors are always on the hunt for the next big thing they don't want to miss out on. You never know; your idea might be the one that finally gets them off their email and excited about a real conversation.
- **Research competitive/complementary businesses.** Look for investors who have invested in businesses related to yours—even direct competitors. Then find the most junior person on the investment team and reach out. These people are often eager to bring fresh ideas to the table and are usually willing to spare 15 minutes to hear your idea on the off chance it's the next Uber.

You've made it to the end of Power Move #1! If your first business idea doesn't get you here, don't give up. No matter what, keep going. Get creative. Figure out ways to expand your product or buyer and try again. It's okay to go back to Step 1 of this

Power Move as many times as you need to ultimately get to the million(s)-dollar idea that will change your life.

And once you've landed on something that ticks all the boxes, stop and soak it in. You're not just dreaming anymore—you've got a business you can bet on and a growth plan that's wired for the future. This is your moment. Take a deep breath, high-five yourself (or your work wife), and get ready to turn that confidence into action.

Congratulations. Time to graduate to Power Move #2.

■ ■ ■

Gut Check

Am I Sitting on a Million-Dollar Idea?

- ☐ Does this idea solve a real problem for someone else, or is it just something I like to do that makes me happy? *(Does it solve real pain points or just soothe yours?)*
- ☐ Can I clearly describe who would pay for this and why they'd pay now? *(Or do I find myself saying "It's for everyone" or "Once I build it, I'll figure it out"?)*
- ☐ If I had to pitch this to a stranger with no emotional investment in me, would they take it seriously? *(Would they start sharpening their pencils to fund me or smile politely and say, "What an interesting idea"?)*
- ☐ Is my plan built around when my kids nap . . . or could it eventually support a team, scale, and still let me be present at home? *(Do I have white space to think big—or am I just duct taping time blocks together?)*
- ☐ If someone offered to buy this business one day, would it be worth anything without me in it? *(Does this business model rely on me being the glue that holds it all together? Or is there a path that it could stand and thrive without me 24/7?)*

CHAPTER

5

Power Move #2: Build Yourself a Kitchen Cabinet

With 24 hours left before our first offer to acquire Clermont Partners was set to "explode" (yes, that's the official term, and yes, it felt just as dramatic as it sounds), we were both a mess. The buyers kept calling, exasperated, asking, "Haven't we hashed out your concerns?"

It was a lot of money. Life-changing money. But somehow, neither of us could bring ourselves to sign on the dotted line. Cue yet another late-night call, where we were locked in debate, circling the same arguments like a pair of punch-drunk prize fighters. Beth was ready to take the deal, even if she had a few reservations. Victoria was dead set against it; she saw too much risk lurking in the fine print. So, while we were fighting each other, we were also sort of shadowboxing the deal itself.

Luckily, we each had one seasoned voice of reason in our mompreneur circle who had been there, done that, and would drop everything to help us break the tie. We knew it was time to phone a friend. Beth reached out to her private equity BFF—a connection forged through a friend of a friend of a friend (the best kind of business intel chain). Victoria sat down with a bestie who also happens to be a shark of an attorney—in the best possible way. Both, independently, told us the same thing: there was too much risk in receiving the final payment two years down the line. Hold out for a better offer. So that's exactly what we did.

Relying on our closest advisors saved us from making a very costly mistake: taking a deal to buy our company for about 35 percent less than the ultimate offer we accepted. It wasn't a happy accident that we had the right people teed up on speed dial at this critical moment. It was a business strategy years in the making. We deliberately built, nurtured, and maintained those relationships for exactly this scenario. And it wasn't a one-way street; we played the same role for them, trading advice, favors, and plenty of coffee (and let's be honest, booze) along the way.

But, early on, our advisor bench, admittedly, was pretty empty. Definitely not the dream team we had built by the time an offer to buy our business came through. It took us a while to figure out what type of "phone a friend" we were looking for, or why they might be willing to help us.

Why would someone who wasn't related to us or hadn't spent a hungover day with us binge-watching HGTV in our twenties suddenly become our go-to confidant? Why would they spend hours on the phone ordering multiple DoorDashes while debating our strategies and helping us navigate tough calls? Or—most baffling of all—why would they hand over access to the valuable business contacts that took them years to cultivate? For free?

It seemed too good to be true. But it turns out, when you find the right people, that's exactly what they do.

If you're flying solo or just leaning on your favorite mastermind group, you might think building a team of advisors is something you'll worry about later. Newsflash—later is now.

We learned the hard way that charging ahead works until you slam into a wall, whether it's a market shift, a funding crisis, or (in our case) an offer you never saw coming. Our first instinct? Double down and bang our heads against that wall even harder, continuing to follow our current plan into the abyss. But there's a better (and far less migraine-inducing) way. Find a voice—or better yet, a few voices—of reason to jolt you into reality and help you see the problem from a different angle.

Enter what we like to call your *Kitchen Cabinet*, a handpicked crew of unofficial advisors and trusted friends who get your business goals, dish out solid advice, and aren't afraid to serve you a reality check when you need it. These people aren't scared to shake you out of your echo chamber and help you see your problem from a fresh angle. No sugarcoating, no yes men or yes women, just straight talk that keeps you from making expensive mistakes.

Power Move #2 is going to walk you right down the path to your inner circle of peeps who will play a powerful role in shaping your future business.

Successful women get the power of a strong network. More than 80 percent of senior professional women rely on networking to keep moving up the ladder.[1] And female entrepreneurs who engage in formal networking groups? They're 25 to 31 percent more likely to introduce fresh changes to their businesses thanks to the connection.[2] As for us, we're in our network weekly (sometimes daily), especially when we're stuck in a business hole so deep we can't see the light. You better believe those connections have pulled us out of business and personal spirals more times than we can count.

As we built our Kitchen Cabinet over the years, we realized that our go-to advisors always fell into one of three key categories—Champions, Compensators, and Connectors—each with their own superpower.

Power Move #2: Build Yourself a Kitchen Cabinet

1. **Acknowledge your Achilles' heel.** Start by being brutally honest with yourself about what you can do—and what you can't. No one we know is a master of every single critical skill required to launch a successful business.
2. **Build your empire, one contact at a time.** Don't try to build your cabinet in a single day. Or even month. Cultivating the right relationships takes time and effort.
3. **Turn casual contacts into committed relationships.** You ask for a favor, they deliver, it goes swimmingly, and then you call to say thank you. One thing leads to another, and before you know it, you have a set of advisors that you can call day or night.
4. **Narrow the ask.** You are likely to ask your Kitchen Cabinet members for multiple favors, not just one. The key to making sure the favor gets done—and it's not the last one they will ever do for you—is discipline. Make sure you're asking the right favor at the right time.
5. **Pay it forward (constantly).** It's impossible to pay back our Kitchen Cabinet for the positive impact they have had on our business trajectory and mental wellness. But we are the first to have their backs, pick up their calls, help in a job search, or return a DM within seconds.

Champions

These are the ride-or-die people who simply refuse to let you throw in the towel. You call them when things feel shaky, when you're convinced you've made a colossal mistake, or when the numbers look more like a sad joke than a business plan.

THEIR ROLE	They remind you that you're not an impostor, help you separate the actual problems from the imaginary ones (because not everything is a crisis), and deliver the pep talk that gets you back in the ring.
YOUR JOB	Keep an open mind, take the advice seriously, and resist the urge to argue.

OUR CHAMPIONS: They begin and end with a few incredibly tight best friends who cannot help but support us in every way possible. (We hope we return the favor in spades.) We're also lucky enough to count our brothers among this inner circle. Since they worked in an adjacent business, they understood our offering and market, making them invaluable in helping us stay focused on our goals. Now, resisting the urge to argue with them and give them a noogie? Well, that's a skill we've both honed over time. But we have been known to slip up every now and then.

Compensators

These are the seasoned pros who know your industry or stage of growth inside and out but have a few more years (and wisdom) of experience than you. They're thoughtful, patient, and eerily intuitive guides who fill the gaps in your knowledge and experience. Think of these as the skills you desperately need now but haven't quite leveled up to yet.

THEIR ROLE	They answer those critical questions you're stuck on or guide you toward someone or something who can.
YOUR JOB	Don't waste their time with questions you could figure out on your own. Save them for when you're seriously stuck. (Which you will be. A lot.)

OUR COMPENSATORS: For Victoria—aside from Beth (wink wink!)—she built out her Compensators through her leadership positions at regional and national chapters of our industry's largest professional organizations. These connections helped her pressure-test new products and offerings while gaining valuable insight into our clients' mindsets.

Beth is a failed academic at heart, and she's not shy about calling up every professor who's ever written a research paper relevant to our business to keep us (and our clients) ahead of the curve. Nowadays, both are building their Gen Z network to ask the social media questions they are too embarrassed to ask their kids.

Connectors

These are the human switchboards of your network—the ones who seem to know everyone, everywhere, all the time. They are out on the town seven nights a week, their virtual Rolodex is bulging, and they can't walk into a room without a chorus of name-shouting and bear hugs. Lucky for you, they're also generous with their intros.

THEIR ROLE	Connections, connections, and more connections.
YOUR JOB	Leverage those connections with a healthy dose of gratitude, cheerleading, and returned favors.

OUR CONNECTORS: Our Connectors are an eclectic mix, from sharp investors and seasoned CEOs we've stayed close to over the years to the random-but-amazing like-minded moms we met at playgroups, field days, and hockey tournaments.

Most of them were more outgoing than either of us and were the first to offer an introduction. But we learned to follow up quickly and became skilled at reciprocating with smart, thoughtful connections of our own.

Beth's favorite? A fellow mom she had passed in the school pickup line for years without speaking much to, until one day, they finally struck up a conversation. Turns out she was scaling a services business of her own, and they ended up swapping lessons learned (and plenty of contacts). Victoria's most unexpected win? An incredible mompreneur she met on the sidelines of her daughter's volleyball game. The connection was instant, and there were favors before the week was out. If there's one lesson here, it's to keep your mind and heart open. Some of your best connections will come from the least expected places.

Our first Kitchen Cabinet members were generally best friends or relatives, so we realized we were stacked with Champions but seriously short on Connectors and Compensators. In fact, our only Compensators at the time were each other. Talk about an echo chamber! As the business grew, two things became clear: (1) we were leaning on our inner circle a bit too much, and (2) we needed to find people, mostly women, with a few notable exceptions, who could fill in the more specific gaps in our knowledge and business styles and, importantly, people we could actually help in return. So, we rolled out the following strategy—tapping into friends and contacts to introduce us to others, making super-specific requests, staying connected and appreciative, and paying it forward whenever we could.

Step 1: Acknowledge Your Achilles' Heel

You've got to start by being brutally honest with yourself about what you can and cannot do. If your business idea has real money-making potential, you're clearly a smart cookie. But no one we know is a master of every single critical skill required to launch a successful business. Most entrepreneurs tend to go deep in a few key areas, but they need a little backup in others. And that's where your Kitchen Cabinet steps in.

Take an inventory of the critical areas required to launch and execute your business idea successfully. Build a skills matrix and leave blanks for any area where you could use a little help or are flying completely blind. (Don't panic, we've got a sample matrix for you.) Include every must-have you can think of for your business as it grows. You won't need them all on day one, but it's good to know what's coming down the pipeline. By mapping out both your current and future skill needs—and spotting the gaps—you'll be ready to scout out the people you'll need in your network now and in the future.

Here are a few skills that were essential parts of our matrix as we launched Clermont and might help you get started on your own matrix:

- **Strategy building.** New businesses need six-month, one-year, and three-year goals, along with a detailed plan for how to achieve them. Keep in mind that strategic thinking and strategy building are two very different things. Having an expert who's done the heavy lifting—whether on their own or while running a division of a larger company—could be key to covering all your bases. Think of them as your strategy GPS.
- **Product or service features.** While you've validated your TAM and sized up your potential competition as part of Power Move #1, it's now time to map out the specific features that will ensure your initial idea (and all the add-ons that come after) is market ready. When you've been deep in your own idea for weeks (or months), the right sounding board will cut through your blind spots and give you a clear read on what will resonate with your audience.
- **Pricing.** Books (really boring ones) have been written on this topic, and you'll hear more opinions than you can shake a stick at on how much your product or service should cost. Do your competitive homework on price points, figure out if you're going premium or playing the price war game, and then ask your Kitchen Cabinet to weigh in on the final price. Chances are, they've all made a few pricing blunders and collected enough feedback to save you from making the same mistakes.

- **Legal/HR expertise.** Writing contracts, applying for patents, drafting partnership agreements, and determining how to collect money in different states and countries without incurring tax penalties are table stakes. So are attracting and managing employees as you scale. Early on, we made the mistake of putting HR last and it forced us to hit pause on scaling because we didn't have the team to deliver the work. Adding a lawyer and an HR expert to your Kitchen Cabinet will save you lots of headaches.
- **Money matters.** Women are notoriously bad at asking for money, and investors are notoriously terrible at giving it to us. Remember, women entrepreneurs received less than 2 percent of total venture funding,[3] so chances are we could use some expertise in this area. Go find yourself a seasoned pro who can help you quickly summarize and sell financial modeling points you haven't considered since your college accounting class. And never stop building your bench of investor connectors. In fundraising, trust and intros open more doors than pitch decks.
- **Scaling.** This might be the most important skill of all, so do not let this potential blank in your skills matrix go unfilled. Eventually, you'll need some real smarties who can share the good, the bad, and the downright ugly of how and when to scale. Don't skimp; cast a wide net to fill multiple seats. Find slow burners, rapid expanders, and the always reliable steady-as-she-goesers. This is hard, and we guarantee you'll have at least 100 reasons a day to speed dial someone who's lived to tell the tale.

Now it's time to turn your skills matrix into a spiffy visual framework to reveal potential matches within your network (or adjacent to it), including friends, family, and next-door neighbors. Bring your contact list and colored pencils and be ready to get creative!

ROLE	CONTACT NAME	CONNECTOR, CHAMPION, OR COMPENSATOR
MASTERMIND MODE: STRATEGY		
Market Research and Analysis		
Competitive Strategy		
Business Model		
Scaling		
SHOW ME THE MONEY: FINANCIAL SKILLS		
Budgeting		
Fundraising		
Cash Flow		
Pricing		
Forecasting		

ROLE	CONTACT NAME	CONNECTOR, CHAMPION, OR COMPENSATOR
MAKE THEM LOVE YOU: MARKETING & BRANDING		
Digital Marketing (SEO, social, email)		
Branding		
Customer Retention		
Public Relations		
Sales		
TALK THE TALK: COMMUNICATION & NETWORKING		
Public Speaking		
Negotiation Tactics		
Networking		
BUILD IT, SELL IT, SCALE IT: PRODUCT & MARKET FIT		
Product Strategy		
Prototyping		
Supply Chain		

ROLE	CONTACT NAME	CONNECTOR, CHAMPION, OR COMPENSATOR
DON'T GET SUED: LEGAL/HR & RISK MANAGEMENT		
Contracts		
Legal		
Staffing		
Risk Management		
Project Management		

Step 2: Build Your Empire, One Contact at a Time

If your matrix is already packed with the perfect blend of Champions, Compensators, and Connectors, then congrats, you can skip ahead. (And please, share your magic formula.) But if you're like the rest of us mere mortals, the thought of building your Kitchen Cabinet from the ground up has you breaking out in a cold sweat. (We see you, extroverted introverts.) Maybe you're just starting out or switched fields recently or your friends are wonderful people who couldn't care less about business or capitalism. If that hits home, you might feel like you're starting from scratch, but don't worry, you can still build a solid Kitchen Cabinet.

First, don't reinvent the wheel. No one we've ever counseled was truly starting from scratch, and you won't be the first. You already have a network, and now is the time to work it. Start by mapping your existing relationships to your skills gaps. Look at your inner circle first: family, friends, and colleagues who know you. Next, export your LinkedIn contacts (yes, all of them) and, while you're at it, your email address book, too. If you're a member of any organization you're genuinely engaged with, grab those membership lists as well. Now, dump it all into Excel and start sorting—who's easy to reach, who's a long shot but worth trying, and who's an absolute moonshot but could be game changing?

Next, prepare to lose a few days going down the LinkedIn rabbit hole, playing the "Six Degrees of Who Knows Who" game. Scroll through your contacts' connections, see who's in their orbit, and start expanding your potential connection list. We found that colleagues in and around our industry were generally open to a cold connection. Connections with other college alumni, past employers, or charitable organizations gave us an even better chance of turning a cold outreach into a warm conversation. (Both of our universities are strategically located in Indiana, though one was way more fun than the other—let's go Hoosiers!—and both turned out to be gold mines for new connections.) For first-level contacts, don't just click and send a generic message.

Be thoughtful and specific about why you're connecting. Remember, the goal is to expand your circle with quality relationships, not just collect a list of names. A little effort in personalizing those outreach messages can go a long way in turning a connection into a meaningful conversation. (More on this in the "Narrow the Ask" section.)

Second-level contacts require a bit more finesse. We have a straightforward strategy to increase our chances of receiving a response. With permission, we referenced mutual connections to smooth the introduction. But first, we made sure they were consistently active on the platform—sharing smart ideas, events, or perspectives regularly, not just popping up once a year with a "humbled to be named" post about their latest industry accolade. Next, we checked for signs they were open to networking, which we guessed from event photos, personal invites, or posts about connecting job seekers in their network with potential employers. (Fun fact: We discovered that having a vast number of connections didn't necessarily correlate with someone being open to a cold networking call.) If they checked these boxes, we thought the outreach had a greater chance of success and went for it. These kinds of filters might seem a bit picky, but trust us, we learned the hard way. More than once, what seemed like the perfect contact ghosted us completely. And the worst part? We had already cashed in a favor to make the intro, only to walk away empty-handed.

Our intro connection notes were simple:

> *Hi—we both know Grace, I am launching an [XX] business, and she said you were a go-to source for her on X. Could I pick your brain over a cup of coffee at a time and place that would best work for you?*

That was it. No pitch deck, no long-winded backstory, just a direct, respectful ask. Most people like being seen as the expert and truly want to help other people, if they have time. So, if they tell you to follow up in two weeks, don't ghost them, but don't pester either. Set the reminder and circle back on their terms. We promise, this is how powerful networks get built, one coffee at a time.

Sometimes the initial outreach or meetings we had were absolute trainwrecks: awkward silences, excessive watch-checking, and a general vibe of *why are we here?* But just as many were downright mind-blowing. Halfway into a cup of coffee, our new friend would start mentally rifling through their network or launch into stories of their own past business successes and failures that made us quickly reach for our phones to take notes.

What we realized was this: the more we brought to the table in those early meetings, the more we learned and the more likely they were to take our next call. Showing up with the right mindset is the secret sauce for successful conversations. Bring these qualities along—in equal doses—and watch the magic happen:

- **Humility.** This is not the moment to roll out the red carpet for your accomplishments or overstate where you are in your business. In fact, doing so could have the opposite effect and make someone less inclined to help you. Be up-front about being early in your journey, facing a few challenges, and genuinely needing some guidance. Tell them how grateful you are that they took time out of their busy schedule and how much you respect their knowledge and what they have achieved.

  The biggest don't? Name-dropping and pretending you don't need the favor (when you most definitely do). Take the case of a very young woman who approached Beth, asking for a connection to one of her CEO clients. She proceeded to name-drop some bigwig CEOs for a solid 10 minutes before asking Beth to introduce her to another CEO because she had "a few spots left" in her team's innovation consulting practice. Mind you, the CEO led a multibillion-dollar company with consultants coming out of the woodwork. So why on Earth would Beth help her make an intro just to watch her pull the same "posing" stunt on one of her top contacts? Needless to say, Beth declined.

- **Clarity.** Make sure your elevator pitch is tighter than your favorite pair of jeans from the early aughts. Explain what your business does and where the gaps are, fast. Time is precious, so in just a few sentences, you've got to prove you have a vision, you're executing on it, and, if they help you out, you won't squander the opportunity (or, heaven forbid, make them look bad). The last thing you want is to come off unprepared or fuzzy about your own business. Nail down the industry, the need, your solution, and how your experience backs it all up. It's a lot to fit in, so practice, practice, practice. Ours? "Two serial entrepreneurs with multiple millions in exits help women conceive, launch, and scale seven-figure businesses through online and in-person courses, connections, and community."

If you are struggling to find your messaging groove, we recommend a quick read of *Find Your Red Thread* by Tamsen Webster. She breaks down how to craft a brand narrative that's not only compelling but sticks.

- **Directness.** Don't beat around the bush about what you need. Be clear and direct and tell them exactly what you're after and why you need it. The best pitch we ever got came from someone who was a friend-of-a-friend contact, and it went like this: "I've been an interim CFO for Consulting Company XX for 10 years, across every tech sector imaginable. I've written a playbook on how companies can get the most out of this interim role while searching for a permanent replacement. I know the exact CV of the ideal candidate, how long it takes to onboard them, and how to ensure both sides get what they bargained for. All I need is a CFO board of advisors to help me build contacts in the business. In exchange, those CFOs get access to a small, exclusive community they can engage with as much or as little as they'd like." We introduced her to two of our favorite CFOs in the blink of an eye.

Now it's time to let those relationships percolate—slow and steady, like a good moka pot. But don't just set it and forget it.

Step 3: Turn Casual Contacts into Committed Relationships

You ask for a favor, they deliver, it goes swimmingly, and then you call to say thank you. One thing leads to another, and before you know it, you're at dinner or drinks. Or maybe they're swamped, so you keep them on your call list, invite them to an event they might like, and keep the conversations flowing. Every few months, you reach out a little more, remembering that patience is a virtue.

In the beginning, it's like walking a tightrope and balancing between overdoing it and leaving the trail too cold. The trick is figuring out how and when you can be valuable to your contacts in return. Always keep the door open so they know your "ask" isn't a one-way street. We often tapped existing Clermont Partners clients for an intro to a colleague in their company who might benefit from another service we offered. In exchange, we gladly shared tips and made introductions to headhunters when they started looking for a new position. But a word of caution: don't go asking for big favors from heavy hitters and then try to come up with an appropriate return favor. Beyoncé and Mel Robbins don't need your help; a simple thank-you note and good vibes to the universe are the best you can do.

Speaking of a simple thank-you note, write one. It isn't just good manners—it's the glue that strengthens relationships and keeps your network engaged. An email will do the job, but a quick phone call is usually better. Let them hear the genuine gratitude in your voice. When we do favors for others, the best part is hearing how our help made a difference. If things went well, we're thrilled. If they didn't, we're invested, which means we'll likely brainstorm other ways to help.

We've always been amazed at how easily women let valuable connections slip, especially after working so hard to build them. Right after someone did us a favor, we'd go all in on the thank-yous—flowers, wine, fun invites—whatever it took to show our gratitude. But we didn't stop there. As the relationship matured, we stayed just as committed to keeping in touch and making sure they knew how much the connection meant to us. A man who worked with us years ago does the absolute best job we have ever seen with this routine communications approach. He and Victoria met more than 20 years ago. Even though they worked together for only two years, he has spent the last 20 years checking in like clockwork, every six months. He always has a positive word to say—and sometimes he has an ask for her, and other times she has an ask for him. They've traded introductions, opened doors, and celebrated each other's successes and failures. The takeaway? Not every great relationship comes from a perfectly calculated networking strategy. Sometimes the strongest connections come from unexpected places. But the ones that last are built on genuine support, a natural give-and-take, and consistently showing up for each other when it counts.

Don't be the person who comes around only when you need something. We can't tell you how many times people ghosted our emails or invites for months (and even years), right up until they found themselves needing a favor, usually during a job search or asking us to hire their third cousin's son. We still tried to help those people but not with the same level of effort we applied to those who kept up with us regularly. Building genuine, ongoing relationships is the key to ensuring your network is there when you need it most.

Step 4: Narrow the Ask

You are likely to ask your Kitchen Cabinet members for multiple favors, not just one. And the people you are asking are just as busy as you are—juggling businesses, careers, kids, aging parents, hobbies, service projects, and who knows what else. They've likely agreed to work with you because they like you, think you're smart, and/or believe they can help. But here's the catch: they also know exactly how much time they can spare and how far they're willing to go to help, especially in the early stages when they're still figuring out how to engage. Don't take that trust for granted. Lose it, and you might just lose a valuable member of your cabinet.

The key to making sure the favor gets done, and it's not the last one they'll ever do for you, is discipline. Make sure you're asking the right favor at the right time. Ask for help only if it meets these conditions:

- **It's in their wheelhouse.** Don't ask someone important for a favor unless you're absolutely sure they can deliver. If you're asking for an introduction, know beyond a shadow of a doubt that the person you're asking knows the person you want to meet. Do your homework. Stalk their LinkedIn contacts like it's your full-time job. Revisit, as best you can, those murky wine chats where your target contact was discussed. Don't waste an ask on a dead-end "I wish I could help" response.
- **It's as specific as possible.** We appreciate it when people ask for an introduction to a specific person or entity. Or at the very least, give us enough details about the type of person they want to meet so we can zero in on the perfect match. Avoid fishing expeditions and don't ask for general introductions to "smart people in the retail industry." Instead, aim for something like, "I'm looking for someone with a proven track record of scaling women's perfumes in the western United States." The more specific you are, the easier it is for your contact to say yes. The same goes for investor intros. Research first! Know whether they invest in companies at your stage, what they look for in an ideal investment, and whom they've already backed in or near your space.

- **It's timed right.** Be mindful of how much time it's going to take them to do the favor you are asking. If you make it hard for your contact to fulfill your request, don't expect a quick response. From our experience, any request that could be knocked out in three minutes or less got done almost immediately. But if it took multiple steps or a few days to complete, it might slip through the cracks. We eventually realized that while our go-tos genuinely wanted to help, if saying yes meant missing a meeting or skipping a SoulCycle class, the favor would be postponed—and postponed—and postponed.
- **It's not an overreach.** Don't overstep. This one is a no-brainer: don't ask someone you don't know really well for a connection. Their network was as tough to build as yours, so respect it. Instead, try to get to know the person better before you ask them a favor.

You might do everything right and still. . .crickets. Or your contact makes a promise, and then you never hear from them again. Don't let this bring you down. Inevitably, some of your queries won't get responses, even from people you were sure would be lifetime members of your Kitchen Cabinet. People are busy. Give them the benefit of the doubt. But if several attempts to connect go unanswered, start the hunt for another contact who can replace that skill gap on your matrix.

Step 5: Pay It Forward (Constantly)

It's impossible to pay back our Kitchen Cabinet for the positive impact they have had on our business trajectory and mental wellness. But we can and do reciprocate the hell out of them. We are the first to have their backs, pick up their calls, help in job searches, or return a DM within seconds. We cheer, both publicly and privately, their successes and failures. It's this circle of support, along with 24/7 availability—that makes us thick as thieves. Here are a couple of really easy hacks to keep the communication lines open and enhance your relationships in the process:

- **Show them they're on your mind.** Forward smart, relatable content, or just plain interesting stuff, whenever it makes sense. We got into the habit of sending articles to individual members of our network along with a quick note explaining why the piece made us think of them. This might be stating the obvious, but steer clear of politics. You never really know where someone stands—until you do, and by then, it might be too late. Case in point: we once assumed a contact in our network was on one side of the political spectrum, until he casually mentioned that some of Beth's comments didn't sit right with him. Surprise! Turns out, we guessed wrong. Luckily, he was honest with us. Beth took the hint and became a lot more intentional about what she said around him.
- **Share your own related work.** Beth loves writing thought leadership and research snippets. In our consulting business, we leveraged them for marketing purposes, but in general, we use them to be provocative and get our network talking and commenting. We cherry-pick the smartest stuff and most relevant topics for each member of our crew before we send it along. This might take an hour per week to customize, but it's rare that we don't get an immediate "thanks for thinking of me" in return.
- **Spread your (relevant) good news.** If we have good news about ourselves or our business that is pertinent (and if we haven't been beating our connections to death lately), we send out brag sheets. If it's not so relevant or if we've already filled up their inbox that week, we leave it to our social media channels to share our news. And the humble brag of "I am honored to be added to. . . " is much better shared by others, not by you.

- **Shout their good news from the rooftops.** Smart women tend to be terrible at taking victory laps. (Many men, ahem, do not seem to have that problem.) Do it for them. When a member of your Kitchen Cabinet does something great, promote the hell out of it. Share their news across your network to help them expand their own. In general, never miss an opportunity to cheer for your peeps publicly and get some much-deserved attention for the amazing women around you.

Keeping in touch and following up is great. Returning the favor? Even better. We've made it a top priority to support the people who share their precious time, contacts, or expertise with us. That means inviting them to events where they can expand their own networks (or at least have a great night out on us). We've given their kids internships, never turned down a charitable donation request (even if we had to bite our tongue on the cause du jour), and showed up for any event at which they were the honoree. Of course, the ultimate favor is helping your network's own Kitchen Cabinets grow. When we meet someone with a skill set or network that could benefit a member of our Kitchen Cabinet, we don't wait for permission. We make the introduction.

Beth had a friend who seemed to have it all: thriving business, endless connections, and a generosity with his time that made him an invaluable ally. But even he had a gap to fill. He needed to hire a firm in our industry but couldn't work with us due to conflicts. So Beth rolled up her sleeves. She sent him a sample RFP, a breakdown of the best firms, direct contacts, and key insights on how to engage them. Then she made personal introductions to the top players in the space. It wasn't rocket science, but it saved him 10–20 hours of research, gave him the confidence to hire the right firm, and provided a few additional contacts he could use when these situations arose again. Years later, he's still a strong ally in Beth's network.

Don't stress if your first draft of a Kitchen Cabinet isn't stacked with A-list heavy hitters. Building a strong network takes time. It took us nearly three years, and to this day, it continues to evolve. If you're just starting out or have spent years in a single job, your connections may be more limited, and that's completely fine. Stay in touch with the people you meet and let the group take shape naturally. The key is consistency. Each week, make an effort to connect with current or potential Kitchen Cabinet members. We dedicate Fridays to nurturing our network—sending LinkedIn messages, personal emails, and event invites to strengthen relationships. Victoria's tennis prowess has even helped expand her list of contacts, proving that networking happens in more places than just packed business events.

A final note, since we know you are all thinking, *How could they have ignored the traditional in-person networking circuit?* This might be a matter of personal preference, but we believe forced networking at events has a very low hit rate. Of course, there are exceptions. While we found general "Women in Business" empowerment events a time suck with little to show for it, events tailored to women scaling businesses were more promising. Even better, events connected to industry, cultural, or community groups that we actively engaged in throughout the year yielded people who were friendlier and had a greater appetite for longer conversations. If possible, we would get an attendance list first so we could be more intentional with whom we approached. Our lesson? Be authentic; try to find common ground to share a feel-good moment or a wicked laugh. Your goal should be to find a reason to have a second conversation. Worry about the third conversation and a possible ask later.

The best events on the networking circuit were the ones we sponsored ourselves. In the early days of our business, we began hosting quarterly women's events, which proved to be game changers in building our Kitchen Cabinet. But here's the twist: they weren't stuffy, hard-hitting "let's talk business," business-card exchange marathons disguised as networking. Nope. We threw fun, memorable gatherings where we could let loose and get to know each other beyond the elevator pitch.

Our first event was a barn burner. We brought in an up-and-coming Instagram influencer—an ex-college cheerleader with a sharp eye for fashion, specializing in clothing for petite women. Keep in mind, this was more than a decade ago, back when "influencer" wasn't a career path and social media strategy wasn't a zillion-dollar industry. She walked us through how she built an audience of more than 20,000 followers and turned it into a successful business. (Fast-forward to today? She's closing in on 300,000.) Another favorite event was a private dinner and movie screening at the New York Film Festival. We provided popcorn and Twizzlers and in return, had a lot of fun, and forged some priceless connections. No matter how you do it, forget the cookie-cutter approach of exchanging business cards and sending flowery but generic emails. Focus instead on building authentic relationships. Trust us, that's the secret to a *fierce* Kitchen Cabinet—and it will take you much further than any networking script ever could.

Building our Kitchen Cabinet is the secret sauce that saved us from costly mistakes and kept us sane when the stakes were sky-high. Surrounding yourself with the right mix of Champions, Compensators, and Connectors means you're never flying blind, no matter how wild the ride gets.

Now that you've got your advisors, mentors, and allies lined up, it's time to turn your attention to the next challenge: growing your business. The upcoming Power Move dives into how to scale strategically, avoid burnout, and turn your vision into unstoppable momentum.

Gut Check

Am I Trying to Build an Empire Without Backup?

- ☐ Who is the first person I call when I am stuck on a major business decision, and are they qualified to help? Whom do I *wish* I could call when I am stuck? *(Before you speed-dial your bestie or your spouse, ask yourself, do they have the experience, objectivity, and industry know-how you need right now? And if you don't have that person yet, what would it take to find them?)*
- ☐ Do I have at least one Champion, one Compensator, and one Connector in my network right now? *(We know you do. But make your list so that* you *know you do.)*
- ☐ Which gaps in my skill set do I need help with? *(No one has all the answers. Are you DIY-ing legal, pricing, or financial forecasting because you love a challenge or to avoid the discomfort of asking for help?)*
- ☐ Am I holding back from reaching out to someone impressive because I feel like I haven't "earned" the right? *(Let's debunk that myth: you earn the right by being prepared, direct, and respectful. You don't need permission to ask a favor.)*
- ☐ What's one relationship I've let go cold that deserves a thoughtful reconnection this month? *(This isn't about fake networking—this is about reconnecting with someone who once helped you or inspired you and simply needs a reason to hear from you again.)*

CHAPTER 6

Power Move #3: Make the Money Moves That Matter

There's a magic number in your head, the milestone that screams, "You've made it!" But here's the kicker: when you finally hit it, you'll probably barely notice. You'll just be too busy chasing the next one. On to the next goalpost.

The truth about growth is that it's not a finish line; it's a moving target. Scaling your business means more than just adding customers or revenue. It's about building a system that can handle the chaos without breaking you. In this chapter, we're diving into how to grow with grit, discipline, and a strategy for taking the calculated risks so your business takes off.

Our first big financial goal was to break seven figures at Clermont. A win so memorable, in fact, that neither of us can recall the exact moment we crossed that line. What we do remember is that when we doubled it—and then some—we hit a fork in the road. Growth was stalling, our current customers were tapped out, and our easy marketing wins had dried up. Suddenly, we were stuck brainstorming (sometimes together, sometimes solo in carpool lines or on boring calls) about what came next. Do we play it safe with steady, predictable wins? Or do we go all in, risking it all for explosive, double-digit growth?

If you have been reading this book even a little, you already know how this story goes. We did *not* stick to the "steady as she goes" path, sleep soundly at night after tucking our kids in, and settle for a modest payday. Nope. We went all in, pushed for scale, and pursued the kind of financial freedom we had set out to achieve in the first place. Or, as Victoria so eloquently puts it, "balls to the wall."

Before we took our own swing-for-the-fences leap with Clermont, we were nestled comfortably in our financial safety zone. We had a steady stream of retainer clients—our reliable monthly income with predictable billing and those ever-comforting 60-day-out clauses. Then there were the project clients, which were short-term gigs that paid more, but it was a crap shoot if they would turn into more work. To keep things sane, we made sure our expenses never exceeded our retainer income. Projects were great when they landed, but they had serious feast-or-famine energy, and we knew better than to bank on them.

You'd think hitting that financial safety zone meant calmer nights and more family time. It didn't. The more high-retainer clients we landed, the more likely that we'd get a "just one quick thing" call during bedtime or find ourselves cramming on Sunday nights for a Monday of back-to-back "check-in" calls with clients or fielding "urgent" emails that turned into conference calls in the middle of a Disney vacation with the kids.

Beth still winces when her twins bring up the time she missed the Brownies induction ceremony. She had to tap one of her ride-or-dies—this time, her amazing cousin Licia—to stand in. While Licia held her kids' hands at the ceremony, Beth was stuck on the tarmac in Detroit, grounded after a client trip, listening over the phone as her kids crossed some imaginary promise bridge, and even they can't recall what it promised. For the record, they hated Brownies and never went back. But somehow, the trauma lives on.

Victoria's cringiest moment? Missing Ali's preschool Mother's Day tea to be at a client's investor day in New York. She did her best to steer the date, but when the CEO finally had a window, his schedule won. The knockout punch came later that night on FaceTime, when Ali said, "You were the only mom not there." Silver lining? Ali, now 14, read this over Victoria's shoulder while she was editing and said, "I don't remember that." They never do. (Consider this your cue to flip back to Chapter 1 and let the mom guilt go, again.)

We were burning out, and we knew it. If we were going to keep growing without losing our sanity—or missing another school ceremony—we needed leverage. That meant clients who didn't demand our every waking hour and were willing to work with our team, not just us. The ESG segment had real potential to do just that. It came with a software angle, which meant high margins and less of us in the weeds. And after years of white-knuckling every client fire drill, that sounded like salvation. The catch? We needed more capital. So we did the unthinkable: we tapped into our project-based revenue stream to help fund it. We let expenses rise to match total revenue, not just retained revenue, something we swore we'd never do. It was a calculated gamble that gave us the time we needed but left absolutely no room to screw up. This decision cranked up the pressure, not so much in a "we're about to go under" kind of way but more the mental vice grip of knowing that we might have to forgo salary and bonuses to cover ongoing expenses if project revenue dried up. We shot way past our comfort zone.

You know the rest of the story. That gamble paid off. And we learned something really important: sometimes you have to step outside your comfort zone and bend your own rules. So how do you accomplish this? How do you grow smarter, not just bigger, so you can keep your sanity and your family intact?

This Power Move is all about getting brutally honest with yourself, knowing what you're willing to do to win and where you draw the line. But here's the cold, hard truth: too many female founders choke, or at least hesitate right at the moment that matters most. Instead, we want you to recognize those key moments and lean in, hard. When the next step feels scary, that's often the sign that you're exactly where you should be. Don't pull back. Don't overanalyze the spend or bootstrap yourself into burnout. Take the (well-considered) leap instead.

To help you push past your doubts, do the hard stuff now. To help, we have broken down this Power Move into more manageable steps.

Power Move #3: Make the Money Moves That Matter

1. **Building takes emotional and financial capital. Budget for both.** Before diving headfirst into any scaling plan, create a checklist. List your biggest fears and exactly what you're risking, personally and financially, and then stack that against what you hope to gain.
2. **Get clear on what you will—and won't—do financially.** At some point, you'll come face-to-face with an unexpected opportunity that wasn't in the business plan, and chances are, it will come with a serious price tag. You'll need to decide whether to raise outside capital, walk away, or bend your own rules. Whatever you decide, one thing's certain: knowing your financial parameters keeps the decision intentional, not emotional.
3. **The right opportunity is worth the wait.** You're probably itching to dive in and start moving toward launch. But you will likely need to wait—and wait some more—until that golden opportunity finally appears.
4. **Swing big at the right time.** As entrepreneurs, we must be mentally prepared not just to recognize the golden opportunity when it arises but also to seize it without hesitation. If we doubt ourselves or overthink it, a competitor will swoop in, and we'll miss our shot.
5. **Share the field, win the game.** Even though we're taught to share, sometimes we just don't want to. Our instinct is often to maintain full control so that we can claim the largest share of the pie. But as entrepreneurs, we frequently have to give up equity in exchange for capital to fuel our leap to the next level. The paradox? Sharing the upside often increases your take-home returns.

Step 1: Building Takes Capital—Emotional and Financial; Budget for Both

No one warns you about the emotional tax you'll pay as a mompreneur. Especially as you enter building mode. Every day, you're making trade-offs—missed bedtime stories, skipped field trips, or just plain exhaustion from juggling it all. You might feel guilty or like you're failing at both business and motherhood. That's normal. In fact, if you're not feeling at least a little bit guilty, you're probably not paying attention. These emotional trade-offs are the real price of admission. If you're not willing to feel all the messy, hard feelings that come with chasing your dreams, you're not ready to play in the big leagues. Embrace the discomfort. Name it. Own it. And then get back to work, because the women who win are the ones who refuse to let guilt or doubt call the shots.

We both wrestled a lot with our personal balance sheets when we decided to launch Clermont Partners. For Beth, the hardest part was feeling like she was taking a massive pay cut just as her career was hitting its stride. For Victoria, it was the sheer terror of draining her savings (including retirement) to bet on a future that could either be "early retirement in Tuscany" or "ramen for dinner every night for the next five years," especially with a house full of kids who somehow needed new shoes every other week.

We also knew to really embrace growth and scaling meant we had to make peace with missing a lot of traditional mom milestones. We weren't going to be "room moms." There was zero chance of us assistant-coaching our kids' sports teams. And we were definitely out of the carpool rotation. More often than we'd like to admit, it was our moms or our nannies who knew more about our kids' days than we did. We didn't blow past that reality blindly; we knew exactly what we were signing up for. Instead, we made a pact with ourselves: be fully present when we were there and fiercely intentional about carving out one-on-one time with each kid. We leaned on each other—and had each other's backs—to make it all happen. But sometimes we fell short. We weren't always fully present and get reminded of that still today. Case in point? Billy, Victoria's son, just got his first iPhone. The other day, mid-conversation, his phone rang. He held up a finger to her and said, "Hold on, I have to take this call." Yep. We all do our best.

And for those wondering how we managed to squeeze in friendships and self-care? We didn't. Loneliness and feeling left out were normalized for us. The one thing that kept us afloat was having each other—to vent, to tag in, to get it without judgment. That was our lifeline. And some days, it was the only thing that kept us from drowning.

Launching a business isn't just about crunching numbers. It's about staring down your fears, your doubts, and your personal limits—both emotionally and financially. That's why, before diving headfirst into any scaling plan, we've learned to run through an emotional checklist. And yes, we recommend putting it on actual paper. There's something about physically writing it out that makes both the fear and the upside feel real. List your biggest fears and exactly what you're risking—personally and financially—then stack that against what you hope to gain.

Here's Beth's 30-year-old starter list for you to kick things off. (And, please, do not let this scare you straight out of launching and growing the hell out of your business.)

WHAT I MUST GIVE UP	WHAT I WILL GAIN
Validation from my corporate peers as my career continues to advance	Daily dopamine hits from the excitement of running a start-up
Advancing rapidly at my corporate job	Autonomy from having more control over how I spend my day
Paying off the family loans that helped me start my business	Confidence that I am finally meeting the entrepreneurial expectations of myself and my family
Peace of mind that comes from having savings and making ongoing regular contributions to my 401(k)	Increased probability of building a major nest egg and reaching early retirement
Time for hobbies and self-care	A small hope and dream that I hit it big beyond my wildest dreams

When we made the decision to break out on our own, we decided to stress-test our decision by writing down in black and white what we stood to gain (and lose) by going "balls to the wall," because let's face it, we weren't going to half-ass the next business. We met in Victoria's kitchen, which was peaceful if your definition of the word includes shrieking two- and four-year-olds who kept interrupting her every five minutes, nanny or not. As we compared what we were willing to lose, our lists were eerily similar. But when it came to what we each hoped to gain? That's where things wildly diverged. Victoria's list was all about what she could build for her family. Beth's? Hers was all about trying to overcome mom guilt that crept higher and higher in lockstep with her growing responsibilities at the large consulting firm that had bought Ashton. It made sense; Victoria was still at the beginning of raising her family. (Three more kiddos would come during the early years of Clermont.) Beth, on the other hand, was deep in the emotional trenches of middle school parenting, watching the moments fly by and feeling like she was missing it all.

Our tipping point wasn't what you'd expect. The one thing that trumped the entire risk side of the risk/return list and made us see clearly that we had to do it again, surprisingly, wasn't money. It was about control. Control over our time and who got to decide how we spent it. The nature of our high-stakes consulting work meant our clients paid for, and deserved, 24/7 access to us. But our corporate overlords didn't. The higher we climbed on the corporate ladder, the more relentless the demands became. And many of those demands revolved around bureaucratic projects and related internal meetings that bored us to tears.

We didn't want to answer to anyone else's calendar chaos. We wanted to be our own top brass and HR team, deciding when admin tasks needed urgent attention and when they could wait until after school pickup or after we'd given ourselves a millisecond of self-care. So, after yet another mind-numbing week of "all hands on deck" meetings that accomplished exactly nothing, we looked at each other and said, "That's it. We're doing this." And we never looked back.

These kinds of decisions are brutal and important and not to be taken lightly. Expect to have to rewrite and reprioritize your own list a bunch of times. It's never going to feel great because short-term pain is part of the launch process. If, in the cold light of day, the cons outweigh the pros, maybe it's best just to stay the current course for a while. For good measure, run the list by someone who knows you best—partner, mom, ride-or-die—just to make sure you aren't glossing over any red flags. Then make the leap, whichever direction feels right. Because one way or another, staying frozen in the middle isn't an option.

Once you've sorted the emotional trade-offs, it's time to take a hard look at the financial side of the equation. Thinking about giving up future income is one thing. Actually draining your savings or raiding your retirement fund to launch your business? That's a whole different level of stress. And there's no room for wishful thinking or back-of-the-napkin math here. This is the real deal. You need to know—down to the last dollar—how much it'll take to get your business off the ground and keep it flying until it's self-sustaining.

Here's a little tough love. Chances are your slick "My Business" PowerPoint is stacked with big ideas and shiny growth strategies but light on the gritty details—like what your first-year revenue and profit will be. STOP RIGHT THERE. Don't move another inch until you've nailed down your revenue and profit model. Trust us, you don't want to be the mompreneur who realizes halfway through launch that she can't afford to keep going. Whether you're pitching family, VCs, or just your own inner skeptic, you need to be able to answer the big questions: When will revenue start rolling in? When will you hit breakeven?

Take it from someone who'd never built a revenue model before (ahem. . .Victoria. . .15 years ago); it's not as intimidating as it sounds. Your model doesn't have to be a complex, multi-sheet Excel nightmare. It can be as simple as a monthly waterfall showing expected revenue impacts—timing, amounts, and velocity—based on your sales and marketing investments. Think of it as your business' road map, one that'll help you avoid the financial potholes and keep you squarely focused on the revenue number you need to take home real profits.

Here is a basic version of the model we used to forecast Clermont's annual revenues in the first year. We started with a lot of assumptions, backed by market research, sales data, and seasonality trends. (Remember all the work we did in Power Move #1? This is a great time to use it.) Our clients were going to be mostly retained (steady, recurring revenue), with average monthly billings between $8,000 and $12,000. We knew it would be a slow and steady build, i.e., no major seasonal spikes to worry about.

Revenue Forecast

	JAN	FEB	MAR	APR	MAY	JUN	JUL	AUG	SEPT	OCT	NOV	DEC	
Client 1	$8,000	$8,000	$8,000	$8,000	$8,000	$8,000	$8,000	$8,000	$8,000	$8,000	$8,000	$8,000	
Client 2		$9,000	$9,000	$9,000	$9,000	$9,000	$9,000	$9,000	$9,000	$9,000	$9,000	$9,000	
Client 3			$8,000	$8,000	$8,000	$8,000	$8,000	$8,000	$8,000	$8,000	$8,000	$8,000	
Client 4			$8,000	$8,000	$8,000	$8,000	$8,000	$8,000	$8,000	$8,000	$8,000	$8,000	
Client 5				$10,000	$10,000	$10,000	$10,000	$10,000	$10,000	$10,000	$10,000	$10,000	
Client 6				$8,000	$8,000	$8,000	$8,000	$8,000	$8,000	$8,000	$8,000	$8,000	
Client 7					$12,000	$12,000	$12,000	$12,000	$12,000	$12,000	$12,000	$12,000	
Client 8					$8,000	$8,000	$8,000	$8,000	$8,000	$8,000	$8,000	$8,000	
Client 9						$11,000	$11,000	$11,000	$11,000	$11,000	$11,000	$11,000	
Client 10						$9,000	$9,000	$9,000	$9,000	$9,000	$9,000	$9,000	
Total	**$8,000**	**$17,000**	**$33,000**	**$51,000**	**$71,000**	**$91,000**	**$91,000**	**$91,000**	**$91,000**	**$91,000**	**$91,000**	**$91,000**	**$817,000**

Now, as we took on more project work, this spreadsheet got a whole lot more complex as we tried to guess the timing of short-term projects. But for the first year, this was a good start. It gave us the clarity to validate the business, spend wisely, hire at the right time, and measure if we were growing—or just keeping ourselves very busy.

These were the projections, but that was just the starting point. To stay grounded, we regularly compared forecasted revenue to what was signed on the dotted line. Each month (okay, week), we took a hard look—prospect by prospect—at what closed, what didn't, and how well our sales and marketing spend was performing. Over time, we got smarter. The gap between what we projected and what we closed started to shrink, and we made fewer painful mistakes, turning pipeline hopes into real, bankable revenue. This scrutiny of actual versus projected revenue also taught us an important lesson on the value of nurturing prospects already in the pipeline, not just staying focused on adding new companies to the top of the funnel. Over time, we made ongoing tweaks, including the type of salespeople we hired, the tools we equipped them with, and the amount of marketing support we could afford to invest in them. Those tweaks slowly paid off. Our projections got sharper, our expenses (as a portion of revenue generated) decreased, and, slowly, our projections became a lot more reliable.

Top-line revenue is just one piece of the puzzle. Understanding your expenses is just as, if not more, crucial to truly getting a grip on how much capital you'll need. For us, people, data, and sales and marketing costs were our largest expense items—about 95 percent of total expenses. Once we nailed the projections, it was clear: Clermont needed solid up-front capital, but it would hit breakeven fast and start covering its own costs by the six-month mark.

To launch, we needed financial data, a sales system, and marketing dollars to quickly build a brand and attract the expensive consulting agreements that would ultimately be our bread and butter. While these investments were not for the faint of heart, they were critical to early success. Data-driven insights gave us a competitive edge in landing new business and turning that data into thought leadership gave us access to boardrooms where the biggest sales could be made.

For us, breakeven in year one was non-negotiable. Without it, we'd be handing over way too much in equity to outside investors to offset the cash burn. Or worse, turning to friends and family for a loan that would feel too much like a favor. Our expense buckets will be different from yours, but there are a few essentials to factor in when mapping out the path to breakeven:

- **Start-up and ongoing fixed costs.** Think computers, office supplies, and, of course, technology and connectivity. These are the basics. In our case, we got a lucky break: one of us is married to a forward-thinking IT professional (thanks, Bill!) who set us up with a killer deal and future-proofed us with a cloud setup, making the switch to remote work a breeze during COVID-19.
- **Salaries and benefits.** You might need to pay yourself (or someone else) at the start to keep the wheels turning. Victoria did, so it went straight into the expense column. You are likely going to need health insurance as well. Generally, you can deduct health insurance premiums for you and your family as a business expense.

- **Product costs.** These are the expenses directly tied to producing the product, like raw materials, components, and even mailing and postage costs. Basically, anything used to create or assemble your masterpiece. Think of these as the "ingredients" that go into your pride and joy.
- **Sales and marketing.** This includes everything from design and sales platforms to email campaigns and conferences. When you're grinding to hit your first revenue milestones, these expenses can feel like a major drain, but you aren't likely to get there without them.
- **Travel.** Inevitably, you're going to need to hit the road (or the sky). Don't forget to account for these expenses in your budget. Travel costs can add up fast.

Here again is a quick, simple snapshot of what an expense model looks like:

Expense Model

	JAN	FEB	MAR	APR	MAY	JUN	JUL	AUG	SEPT	OCT	NOV	DEC
Total Revenue	**$8,000**	**$17,000**	**$33,000**	**$51,000**	**$71,000**	**$91,000**	**$91,000**	**$91,000**	**$91,000**	**$91,000**	**$91,000**	**$91,000**
Employee Costs	$2,400	$5,700	$9,900	$15,300	$21,300	$27,300	$27,300	$27,300	$27,300	$27,300	$27,300	$27,300
Occupancy Costs	$800	$1,700	$3,300	$5,100	$7,100	$9,100	$9,100	$9,100	$9,100	$9,100	$9,100	$9,100
Insurance and Legal Costs	$400	$850	$1,650	$2,550	$3,550	$4,550	$4,550	$4,550	$4,550	$4,550	$4,550	$4,550
Marketing Costs	$1,200	$2,500	$4,950	$2,650	$10,650	$13,650	$13,650	$13,650	$13,650	$13,650	$13,650	$13,650
Travel Costs	$400	$850	$1,650	$2,550	$3,550	$4,550	$4,550	$4,550	$4,550	$4,550	$4,550	$4,550
Other Costs	$400	$850	$1,650	$2,550	$3,550	$4,550	$4,550	$4,550	$4,550	$4,550	$4,550	$4,550
Total Expenses	**$5,200**	**$11,050**	**$21,450**	**$33,150**	**$46,150**	**$59,150**	**$59,150**	**$59,150**	**$59,150**	**$59,150**	**$59,150**	**$59,150**
Operating Income	**$2,800**	**$5,750**	**$11,550**	**$17,850**	**$24,850**	**$31,850**	**$31,850**	**$31,850**	**$31,850**	**$31,850**	**$31,850**	**$31,850**

Now, there are tons of books out there on financial modeling, but most of them are designed for MBA types building fundraising decks, not scrappy founders just trying to figure out how to afford Canva Pro and some Facebook ads. What you need right now is something simple, actionable, and not completely intimidating. So here are our top three recommendations for figuring out how much your idea will cost to launch and grow:

- **First, phone a friend.** Odds are you've got at least one accountant or spreadsheet-loving pal who thrives on turning chaos into tidy rows and columns. Hand them your list of expenses and let them work their Excel magic. No finance friend? No problem. Try the SBA's SCORE program or check out local incubators, especially those focused on women and diverse founders; they're popping up everywhere and often come with free mentoring.
- **Next, read Bill Aulet's *Disciplined Entrepreneurship*.** He's a professor (not a venture capital wiz with money to burn), and his chapters on expenses are both practical and mercifully well illustrated. Bonus: He includes tools and templates that won't make your head explode. And no, you don't have to read the whole thing. It gets a little bit dense and intimidating, so focus on the modeling.
- **Finally, use AI.** We literally typed into ChatGPT, "Build me a first-year expense model for a content marketing business with one employee using Facebook and Instagram ads to get clients," and out came a solid starting point.

One last loving nudge—if you're a creative soul who's been dodging Excel like it's your high school reunion invite, it's time. Hit YouTube, grab the most basic version you can, and just learn the basics. It's old school, but trust us, everyone still uses this tool, and gaining a basic knowledge of it will make your life (and your finances) a lot easier going forward.

With a combination of learning, favors, reading, research, and a little luck, you should soon have a clear picture of the revenue needed to hit breakeven and the start-up capital costs to get you there. Next tweak prices, costs, and investment timing until you land on the model that gives you the best shot at success with the capital you've got (or the capital you're pretty sure you can raise).

Last, it's time to think about what you will (and won't) do for the money.

Step 2: Get Clear on What You Will—and Won't—Do Financially

It's a big step to finally know the capital needed to fund and sustain the business. But (there is always a but), inevitably, there are going to be moments when you come face-to-face with a new opportunity that wasn't in your business plan and requires serious cash.

Early on at Clermont, we were bringing in clients, and the increasing workload was putting serious strain on our skeleton crew. So, naturally, we started the process of hiring a junior person to help balance the load. Now, before we dive in, remember how we told you we've stepped in it more times than we'd like to admit? Well, this one still haunts Victoria. Everything was cruising along. We were scrolling through LinkedIn, setting up interviews, and eventually found an amazing candidate. We extended the offer, and he accepted. The only catch? We didn't have the revenue to back up the hire. Oh right, we'd been running in the red for months. This was way early in the game. Beth had just joined the firm from her legally enforced garden leave, and Victoria had been out hustling for business, not the partner charged with keeping an eye on the financials. She had zero visibility into our cash flow or, more accurately, lack thereof. The (ex) partner managing the finances had never even made a budget (shame on us for not insisting on one); vendors were getting paid well ahead of due dates, which was draining our cash; and there was no reporting system to sound the alarm that our expenses were outpacing revenue at twice the speed.

You can probably guess where this is going. We had to rescind the offer. Then, we had to make some brutal decisions, including slashing our own salaries. The financial hit was tough, but pulling the rug out from under this bright-eyed, 20-something kid was nothing short of soul crushing. The debacle eventually led to a buyout of the other partners, leaving the two of us to carry the torch on our own. And, most importantly, it came with a non-negotiable rule: never operate in the red again. Ever. If we had to pick the most important Power Move in this book, establishing your own non-negotiable financial rules of engagement would definitely be at the top of our short list. It might seem counterintuitive given the "bet the farm" mindset that we, and all entrepreneurs, need to have. But exercising discipline around finances on a day-to-day basis is what's going to prevent impulse buying and set you up to really go for it when the timing is right.

A quick hit list to consider. How much do you want to keep in cash: just enough to scrape by for a month or a cushy three-month runway so you can sleep at night? How comfortable are you with debt? Would you trade a chunk of equity for faster growth, or does that feel like selling the family treasures? And what are your personal finance non-negotiables—the guidelines that quietly (or loudly) shape how you'll make money decisions in the business? Bottom line: Talk it through—with yourself, your partner, your Kitchen Cabinet members, or the person who knows you best. Then write it down, lock it in, and move forward.

Beth was very affected by what she saw early in her career. She watched smart people drive their businesses straight into financial disaster. It wasn't always bad ideas that wrecked them; it was usually poor timing. Some expanded too fast, hiring like crazy or signing big leases ahead of their "explosive growth." Others put too much faith in a few big clients, only to get burned when one stopped paying. Beth's ex-husband learned that lesson the hard way. His revenue was tied to just a few clients, and when one walked, the business spiraled fast. These experiences didn't stop Beth from wanting to take big risks. But it did make her much more open to following Victoria's annoyingly sensible plan B.

Don't know where to start? Take a look at our non-negotiables—the financial rules we lived and died by. And still do.

- **Lock down your reserves.** We keep at least two months of operating expenses in the bank, no exceptions. To avoid temptation, we strip it from the cash portion of our balance sheet. Out of sight, out of mind.
- **If we can't fund it, we don't do it.** In the early days, we refused to take on debt for new hires or big expenses. Instead, we cut our salaries or distributions first. If our personal take hits zero, hiring stops. No exceptions. As we grew and gained access to more capital, this rule evolved, but the core principle remained: never outpace your financial reality. If you aren't sure you can afford it, build a model that says you can or don't do it.
- **Be collectors first, business owners second.** Without cash flow, there is no business. So getting paid on time needs to be a non-negotiable you are laser focused on daily or weekly. If you have a business that can work by collecting before you deliver, great. If your business is like our consulting one and you can't even bill until weeks after the service is provided, efficient collections become your key to survival. For starters, we almost always locked in net-30 terms with clients, meaning they had 30 days to pay. On the other hand, we encouraged our vendors to accept net-45 payment terms, which provided us with a rolling 15-day buffer between incoming revenue and outgoing expenses. And when our clients went past that 30-day mark, we started (nicely) hounding them. We made sure the invoice wasn't stuck in limbo for some odd reason—the amount didn't match the purchase order was a big one—or that classic corporate excuse that the approving person was on vacation and it never got rerouted to them on their return.

This relentless focus on cash flow wasn't just smart—it was survival. Remember when we told you about that story of the offer we had to rescind? That was because we weren't managing our cash flow properly. We had the revenue, but it wasn't coming in fast enough to cover our growing costs. We never made that mistake again.

- **Match expenses to more predictable revenue.** Clermont's recurring revenue kept our cash flow steady, while the project work was lumpy and harder to predict. To hit our overall revenue targets, we needed both, but we couldn't afford to hire or ramp up expenses based on project revenue that wasn't guaranteed. So we built our expense structure around the recurring revenue. That way, profitability stayed consistent, whether or not a big project landed that month. (Yes, we did make an exception to fund a potentially high-growth opportunity, but we knew exactly what we were getting into and had contingency plans if it went sideways.)
- **No debt made the cut without passing our two-test rule.** Banks were not banging down our doors to lend us money when we first started, but by the end of the second year, we got our first $100,000 credit line. What we drew on the line, it got paid back quickly. And since then, we allow ourselves to borrow only if an expense meets two strict criteria: (1) it must be an investment, not a crutch, and (2) we must personally be able to cover it if things go south. No exceptions.

With your own version of money boundaries in place, you'll know exactly where you stand—what you'll spend, what's off-limits, and how to run your business without blowing the budget or your sanity. Now, it's time to get out there and get investing in your future, right?

Wrong. Timing is everything.

Step 3: The Right Opportunity Is Worth the Wait

At this point, you know how much money you need and where your financial boundaries are. You're probably itching to dive in and start moving toward launch. But you will likely need to wait. And wait some more, until that golden opportunity finally appears. We've learned the hard way (more than once) that it's all about timing. Even the best idea will flop if the market isn't ready, if your business isn't ready, or if your gut tells you it's not the right opportunity.

Waiting for the perfect moment to launch is a little like waiting for your toddler to put on their own shoes. Sure, in theory, it could happen, but in reality, you're probably going to be late for preschool. Being too early for a party also comes with its own special brand of embarrassment and pain. The same applies to being too early with a business idea.

We launched our ESG segment a solid 18 months too early, only to realize our target buyers weren't ready. The trend we were betting on? Barely a blip on the C-suite radar. Sure, it was starting to pop up in their newsfeeds, but honestly, most of them were still trying to figure out what "ESG" even stood for. More importantly, they had to wrap their heads around the steep price tag. Even though these execs nodded along and said all the right things—"Great concept" and "So important"—it was clearly not important enough to them to fit into their annual budgets. . .yet. And as all of you in corporate America know: no line item, no money. Instead, we got a lot of polite interest and vague promises about maybe, possibly, next year. Our big idea was DOA, at least for that round.

Thank God we had our non-negotiables in place. Our core investor relations business was chugging along, bringing in enough cash to keep the lights on and the kids in soccer cleats. So we doubled down on building product 2.0, realizing it needed a software component in addition to the services side. Of course, we were still pulling 100-hour weeks, juggling revenue from the legacy business while building a scrappy new one from the ground up. (Oh—and parenting. Always parenting. Like Victoria taking a strategy call from the parking lot of her kids' elementary school before the third-graders' pumpkin walk or Beth running to catch her daughter's volleyball game the moment the CEO signed off on the final press release.) Exhaustion doesn't even cover it. But without the cash flow from the core business, we couldn't have funded software development, and the ESG advisory would have been a pipe dream.

In our case, the market wasn't ready. But in many others, the market is ready; you're just not quite ready to meet it. If you don't have the bandwidth to go all in on a new idea, it's probably not going to work. So take on only what you can realistically handle between school pickups and sanity breaks, and whatever you do, give it your full attention. Half-built businesses rarely go the distance.

One of our former colleagues is in the healthy snack business and could teach a master class in this. She was absolutely obsessed with perfecting her ingredients, spending almost one year getting the right balance of protein with healthy additives, making sure they were shelf-stable, and then upgrading her packaging until it looked like it belonged on the top shelf of a luxury grocery store. Meanwhile, she steadily built her brand on social media, growing her loyal following one at a time. And then, like a scene straight out of a McKinsey case study, one of those followers came through with an offer to stock her snacks in a niche high-end grocery store. They sold out immediately.

At the same time, she was busy pulling off another major achievement: giving birth to the world's cutest baby. A few weeks into her maternity leave, the industry's biggest expo was happening—across the country. She was torn; should she go, despite the personal juggle and the fact that her newest flavor wasn't ready? Would it hurt her brand to show up with only one product? In the end, she made the tough call to sit this one out, staying local and focusing on making a major splash at next year's show instead. In our view, that's a bold move—confidence in her brand, trust in her product, and the kind of discipline that pays off big time.

At Clermont, Beth was always the one itching to scale at lightning speed mostly because, in her somewhat deluded mind, the business was already much bigger than it was. There was a constant tug-of-war over hiring heavy hitters to help scale even faster. Victoria, especially in the early days, worried these hires would be too expensive or that their personal brands would overshadow the one we were still building. We'd seen it before—a small competitor proudly announcing their flashy new exec with a big press release and a media blitz, only for that same exec to quietly exit within the year. Ultimately, we let our financials make the call; we'd hire only if it didn't break our non-negotiable rule (expenses had to be covered by recurring revenue). The moment the numbers worked, we pulled the trigger.

The second rule of waiting for the right opportunity is to never, ever go against your gut. We got this lesson early on when we tried to fast-track our entry into a higher margin slice of our core business market with a small acquisition. After researching and culling huge target lists down to one firm that was small enough that we could afford it but big enough to have a few marquis clients we thought we desperately needed, we were ready to make our move. Beth sent out an introductory email, and to our delight, there was interest. Before long, we had set up a meeting in New York. It was the start of an exciting new chapter for us, or so we thought.

After our initial set of meetings, we started to have that familiar flutter in our stomach—the kind you get when you're standing at the top of a roller coaster, not quite sure if you're about to scream with excitement or puke from nerves. Two things kept nagging at us. First, all of their employees were remote (this was pre-COVID, so it was an anomaly) and didn't seem too connected to each other. (Think of a world of remote work with no Zoom or Teams.) Basically, everyone was living in their own little work island, and the vibe was more "stranded in a desert" than "team retreat." Additionally, more than 30 percent of their revenue came from a single massive private equity firm. The CEO had all the right answers to our probing questions, but we both couldn't shake the feeling that something wasn't right. We walked away, second-guessing ourselves for months. Less than a year later, that private equity giant—the one that accounted for a third of their revenue—cut ties completely. Crisis (just barely) averted.

Near misses like this won't be a one-time thing. You'll face these turning points until you sell the business or ride off into retirement. And if you're wired for growth like we are, expect plenty of come-to-Jesus debates over how to spend valuable capital. (They're a lot easier when you've got clear financial rules of engagement.) What those crossroads look like will depend on your company's size and whatever chaos your industry is serving up, but one thing's guaranteed: the tough calls never stop.

Trusting our gut wasn't just reserved for big moves like acquisitions. Sometimes it was about taking on a huge new customer. Sponsoring a major conference. Or investing in a high-end product engineer to help us fine-tune our software offering. When these opportunities arose, we always wanted to jump in with both feet. But sometimes, something just felt off. A few red flags? Not being able to serve the new client without taking on key hires, and the client only willing to sign a short-term contract. Or the price tag for the massive conference sponsorship opportunity is not exactly jibing with the top target attendees. Or the product engineer who came highly recommended but keeps delaying the project kickoff meeting.

The point is to look for the red flags. They might be glaringly obvious or just show up as a nagging feeling in your gut. Either way, be willing to take a pause when you notice them.

When something doesn't feel right, it usually isn't. Or when something seems too good to be true, it usually is. But if you're not quite ready to miss a golden opportunity on instinct alone, call in the reserves. Remember Power Move #2? That's when you built your Kitchen Cabinet, and this is exactly why you did it. Unlike you, your Kitchen Cabinet isn't knee-deep in the emotional weeds, so they can see the bigger picture. Bring them in, lay it all out, and listen. They just might save you from a multimillion-dollar mistake.

While letting an exciting opportunity pass you by is never easy, take heart. As impetuous as we have both been known to be, when we passed on an opportunity, it was usually to make space for something even better. So take your time with that big swing. A perfect fastball, straight down the middle, is surely coming your way.

Step 4: Swing Big at the Right Time

On Monday, you walked away from what seemed like a surefire opportunity to catapult your business. Almost. Except, it wasn't the right timing. Or the right person. Or the right feature. Or it was just too expensive. You go home to wallow in it for a bit and read yet *another* book about some other entrepreneur making it big. Then, on Tuesday, the opportunity of a lifetime lands on your desk, right next to last night's empty pint of Ben & Jerry's Phish Food. This time, it truly is perfect.

As entrepreneurs, we must be mentally prepared not just to recognize the golden opportunity when it arises but to seize it without hesitation. If we doubt ourselves or overthink it, a competitor will swoop in, and we'll miss our shot. So how do we control our nerves and avoid second-guessing? We stick to the facts and make decisions with a clear, clinical mindset. But (once again) we also know to trust our gut instincts.

Here are four solid indicators that the opportunity is truly right for you:

1. The investment directly serves one of the strongest growth areas in your TAM.
2. The opportunity seamlessly aligns with your strategic plan to grow the business.
3. You have a real-world example of a similar investment working, whether in your own industry or one you follow closely.
4. Your gut says yes. (Notice how this one is fourth? That's because it has to pass the other tests first.)

The first holy-crap-this-will-change-everything decision we made was figuring out how to structure and price our new service offering. Our first investor relations clients were legacy accounts we brought over from our old firm, and their pricing was low. To convince them to take a chance on our shiny new (and totally unproven) venture, we had to offer a discount. Such a big discount that it became impossible to hit our 30 percent profit margin goal. But this margin was a non-negotiable if we wanted to make real money and scale. So we had no choice but to increase our prices for non-legacy clients. Charge too much and the clients might not bite. Charge too little and we'd be working ourselves into the ground with nothing to show for it. The sweet spot wasn't just about numbers. It was about staying in business.

Victoria, fully embracing her "balls to the wall" life mantra, was all for going high. Beth, who could be surprisingly conservative with pricing decisions, was firmly in the let's-not-scare-them-off camp. To settle the debate, we went back to our TAM research. There were only about 2,000 publicly held companies in our target market, and if we secured 10 percent, our actual addressable market would be approximately 200 accounts. Running the numbers again, it became clear—we couldn't hit our financial goals charging $90,000 per client annually. We had to aim for closer to $150,000. Now we had to validate whether the market would actually pay for it. What were competitors charging? We found that about a third were already operating in that higher price range. That gave us confidence there was room for us, so we went for it.

Did we hit $150,000 across the board? Not quite. But we got damn close—about 50 percent higher than where we would have been if we'd played it safe. It completely changed our margins, our trajectory, and, honestly, the entire game for Clermont. A win by every measure. (Although, full disclosure, sending out that first proposal with the new price tag was a total nail-biter.)

The other time we decided to swing for the fences was when we expanded into ESG, our ultimate growth engine. We understood part of the equation but didn't consider ourselves anywhere close to experts in the area. Competing in this space would mean serious investments in both talent and software. We could technically self-fund it, but just barely. The idea of adding a potentially high-margin, high-growth offering with very few competitors, however, was too attractive to ignore. And then, out of nowhere, the regulatory gods finally delivered—sweeping new disclosure rules were headed straight for public companies—the very thing we'd been warning about, pitching around, and watching get dismissed or delayed by would-be clients. Suddenly, what had been a "nice to have" became a regulatory fire drill.

So, again, we went for it. Because this was way out of our comfort zone, we gut-checked with everyone: our Kitchen Cabinet, our employees, lawyers, consultants, and any academics willing to talk to us to make sure our read of the regulatory tea leaves was right. The consensus was that we were on to something, but the timing was going to be the wildcard. We pulled the trigger anyway. And after plenty of trial, error, and what-the-hell-are-we-doing moments, it turned out to be the secret sauce that added revenue and growth for Clermont. And, in the long run, it was the game changer on how much buyers were willing to pay for us when we put a "For Sale" sign up a few years later.

The same rule applies when hunting for your growth opportunities.

If you want to start small, consider marketing partnerships with slightly bigger companies that align well with your brand. Or take a calculated risk on a hire—whether in sales, product, or finance—that pushes you just outside your comfort zone but has the potential to boost revenue or margins within a few months. (We can always get behind smart marketing or sales investments because these functions are what fuel every business.) Or maybe it's a new product that feels like a natural extension of what you already offer but requires a new hire, a manufacturing partner, or a strategic partnership to bring it to life.

The key? Constantly pushing for the investment that will grow your top line within 12 months, even if it's slightly (or highly) disruptive to your business. Ignore this rule at your peril. Starving your company of growth investment at best will keep you growing at the same pace you are today. But breaking out of your comfort zone can be exactly what you need to fast-track your goal of financial freedom.

Step 5: Share the Field, Win the Game

Even though we're taught to share, let's be honest, sometimes we just don't want to. We want to have our cake and eat it too. A great growth opportunity comes along, and if we've got the cash flow to fund it ourselves, we claim the whole slice. But if we don't, we might have to give away a few slices. In the business world, "sharing" usually means giving up some ownership (equity) to the investor willing to take the risk (loss of capital) that it might not work out.

Many business models will fail (quickly) or flounder (slowly) without some level of investment capital. This is particularly true for businesses operating in a highly competitive environment in which companies constantly innovate and introduce new products and services to gain an edge. These businesses simply won't work without a slug of capital investment from time to time. Your industry might not be this competitive, but there could be a golden moment when an investment can help you gain a toehold in an area poised for growth. Chances are you'll need capital for that as well.

How do you know you are in that moment? Spotting it ahead of time is pretty tough—easier than predicting where the next hurricane is going to hit but way harder than just shaking your Magic 8 Ball. Unfortunately, it can be painfully obvious in hindsight. There are a couple of rules to help you avoid this all-too-common, often fatal mistake. The first and most important one is to be realistic about your investment needs early on. It's helpful to put your business idea into one of the following three buckets before deciding on whether outside investment is a good idea. Sound familiar? It should if you are still musing about your Mompreneur Mayhem Matrix from Chapter 3.

- **Zero investment, slow scaling.** You have decided to white-knuckle, err, bootstrap, your business. This can work well in either a huge marketplace with lots of sellers and low switching costs or a small niche marketplace where your unique expertise will win the day. If your business plan is realistic about the limited amount of marketing and/or product feature investments you will be able to make and still attract customers, you should be fine without a huge investment. Our advice? Focus on a great core product, amazing customer service, and/or a brilliant delivery system for a hard-to-access product. These will help you, month after month, quarter after quarter, build a brand with loyal customers and recurring revenues. Just make sure you are not trying to compete in a fast-changing marketplace where better-funded competitors can eat your lunch in a sales battle.

- **Smallish investment at launch, ongoing investment from cash flow.** Most breadwinning mamas feel safer with businesses that fall into this category. While start-up costs can be high, revenues come faster, and your business can hit break-even pretty quickly. With careful budgeting, you can use cash flow to make limited future investments. Professional services firms (think marketing, content creation, consulting, PR) fit this model well with limited R&D and inventory investment needs. These companies can slowly chip away clients from competitors or in slow-moving industries with small personal or business loans. We know a lot about these types of businesses. —We started two of them!
- **Unicorns with significant investments needed to scale—and keep scaling.** These businesses are few and far between. If you have one, don't hesitate to get an outside investor. (Who are we kidding? If you have a great idea, they are likely at your doorstep already.) These businesses require substantial investment capital to compete effectively. And they need it fast. Think breakthrough new products or the creation of a completely new market. In these scenarios, marketing budgets push seven figures just to launch. If you have this business, hold on tight!

If you fall into business bucket two—or you're in bucket one but want to speed things up—outside investors might be part of the equation for scaling. We've seen plenty of aspiring female founders who either didn't want or didn't think they'd ever need an investor ultimately end up backed into a corner with a terrible choice to make: forgo an amazing opportunity or accept highly dilutive last-minute capital from shark investors to avoid going out of business.

Opportunities are often fleeting, and acting swiftly can be the difference between triumph and a flatlined business. We love how Nasty Gal's Sophia Amaruso puts it: "If it's a good idea and it gets you excited, try it. And if it bursts into flames? That's going to be one hell of a story." It's a razor-thin line between jumping at growth opportunities your business isn't quite ready for and sitting back, waiting for the perfect pitch to land. And moms? That golden opportunity always seems to show up at the worst possible moment, usually when your kid needs you most or when a family member or close friend is in crisis, and you know you want to step up and be there for them.

Beth will never forget watching Victoria pull double duty: working a full day, leaving at 4 p.m. to sit at her mom's hospital bedside, heading home to tuck in her kids, and then logging back on for hours to keep the business on track. There's no caregiver you can hire to dig you out of that kind of grind. That takes grit, the kind only moms seem to carry in spades.

If you have thought about it deeply, though, and you are ready for the wild ride of growth, take the leap. Make sure your safety and sanity nets are in place—your non-negotiables, a tight Kitchen Cabinet, and a few helpful advisors sprinkled in to weigh in on whether you should hit the brakes or floor it. Then buckle up, we guarantee it's going to be a wild ride.

■ ■ ■

Gut Check

Are My Head (and Wallet) Right?

- ☐ What am I risking with the current state of my business? And what do I hope to gain? *(If you don't know exactly what you're risking—and what you stand to gain—you'll make emotional decisions instead of strategic ones. Clarity is what separates gutsy calls from costly mistakes.)*
- ☐ In what areas of the business am I being overly conservative with money out of fear—and where am I playing fast and loose in the name of growth? *(You can't play it safe and scale fast. But blowing money on shiny objects without discipline is the quickest way to end up back at your day job.)*
- ☐ What are my personal money non-negotiables? Do they align with my business goals? *(If you haven't documented your personal financial boundaries, stop and do it now. Disconnects from the realities of bootstrapping don't just slow growth. They fast-track burnout and drive poor decision-making.)*
- ☐ What's the one big money move I'm avoiding because it feels scary but could unlock real growth? *(The only response to fear in business is better data. What information could you gather to get more comfortable or rule out the next potential growth opportunity?)*
- ☐ Would I take outside capital if it meant giving up equity—but gaining real scale? *(Are you ready to give up some entrepreneurial independence to scale faster? What facts do you need to know if this is the moment to take a smaller slice of a bigger pie?)*

CHAPTER 7

Power Move #4: Start Before You Are Ready

We were on fire. It was right before the world slammed shut from COVID and once again, we'd committed to a one-day turn-around from Chicago to LA to meet a major public company CFO. His board was breathing down his neck for an ESG strategy, not because they suddenly found religion on ESG but because their biggest investors were demanding proof there would be no surprises that would tank their stock price, like a trace toxic chemical being used in their kid's snack products or an HR scandal splashed across the local paper.

The poor guy was drowning in printouts from his well-meaning summer interns—hundreds of examples of other companies' disclosures that didn't really apply to his business—while clutching a dense, compliance-laden set of talking points from his overpriced New York lawyer. The suggested language?

> *As of the date of this statement, the Company is not aware of any material violations related to environmental, social, or governance (ESG) matters and remains in compliance with all applicable laws and industry standards to its knowledge.*

It was a legal mouthful that would land like a lead balloon and might even make investors wonder if there was something to worry about. He knew that statement wouldn't cut it. They needed more.

We threw out every recommendation we could think of while he seemed to be getting more confused by the minute. Sweating the close, we braced for the inevitable blowoff: "Okay, send me some references." Instead, he leaned back and said, "Alright. How much is this going to cost me?"

By all accounts, this should have been the easiest question of the meeting. The moment we had been waiting and hoping for. The prospect had finally moved from "possible" to "definitely maybe" (or, if the stars aligned, "yes"). We were *that close* to landing our first ESG client for Clermont Partners!

And yet—dead silence.

Neither of us answered. We just stared at each other, frozen, waiting for the other one to answer. He repeated the question. Beth, channeling some deep, primal sales instinct, blurted out, "$75,000." As she scrambled to justify that completely made-up number, he cut her off.

"Okay, send me the contract."

Waiting for the car back to LAX, we looked at each other, trying—and failing—to hide the grins that were emerging. We did the usual phone triage—juggling a sick nanny, a school project forgotten at home, and Beth's mom's horrifying discovery that the kids were shoving uneaten broccoli and meatloaf dinner bits under the kitchen chair cushions. There was one more call to a frantic team trying to keep a runaway project on track, and then, after one glorious second of silence, came the inevitable "How the hell are we going to do this?"

Yes, we had a multimillion-dollar business and had priced and closed hundreds of deals in the past few years. But we'd never sold this service before and felt like total impostors. And we kind of were. Up until this moment, our offering was conceptual, and we had zero real-world execution.

The first thing we did was call in our brand-new head of ESG, who, minor detail, hadn't even started her job yet. "Hey, congrats on the new role! By the way, we've already sold your first project." To her credit, she jumped in before her official start date, and somehow, we pulled it off.

In fact, we delivered that service—and a whole lot more like it—in the years that followed. But in that moment, things were pretty dicey. Theoretically, we always knew there had to be a first sale. A first client. So why not now? We knew we were hovering somewhere between "work in progress" and "the next big thing." And we also knew we were burning daylight while our competitors were rumored to be hiring up all the available talent so they could deliver similar offerings. We had to get comfortable putting our service out there even when the features, pricing, and go-to-market strategy were, at best, a rough draft, not a final masterpiece. It was uncomfortable. We were terrified of someone finding out that our experience in the field was basically born of Beth's reading on the subject and talking up any expert in the field who had five minutes for her. Oh yeah, and what turned out to be one *very* brilliant hire.

This kind of feeling is inevitable as an entrepreneur. There will always be plenty of remaining i's to dot and t's to cross when introducing a new product.

If you're a type A perfectionist, pre-launch is going to be your personal nightmare, because the name of the game is to get it out there, learn from feedback, and brace yourself to lose some money (or dignity) in the process. Starting before you're ready will always be nerve-racking, but it's also the only way to push your business toward that seven-figure horizon.

So, with that in mind, let's take a look at the steps in this nail-biter of a Power Move.

Power Move #4: Start Before You Are Ready

1. **Undercook your first product.** While you are still perfecting your masterpiece, putting it out there for the world to critique can feel completely terrifying. Launching a not-quite-finished product makes most would-be female founders twitchy, but the truth is, almost every new business starts out with a little "softness in the middle."
2. **Swipe right on the ideal target audience.** More than half of product launches belly flop straight out of the gate, usually because they're aimed at the wrong crowd. In our experience, founders often tumble into the "everyone" trap.
3. **Keep calm and carry on with customer feedback.** The truth is that we entrepreneurs can be a bit delicate when it comes to feedback. The trick is finding that sweet spot and learning to listen. It's not about taking every comment as gospel; it's about spotting patterns that can sharpen your idea and your pitch.
4. **Accept that the price won't be right, at least not yet.** You've got a product that's caught the eye of a select group of customers and a few features they're slowly finding they can't live without. How much are they ready to shell out for it?
5. **Chase good enough, not perfection.** Most of us are perfectionists. But perfection really is the enemy of progress. Don't channel Marie Kondo; channel MacGyver. Be ready to fix what's not working, get crafty, and move fast.

Step 1: Undercook Your First Product

Let's call a spade a spade—95 percent of new products fail.[1] Yours, in its first iteration, probably will, too. Sound harsh? It's meant to. The reality is that your first product or service is bound to be a bit messy. You'll be figuring out what you're actually selling while simultaneously building the delivery system, crafting buyer personas, and hunting down the people most likely to give it a try. It's where you channel your inner Entrepreneur Like a Mother: cooking dinner, defusing your nine-year-old's playground drama, folding laundry, and firing off a client email, all at once. You do it daily at home—lunch money instead of the healthy chicken wrap you planned, half-checked homework, and the permission slip jammed in the backpack as your kid's walking up the bus steps—so why not bring that same magic to your business? Debuting an under-cooked product is a necessary evil. Would you rather have a product that's a bit rough around the edges but is already out there earning its keep or one that's being polished to perfection while quietly draining the corporate bank account?

We'll answer that question for you. You would rather have your product out in the wild. Why? It might be missing a crucial feature that you didn't initially think was a big deal, but your customers disagree. Or maybe the perfect buyer you initially envisioned isn't interested, while another one with deeper pockets can't get enough of it. Maybe a more established competitor swoops in with a similar product, forcing you to adapt on the fly. A "good enough" offering that can bring in feedback from actual, paying customers will give you insights you'd never unlock on your own. Ever.

So, instead of chasing perfection from the start and refining your idea in your lab or office or garage or whatever, you're going to build your minimum viable product (or MVP, for those of us with no time to spell it out)—a.k.a. the "good enough for now" version of your big idea. Think of this as your idea's first draft, not its final form. An MVP is the simplest version of a product or service that lets you test your core concept with real users *before* blowing a fortune on a full-scale launch. It's about launching with just enough features to attract early adopters, validate assumptions, and gather feedback—so you can tweak, pivot, or scrap it entirely before the budget runs dry.

Some of our favorite MVPs? The Airbnb founders tested their ground breaking concept by renting out their own apartment first. The Dropbox team? They didn't even build the product at first; they just made a simple explainer video to gauge interest. And Zappos founder Tony Hsieh started by listing shoes online and literally buying them from stores in real time as orders came in. Talk about testing the water before diving in.

For Clermont, our MVP began with a single PowerPoint slide, and (we couldn't make this up) it was a wagon wheel. It showcased our MVP "offering" (or at least what we thought public companies needed to start doing around sustainability). And we built it in a New York taxi on the way to a sales meeting. Now, the wagon wheel was actually a hub-and-spoke model depicting our firm as the central hub, connecting all the wild, unruly parts of a company's internal and external financial reporting on sustainability. The spokes? A set of chaotically gathered inputs and outputs of this data—none of which lived in the same place, most of which wasn't audited, and all of which was now being demanded by a disparate set of external audiences. It was, in Beth's words, the world's ugliest slide. The second it hit the boardroom screen, she winced, handed the clicker to Victoria and shut her eyes, waiting for the blank stares. It was busy and cluttered and couldn't feel less like it came from a company setting the pace for the industry. But somehow it did the job. It helped future clients see just how hard it was to gather this kind of intelligence and how wildly different audience segments wanted the same info served up in totally different ways. They realized this wasn't an inside job. They needed real experts. Like us. (Okay, eventual experts.)

Now it was time to promote the hell out of that MVP and get the word out in a big way. We hit the speaker circuit hard, enthusiastically talking up what we were still in the process of beginning to do for our ESG-keen corporate early adopters. (And yes, using that damn wagon wheel slide.) We gave enthusiastic TED-adjacent talks about all the shiny features of our solution and then circled back with small focus groups to find out which ones they wanted to use right now. We built a website packed with best practices (generously borrowed and fully credited to the companies that published them). We hosted webinars with extra-long Q&A sessions, not just to sound smart but to really listen and catch in-the-moment reactions to our consulting recommendations. It worked. By the time we officially launched, people paid attention when we spoke because they knew our advice was grounded in solid research.

Your approach might be different, depending on your offering, budget, and market timing. Consider any of the following as you take your own MVP out for a spin:

- **A small-scale pilot program.** If you're an exercise and wellness coach, think about running a short cohort—a few weeks of live Zooms or a couple of snappy Loom videos to get potential clients walking through an eating reset with you. If 10 people sign up, *voilà*, you've got the start of an MVP. When we were in the second stage of testing our sustainability software, we launched just a small sliver of the product. Clients could ask basic questions through the platform, but most were answered manually behind the scenes. The more questions we got, the more we learned about the hot topics that needed to be built into our second-gen product.

- **A basic website (or even just a landing page).** You've seen this type of landing page a million times: a single page full of questions and promises, meant to resonate with something you or your business has really been wrestling with, and at the bottom, a big red "Book a Free Discovery Call" button. If people click it, you're in business (literally). That's your MVP. When we launched, we spun a one-pager outlining what our software would do, kept a blog to nerd out on all things sustainability and offered beta tester spots—for free. People signed up. A lot of them. We didn't have a full product yet, but we had a website chock-full of good information and, even better, proof that people wanted it.
- **A product itself.** Yep, this one's the obvious MVP. You've got a prototype, a sample, a test run. Maybe it's edible, breakable, washable, or toddler-proof (ideally all four). You put it in people's hands for free or next to nothing and watch what happens. Do they come back for more? Beg for restocks? Ask if it comes in beige? Congrats, you've got something. MVP achieved, with crumbs, cracks, or chaos to prove it.

The point is to start with something, no matter how small. We guarantee you will keep adding and learning, and your MVP will be the thing that brings in all that helpful intelligence.

Be Ruthlessly Disciplined with Your Feature Set

It's fun to imagine every shiny feature your product might one day have—complete with all the bells, whistles, fireworks, and AI-generated holograms guaranteed to dazzle tens of millions of potential users. But to get to the MVP stage, you will likely need to ruthlessly cut 85 percent of your ideas from your original design or offering. File them away under "Future Plans" (which you may ultimately rename "Things to Laugh About Later"). To keep your laundry list of features in check, start with your competitive grid. What features do you absolutely need to deliver that perfect product (or at least a better mousetrap than your competitors)? And we mean one or two. That's it. These are features of your product or service that your customers will pay for because they address a pain point in a different or better way than whatever else is out there. Features that fall under "need to have," not "nice to have."

As you design and refine, always stay laser focused on your core value proposition—that one crisp, compelling reason someone should pick you over the other dozen tabs open in their browser. Maybe it's a better product, lightning-fast delivery, or a process so simple it feels like magic. Whatever it is, it needs to make your customer's life easier. And it must be something you can describe in a single, concise sentence.

Your value prop should solve a specific problem for a specific audience, and make it very obvious that your way is the upgrade. Sometimes it's a long-awaited fix. Other times, it's a quick Band-Aid for a curveball they never saw coming, at least until you can swoop in with the full solution. That's where we found our golden ticket.

Remember that first sale we opened the chapter with? Put that specifically in the "quick Band-Aid" category. The company's investors, think banker types in wingtips, had started demanding public disclosures on things like toxic chemicals used in manufacturing, supply chain practices, and ethical sourcing. One of their competitors had just been caught using a cheaper supplier with notoriously poor lab sterility standards. And before you start thinking these investors suddenly turned into tree huggers, the reality was their clients (the people who had given them money to manage) were starting to ask tough questions about the safety of certain product inputs and the potential for recalls. The last thing they wanted were bad headlines and a nosediving stock price.

We were way ahead of our anxious CFO because we had been talking to those same Brooks Brothers–wearing dudes who we made it our business to interview every chance we got. Sustainability reporting was quickly being added to the long list of mandatory corporate disclosures investors expected and CFOs had to deliver. At the same time, most public companies didn't have the internal tools to measure, track, audit, or share any of this information. That's where we stepped in with two options. One was low cost: license our software and handle the disclosures in-house. The other was premium: hire us to manage the entire process for you.

But we didn't start with two products. We started with one, clunky version. This first offering was a painfully manual, high-touch service hand-curated by our consultants. (It was pre-AI, mind you.) It didn't take long to realize we could streamline everything by building a centralized database and layering in automation. Same quality output but delivered in a fraction of the time. We traded the manual grind for a turbocharged shortcut and never looked back.

Once the first offering started getting traction, Beth wanted to kick it into overdrive with new features, bold expansion, the works. Thankfully, Victoria stepped in with the voice of reason: "Let's make sure this actually works first." But the MVP stuck the landing.

Your debut product could be a whole lot more fun (and way less headache inducing) than ours—maybe a must-have fashion piece, a genius event app to keep your friends in the loop, or a smarter way to track the latest workout fads. It could also be a lot smarter than ours—say a high-end biotech app aimed at early detection of cancer. Either way, make sure every single product or service feature ties directly to your core value proposition. And then get ready to listen with both ears if you hear anyone complain that your offering is messy, confusing, or overly complex. And act on that intel. Stat.

Get Ready to Take More than One Swing at Success

You might think you won't need a version two (or three, or four) of your MVP. We sure didn't. We were convinced we had the perfect ESG service right out of the gate and fully expected buyers to trample each other just to get to it. And then reality hit. Hard. That first consulting offering we sold? We lost our shirts on it. Worse, the client used only about 30 percent of the valuable insights we painstakingly put together. But the real gut punch was when he casually said, "Oh, I haven't even read the back half of your report; I got everything I needed in the first ten pages." Ouch. Knowing how much blood, sweat, tears, and cash went into that work, we wished we'd had that feedback before pouring our souls into an over-engineered, underappreciated masterpiece.

Our software product journey was similar. We, once again, didn't hit the mark with our customers. Our product hit the market early, and its first iteration was missing a critical feature: a reporting component. We'd packed it with features focused on background, education, and top-tier disclosures, aiming to be the "Wikipedia of ESG." Turns out, not everyone shared Beth's enthusiasm for deep data dives. Most users weren't looking to nerd out; they just wanted to hit a button and get a "good enough" report.

Unfortunately, that report-generating feature wasn't baked into our first-gen tool. We ended up manually creating reports, bleeding money with every new purchase. We retooled, built a better (and simpler) software product, and formed partnerships to speed up data acquisition. When we relaunched, we were still early enough to have a leg up on competitors (though not as much as we'd hoped), but now we had an offering that actually met users where they were in their sustainability journeys.

We learned very quickly to check our egos at the door. We also learned to stay focused on creating must-have product and service features and supporting them with a very targeted marketing strategy. Victoria has a saying borrowed from her brother's perfectly timed high school wisdom to make her feel better after a test gone wrong: "Cs get degrees." She pulled it out again during beta testing. A solid C+ from testers? That was a win. It meant people liked it enough to use it. It wasn't perfect, but it was progress. And that's exactly what we needed. From there, we just kept tweaking it to go from a C+ to a B–, then a B+, and so on. We were lucky enough to have a little budget to run focus groups with early users, which gave us the chance to pitch new features and let customers vote useless features off the island. (Does it surprise you that these were the very features we thought would knock the product out of the park?)

Think of the MVP like sending your kid off to kindergarten for the first time: nerve-racking, a little messy, and full of unexpected surprises. Things will go wrong. But you'll be there to handle the first-day hiccups, make adjustments, and send them back out even stronger the next day. (And hey, at least your product won't come home with glitter glue in their hair.)

Step 2: Swipe Right on the Ideal Target Audience

Remember that terrifying stat about 95 percent of new products failing? We've got another. More than half of product launches belly flop straight out of the gate because they're aimed at the wrong crowd.[2] In our experience, founders often tumble into the "everyone" trap. They're convinced their product is so good, the masses—yes, even the folks blissfully unaware they have a problem—will come running. They won't. Instead, the fastest path to sales is to start with the people who already know they need what you're offering. Trying to educate an audience about a problem they don't feel yet is a tough way to launch a blockbuster. Sell it to the guy who's already Googling solutions at 2 a.m.

We get it. From the entrepreneur's perspective, the goal is simple: don't leave money on the table or a single stone unturned. But in the quest to make everyone happy, we end up making things murky. Suddenly, it's tough to validate whether the product actually solves a real problem for anyone in particular. If you're trying to capture too broad an audience with your offering, this problem becomes readily apparent when those who test it are lukewarm about it. (You need them to love it or hate it. Both types of feedback are helpful.) If you get that kind of feedback on your MVP, for the love of all things holy, do not take it as a sign to pile on more features just to please everyone. Instead, do the opposite. Narrow your audience and let them weigh in.

It's the same trap we fall into on a random day off from the grind, trying to entertain a five-year-old and a thirteen-year-old with the same activity. A trip to Sephora? Heaven for your preteen. But for your five-year-old? Pure torture. Cue the meltdown. Or worse, a chaotic game of tag through the aisles. The lesson? Don't aim to please the crowd; go deep with one.

If you don't believe us, believe Vilfredo Pareto, an old-school Italian economist who accidentally became a business school legend. The guy's principle is taught in Ivy League classrooms and probably scribbled on the back of every start-up napkin business plan.

Eighty percent of your traction will come from 20 percent of your audience. The good old 80/20 rule. Win the smaller segment. They're your early adopters, your power users, the weak but discernible voices in the wilderness.

More than half of product launches belly flop straight out of the gate because they're aimed at the wrong crowd.

With Clermont's new ESG service offering, we first went to buyers within public companies that we knew best: CEOs, CFOs, and investor relations officers. Folks we'd known from back in the Ashton days and continued to work with through Clermont's early years. Many knew us and the type of service we provided, and the ones who trusted our counsel knew that when we flagged an emerging topic, it was usually worth paying attention. The problem? In the early days of ESG, those people weren't the buyers. In fact, they weren't interested because it was a cost and a real irritation to provide more public data on any topic. They kept passing us off to the general counsel (GC) who was left holding the sustainability hot potato. We spun our wheels for a while, getting relatively useless feedback from the audience we knew instead of finding ways to tap into the audience we didn't know but actually needed, the GC.

Train yourself to zero in on the insights that align with your product's core value and tune out the rest as noise. Sometimes, the feedback is aspirational—customers want you just a little closer to solving their problem. Other times, they love what you've built but can't help day-dreaming about a few of the sparkly bells and whistles your competitors are showing off. Either way, don't dismiss it. They are handing you a product road map.

Maybe it's a missing feature, clearer instructions, better packaging—whatever it is, follow the trail. Then circle back to your audience. Ask again. Tweak again. Rinse and repeat. Are you seeing the pattern here? Welcome to product-market fit, one iteration at a time. When we tested our ESG software, it became clear that our product wasn't enough for the GC's "doer"—the young lawyer actually responsible for delivering the lion's share of the work. Most were starting with a blank page and had very little familiarity with the various types of sustainability disclosures or the standards they were expected to follow. They didn't just need a tool but guidance, context, and a clear starting point. They clearly were not our low-end software buyer; instead we had to figure out a way to pivot them to our high-touch consulting product. This helped us realize we needed two distinct marketing messages so that potential buyers could see the price and use case differences between our software and our consulting services. Our software had to speak directly to scrappy internal teams with lean budgets and little need for bells, whistles, or customization. Meanwhile, our consulting services needed to woo the companies looking for a full-on outsourced brain trust—think strategy, support, and maybe a little hand-holding.

With this understanding of our two distinct audiences and armed with our two shiny new messages, we headed back out to the market in search of early adopters. Remember that, at the time of launch, most corporates were treating ESG as a "yeah, we'll get to that. . . eventually" kind of issue. We needed to find first movers who couldn't afford to kick the can down the road. That meant targeting companies where ESG actually moved the needle. Think e.l.f. Cosmetics and their "we-don't-test-on-puppies" strategy. It wasn't just values driven; it sold more product. Or the, ahem, less virtuous examples, like companies that had previously found themselves in hot water for polluting, say, a river where kids play. Suddenly, ESG wasn't optional; it was PR rehab.

That intel wasn't too hard to find. We quickly had gathered a pretty hefty list of these "ESG-aware" companies. Only then did we tap into our network, leveraging LinkedIn for some detective work to see who in our network had connections with our list of "ESG-awares." Lucky for us, the GC's desk was already overflowing, they generally had a decent consulting budget, and there was not a single other ESG expert in sight.

You probably won't need to endure the focus group gauntlet like we did. A simpler (and frankly, smarter) way to find your early believers? Build an online space—a community, some irresistible educational content, or just a low-friction way to connect—that draws in the folks already hunting for what you offer or, at the very least, gets them hooked the moment they stumble across it.

You might find your ideal users in online forums, Slack groups, Reddit threads, or LinkedIn and Facebook groups. These specialized communities can be real jackpots. Selling a new, ultra-light zombie tool blade (yes, that's a real product)? The 18,000-strong zombie-apocalypse preppers community might just be your dream audience. Got a genius fix for "yarn vomit" (yes, also a real term for tangled yarn)? The 11 million members of Ravelry's online knitting empire could be *very* interested in what you're untangling.

Once you find these groups, offer exclusive early access in exchange for feedback. Post about your group on LinkedIn, Twitter, or Instagram with behind-the-scenes updates, sneak peeks, or CTAs for testers. If you are one of the lucky unicorns out there who has a budget to work with, targeted ads on Facebook, LinkedIn, or Instagram can also be gold. Or keep it simple: set up a waitlist on your site or social media and use a referral system where testers can invite friends for perks.

You could also just go old school and find local, in-person networking groups that align with your industry or product and/or connect with other women founders on the same ride. You'd be surprised how many are willing to swap real feedback for real feedback. One of our favorite examples? That brilliant founder we mentioned earlier building a mini-muffin snack empire networked her way into a Kitchen Cabinet chock-full of consumer-packaging specialists with this strategy. Here's the irony: so many of us women entrepreneurs are introverted extroverts. (Cue Beth and Victoria sheepishly raising their hands.) The idea of getting out there, making connections, and talking to strangers is exhausting. But trust us, done strategically it can pay off.

Of course, working all day and then spending your kid's final waking hours at an evening networking event—hoping to meet someone who might help your business—only doubles (or triples) the stress for working moms. Beth remembers coming home well past bedtime, tiptoeing into each kid's room to kiss them goodnight while they slept. All except her number three. She was wide awake, waiting, asking why it took so long. What really broke Beth's heart? Learning years later that her daughter had been hiding her nightmares, just waiting for her to come home, because that's when she felt safe again.

Many of our aspiring mompreneur friends think competitors' customers make great focus group material. On paper, it sounds genius: target your rival's loyal fan base, swoop in with your shiny new product—maybe even at a lower price—and watch them jump ship. The reality? Not so much. We've found that introducing a new offering to customers who are already cozy with a competitor is a major uphill battle and may even prove detrimental to your launch. Customers who are loyal to your competitors will often share intel with those competitors. Brand loyalty is real, and asking someone to ditch a trusted vendor, navigate procurement red tape, and onboard a new solution (even a cheaper one) is often more trouble than it's worth—for them and for you.

There is one exception to this rule. If you're one of the rare few who have launched a product based on actual, verified customer frustration with existing offerings (think legit market research, not just a hunch or a few spicy tweets), then, by all means, ignore everything we just said and go for it. When buyers have been burned by clunky, overpriced, or overpromised products, they're often desperate for a better alternative. And when you show up with a solution that actually works? They don't just switch; they become your loudest cheerleaders, brand evangelists, and possibly your new best friends. Don't stress if the first audience you choose for your MVP testing doesn't quite hit the mark or if you cast your net too wide and end up with vague, unhelpful feedback. That's part of the game. The key is to treat it like an experiment, not a failure. Simply carve out a new, more specific target group for your MVP and run it again.

If you're using focus groups, don't just ask if they're the right fit, ask who in their world might be. You'd be surprised how often the right user is just one desk (or Slack message) away. If you're testing through a landing page or website, your best move is to play with the messaging, positioning, or offer and see what actually sticks. The good news is these tweaks are about as low-risk as it gets—just a few keystrokes, a little copy magic, and you can try again. You can also try what is called *A/B testing*, which is where you compare two versions of something—like a web page, email, ad, or product description—to see which one performs better.

The bottom line is you don't need to get it perfect; you just need to get it in front of the right people. Keep refining, keep testing, and stay close to the problem you're solving. The right audience is out there, and when your MVP clicks with them, you'll know.

Step 3: Keep Calm and Carry On with Customer Feedback

Don't think it was all smooth sailing the moment our target customers started showing interest in our ESG offering. Oh no. They had plenty to say about what they needed, and according to them, it wasn't what we were offering. (In our defense, a lot of it actually was in the offering; they just didn't know how to ask for it. And we hadn't quite mastered the art of translation yet.) It took weeks—okay, months—before they finally felt like what they were getting was closer to their expectations.

During that time, we got a crash course in the fine art of hearing and leveraging feedback. Listening without bias is (a) ridiculously hard and (b) completely nonnegotiable. Putting on your big-girl pants and tuning in—with an open mind and a finely tuned BS detector—to what your very first paying customers are saying is a must.

But it's not exactly a confidence boost. We entrepreneurs can be a bit delicate when it comes to feedback. We either spiral into people-pleasing mode or throw our hands up, muttering, "They just don't get us," and start feverishly searching for a different target audience who will. The trick is finding that sweet spot, where you're not bending to every opinion and adding features a mile a minute to placate them, yet you're not ignoring the golden nuggets of suggestions either.

Our approach to customer feedback begins by channeling the meticulous spirit of a certain obsessive detective, Adrian Monk. Sure, some might call him "detail oriented," but we love him because he makes us feel like there is someone out there just slightly crazier than we are. His methodical style is the blueprint for dissecting and analyzing feedback with laser focus. No detail is too small to scrutinize. So let your inner obsessive-compulsive tendencies shine.

Categorize every nugget of feedback you receive by feature. Because whether you're creating a product or service, you want your finished offering to flex on the features your customers or clients cannot live without. Once you've sorted each input by feature, tally how often you've heard each type of feedback and assess the emotional intensity behind it. Pick what works for you, whether you use a one-to-five scale, a happy-sad-face system, or the trusty red-yellow-green approach (our favorite back in the day). The goal is to spot patterns without letting your personal bias run the show. It's our instinct to hear feedback the way we want to hear it, especially when a favorite product feature is getting a bit of side-eye (as Victoria's youngest, Evelyn, has mastered). This is why, although it's a bit more expensive, it's often better to have someone else collect the feedback. When we were especially stressed, it was way too tempting to interpret every piece of feedback as a personal attack on that one feature we personally loved. Not exactly a productive strategy.

With our burgeoning ESG offering, we couldn't afford to hire a fancy third-party firm to run our focus groups. But we did tap a separate team within our own firm to handle the process, and we kept our hands completely off. That distance was intentional. And it turned out to be critical. We were the ones who were going to live or die by the success of this product, and as a result, we had every reason to take a heavy hand in its development. Every dollar going into it was ours, and we felt the pressure to get it right. But we also knew that being too close—too emotionally invested, too wrapped up in our own assumptions—was a risk. It would cloud our judgment.

So we stepped back. Yes, we couldn't quite keep our mouths shut and tried to offer our perspectives on the target audience, the buyer personas, and why certain users might react a certain way. But beyond that, we let the team do their thing. And the feedback that came in ended up fundamentally reshaping the product. Features we thought were must-haves got tossed. Blind spots we didn't even know existed came into focus. That breathing room and objectivity made the product better. Way better.

Address the Squeaky Wheel Issues

Don't try to tackle everything at once. Focus on the recurring themes that matter most. You can always reflect on minority opinions during those late-night brainstorming sessions or panic dreams. Perfect the features that your customers love, and when you've made improvements there, gather more feedback. Repeat this process until you consistently receive positive feedback on these core aspects of your offering and are ready for the big launch.

We got lucky. Once we zeroed in on the right target customer, the general counsel, the feedback mostly revolved around tweaking what we were already offering rather than implementing a big fix. This was a major win, as it confirmed we were tapping into exactly what our customers wanted—a solution for tackling poor sustainability disclosure practices that the government was about to mandate. Even a few of our "maybe later" ideas turned into pure gold. Our beta customers proved we were on the right track by saying "You know what we wish your current offering also had . . ." and then listing features we already had tucked in our back pockets.

Some features we thought would be blockbusters ended up being duds. Public companies, for instance, weren't exactly lining up for wide-reaching, aspirational disclosures. They preferred a slower, more measured approach. (We know, shocking, since our buyer persona ended up being lawyers. And no offense meant; Beth is a lawyer, too.) We also learned that any "step-by-step" advice with more than five steps quickly became "ignore-by-ignore" advice. A more *Glamour*-style "Fashion Dos and Don'ts" format worked better for clients with microscopic attention spans. And our grand plan to show companies how they measured up in the ESG department against the crème de la crème outside their industry? We thought it would inspire some lofty, nosebleed-level ambitions for sustainability. Turns out, our target clients were perfectly content being C students in this area and blissfully ignored our advice. (Don't worry; Victoria shared her "Cs get degrees" line on more than one occasion.)

So yes, some of our "brilliant" ideas flopped, but each miss taught us more about what our audience wanted (and what made them instantly tune out). The moral of the story? Fall in love with the problem, not your pet ideas, and don't take it personally when your brainchild gets met with a shrug. Just focus on your potential client's priorities and you can't go wrong.

Step 4: Accept That the Price Won't Be Right, At Least Not Yet

Finally! You've got a product that's caught the eye of a select group of customers and a few features they're slowly finding they can't live without. Now how much are they ready to shell out for it?

For one of us (Beth), pricing is the ultimate nemesis. Meanwhile, Victoria could easily give Bob Barker or Drew Carey a run for their money. She will ask any price for any product and, most of the time, gets what she asks. (She is the first to lean into her stupid confidence at the perfect time.) But even with her wily skills, we still mispriced out of the gate. Flexibility, creativity, and patience will be your best friends in the early days. When you've got plenty of data, pricing becomes a science. But in the early days? It's more of an art form, especially when you're trying to introduce your shiny new product or better mousetrap to the market. Don't stress too much at this point; your pricing strategy will evolve, as it should, with time. Here's some advice to keep in mind as you get started:

- **Be willing to spin the wheel.** There are plenty of pricing strategies out there, and at first, it can feel a bit like playing roulette with a dizzying array of bets you can make. Maybe you kick things off with an irresistible introductory price to lure in early adopters, opening the door to that critical early feedback. Or perhaps you go bold with a premium launch price, planning to dial it down later when you're aiming for mass appeal. Some get clever and bundle their shiny new product with others (sometimes through a partner, or in our case, with our consulting services), so the customer barely notices the price increase.

We priced our stand-alone software low, thinking we were building a subscription model for budget-conscious DIYers. But in our data-heavy industry, that low price backfired; it signaled the product wasn't robust enough. In hindsight? We should've priced high from the start to position it as a premium, scalable alternative to our consulting services.

Turns out a lot of successful companies pivot on pricing as a strategy. Tesla, for example, initially set higher prices for its electric vehicles to attract early adopters willing to pay a premium. As the market matured, they introduced more affordable models and reduced the prices of their higher-end options to appeal to a broader audience. Amazon Kindle used the same approach, starting with high prices only to lower them later to reach the mass market better. Meanwhile, Chipotle did the exact opposite, raising prices on premium products and then giving higher loyalty rewards and limited-time promotions to encourage customers to try them.

Generally, the best bet is to follow these somewhat amorphous guidelines to ensure your initial pricing is at least in the right ZIP code, if not exactly where you'll end up. Think of it as a warm-up lap before the real race.

- **Review the pricing of similar products or services.** For us, this was a bit of a challenge since we didn't have a direct competitor. So we did the next best thing: we checked out the pricing of other consulting services targeting our ideal buyers.

It wasn't perfect, but it gave us something to work with, kind of like using a paper map when you don't have a GPS.

- **Analyze your costs.** In our case, staff salaries and benefits were the big-ticket items, but we also factored in the technology and data our team relied on to do their work. At first, we made the rookie move of excluding R&D costs from the price, hoping to recoup them once the product took off. (Pro tip: Check your state's tax guidelines. Some, like Illinois, let you deduct certain R&D expenses. This saved us a bundle at the end of each year, retroactively in future tax years.)
- **Consider market conditions.** If inflation is high and budgets are tight, you might need to dial back pricing. Or you might be looking to outrun a competitor, in which case a lower price can help. When we launched during a time of low inflation and booming budgets, our low-price strategy was basically a bad idea. Companies had the budget to pay us larger fees. Cue the quick pivot.

Expect Pricing to Be a Moving Target

Ultimately, you'll be experimenting with several pricing strategies as you hunt for your ideal customer—the one with the lowest cost to serve and the willingness to pay the highest price. Until you get there, adopt a survivalist mindset; make your primary goal to avoid running out of money before you find your people. A postscript to our pricing story? A few years after launching the offering, we figured we had pricing all figured out. But after we sold the company, our new PE-backed owners decided to spend some real money on a pricing strategy consult. Their big insight? We were leaving money on the table. And, as it turns out, they were right. They jacked up our prices, took a hit with some lost clients, and walked away with a much higher recurring revenue. We can't let ourselves dream about how much more we could've made with the right pricing strategy!

Step 5: Chase Good Enough, Not Perfection

We've come a long way with Power Move #4, and we will close it out with a doozy of a step: chasing good enough, not perfection. We can almost guarantee most of our fellow type A female founders are going to have a hard time with this one. We know we did. Accepting "good enough," well, it sucks. Most of us are perfectionists who became entrepreneurs because we were sure we had a better idea than the other guys. But perfection really is the enemy of progress, especially in the entrepreneurial world. Getting hung up on every tiny detail can stymie creativity and bring progress to a halt. It's time to get out of your own way and give your brilliant idea the shot it deserves.

As women, we're practically hardwired to overthink—it's in our DNA. A whopping 72 percent of us display perfectionist traits, and we stress more about making mistakes than men do.[3] Add that we set the bar higher and feel worse when we don't clear it, and you've got a perfect storm: perfectionism, fear of failure, and the craving for external validation. For us, it was like slamming into a mental brick wall. We were paralyzed, literally stuck for weeks, constantly rethinking everything and pushing back our launch date. We tweaked, re-tweaked, and overanalyzed, all while losing sleep, eating too many Baked Cheetos (hello, permanent orange fingers), and trying to bury our feelings by helplessly doomscrolling.

We learned that the only way to get through it is to make peace with your product being "pretty good." Solid. Respectable. Maybe even borderline impressive. But not flawless. Just remind yourself that you're not abandoning perfection forever; you're just putting it on hold. One day, sure, you'll launch that dream product, feature packed, perfectly priced, wildly profitable, and showered with glowing reviews. But for now? "Pretty good" is more than good enough.

We would be lying to you if we said we'd gotten this step down pat; we haven't. We are, however, a bit more self-aware of our past mistakes and how they might have slowed growth for us at times when we were stuck on the development hamster wheel. This time around, we remind each other—sometimes daily—it's about getting things done and out the door versus perfection. The real truth is that you'll never have all the answers, all the cash, or all the confidence you think you need before you hit launch. The only way to win is to start, even if your hands are shaking and your PowerPoint is a little rough around the edges. And when the market throws you a curveball, because it always does, remember, that's not the end of your story. Sometimes, the biggest breakthroughs come from knowing when to pivot, not just push. Speaking of which, next up: how to spot a pivot-worthy moment and turn your "almost" into a "hell yes."

Gut Check

I'm Not Ready, But Should I Start Anyway?

- ☐ What's the one feature that, if missing, would make my product or service a nonstarter for my customer? *(By forcing yourself to identify this single, must-have element, you'll gain clarity on what truly drives value—and avoid overbuilding a bloated list of "nice-to-haves.")*
- ☐ What's the one feature that clearly differentiates my offering from what's already on the market? *(If you can't articulate this in one sentence, you're not ready for launch. Back to the drawing board you go.)*
- ☐ Have I identified at least one buyer—outside my inner circle—who would pay for this tomorrow? *(If not, it's time to find a real early adopter who can provide objective, market-tested feedback, not just well-intentioned support.)*
- ☐ What's the worst-case scenario if I launched today? *(Write it down. Then ask yourself: Could you survive it, learn from it, or laugh about it six months from now—ideally while watching your Stripe account tick toward six figures?)*
- ☐ What specific feedback am I afraid to hear about my idea? *(More importantly, what could you learn if you listened? The critiques we avoid often contain the most valuable insight. Avoiding them doesn't protect your business—it stalls its potential.)*

CHAPTER 8

Power Move #5: Respect the Pivot

We were four weeks deep into COVID lockdown, running on caffeine and chaos, clocking 80-hour weeks while fielding a nonstop barrage of panic calls from clients who were losing their minds over Wall Street's meltdown. (Remember when the S&P tanked 34 percent in a single month?) Meanwhile, those same clients—billion-dollar behemoths with more lawyers than we have houseplants—were suddenly "forgetting" to pay us on time. They were clutching their cash like it was the last roll of toilet paper at Costco, desperate to keep their balance sheets looking just healthy enough so investors wouldn't catch a whiff of trouble. (And yes, these were Fortune 500 giants trying to stiff a scrappy, growing business out of five-figure monthly payments. No hard feelings. Well, maybe a few.)

Our formerly thriving new business engine was dead in the water. Sales emails went unopened. Virtual pitch invites were declined. Our pipeline was completely dry. Meanwhile, Victoria spent her days on the phone with our accountants, trying to untangle the maze of COVID-relief funding—because if we didn't crack that code, we were going to have to dig into personal savings to meet payroll. Her nights as well as every break between calls and press releases were spent juggling a sleepless nine-month-old, twin preschoolers, and a kindergartener who was "learning virtually" (yes, air quotes fully deserved), all while putting just enough pressure on her third grader to keep the younger ones quiet while she jumped on yet another conference call with the bank. It wasn't balance. It was survival, COVID style, with no childcare and five kids under eight.

Just a few months before the world shut down, our ESG practice had finally started gaining traction. We were deep in the build-out (read "spend") of our ESG intelligence software, staying focused, remaining optimistic, and betting big. But now, our marketing strategy of challenging potential clients to get ahead of the curve in disclosing this data before the government made them was a total bust. Companies were scrambling and reverting to the basics while clinging to the herd, anything to avoid standing out. While we had managed to hold on to our client base through the initial chaos of lockdown, we knew that wasn't enough. If we couldn't crack the new business challenge in this bizarre, prolonged COVID landscape, all the time and money we'd sunk into building our growth engine would be for naught.

Then came an especially brutal morning in early May 2020. The corporate world was starting to come back online, slowly and cautiously. Clients were paying us a little faster, and a few were even dipping into new projects. But fresh leads? Crickets. We hadn't added a new client name to our pipeline in months. We were burned out (again), under pressure (again), and staring down a wall. That's when we decided to pivot and figure out what we could do differently.

This is a moment every entrepreneur meets over and over—the brick wall. You'll hit it hard, and then have to go over it, around it, or blast right through. The only real option? Pivot. Fast and without ego. Because if you don't, odds are you won't make it. Thirty-five percent of start-ups fail because they are tackling problems that are interesting to solve rather than pivoting and to serve a real market need.[1]

So we asked one simple question, "What can we do differently?" Immediately, we started on what ultimately became a very profitable pivot. We still believed in the power of an ESG business, but we knew we had to change our marketing strategy and go back to the basics. Early on, we learned that giving our extremely busy clients smart, thought-provoking research to read on long airplane flights was the key to long-term buying. In fact, many told us they'd been reading our stuff religiously for months before finally picking up the phone. We poured our energy into deep research that filled a gaping hole left by Wall Street analysts who were mostly busy screaming that the sky was falling. And in true rebel fashion, we didn't even include a call to action (marketers everywhere just gasped in horror). We just focused on putting the smartest stuff we could write out into the world.

As the slow COVID months rolled by, we tapped team members with lighter client loads to track trends, curate insights, and write their brains out. By late summer, when management teams finally came up for air and were ready to get serious about ESG strategy, they knew exactly who to call—us. And here's the wildest part: the sheer volume of content we pushed out, even the most basic stuff, lit up our SEO like a Christmas tree. Thanks to our marketing team's genius, we snagged the number-one spot on Google in our niche.

Yep, we leapfrogged over firms 10 times our size with bigger marketing budgets that looked great on paper but didn't have the breadth of smarts we did. We even outranked searches for updates on the SEC's impending rule changes. For anyone Googling "ESG consulting" or "ESG communications," we were the top hit, and with search volume exploding by the day, that visibility paid dividends for years.

We've become pros at pivoting through faceplants and flops, because entrepreneurship is basically just a masterclass in screwing up, dusting yourself off, and figuring out a new game plan before anyone notices you're bleeding. We got really good at picking ourselves up and changing course, usually with a little nudge (or a swift kick) from our own kitchen cabinet.

One of our all-time favorite gurus, Dolly Parton once said, "We can't direct the wind, but we can adjust the sails." That quote perfectly sums up one of entrepreneurship's most brutal truths: just when your business plan is finally working like a dream, reality will throw you a curveball, and you'll be forced to adapt. (Side note: Dolly isn't just a national treasure with a killer voice, she's a business ninja. At just 20 years old, as her music career took off, she launched her own publishing company. That power move, by the way, allowed her to retain the rights to her songs and made her a centimillionaire.)

Sadly, we mere mortals can't expect to have Dolly's foresight. You'll face business challenges that you won't nail on the first, second, or even third try. But slowly, you'll start spotting the red flags of a failing strategy faster and stop pouring energy into the wrong things sooner. When this happens, a light will flip on in your perfectionist brain, and you'll realize no decision is carved in stone. Tinkering becomes second nature, and you'll be more surprised when you don't have to tweak something. MBA types call it *continuous innovation*. We call it business as usual. It's all part of the process, and we promise, you will get used to it.

In our case, we've had to pivot every element of our business you can imagine—plans, products, leadership, sales strategies, you name it. In fact, we did it so often, our team eventually insisted we switch from annual to quarterly strategy updates. Apparently, our "real-time" pivots were starting to feel more like whiplash. We tried to defend ourselves by reminding them that many successful companies made significant shifts in strategy over the years. Tiffany's started as a stationery store. The Gap was a record store that sold jeans in the back. Slack? A now-massive community app with 350,000 employees was once a near-defunct gaming company.

The "always be pivoting" mindset didn't just live in our businesses; it seeped into our homes, too. Our families heard the muttering, saw the late-night Googling, and got pulled into the strategy sessions disguised as dinner conversations. Spouses became sounding boards. Carpool runs doubled as informal market research. If something wasn't working, we were wired to fix it, fast. And whether they liked it or not, our kids got front-row seats to the start-up roller coaster and started picking up the playbook themselves.

> *Thirty-five percent of start-ups fail because they failed to pivot to serve a market need.*

Beth's daughter, a natural behind the camera lens, realized her small school had a woefully underfunded media department. So she did what any resourceful teen raised by a serial pivoter might do: she pitched her own course for credit. Bonus twist? She roped in a teacher who was just as eager to level up his own skills, turning it into a win-win mentorship. Another daughter walked away from three years of competitive tennis and the dream of playing in college after realizing her toxic coach could teach a masterclass in mind games. One proudly gave up meat for years, until she moved to Texas, land of brisket and BBQ, and reversed course almost overnight.

Beth's kids grew up changing friend groups, hairstyles, and even wall colors like most people change their passwords. And now that they're older, the payoff is clear; those tiny pivots added up to real-deal resilience. When the family unit they'd known for more than two decades came undone, they adjusted with grace to Family Unit 2.0. These days, Beth gets regular calls that begin with, "So. . .this isn't working. Would it be insane if I tried [insert crazy thing] instead?" Sometimes they make the change, and sometimes they're just floating the idea; but every time, they see another path. Or at the very least, they're willing to find one.

We're not just proud—we're downright smug—that we've taught our kids life isn't a straight line. If the road ahead turns into a dead end, you don't just sit there and pout; you grab a Sharpie and redraw the map. That's the kind of strategic flexibility that's saved our butts more times than we can count, and it's the same mindset that will keep your business (and your sanity) intact when things go sideways.

The only guarantee in entrepreneurship is that something will go off script. The real winners aren't the ones who never mess up. They're the ones who spot the detour, pivot fast, and keep moving forward. Embracing the pivot isn't just a survival skill; it's your ticket to long-term success, creative problem-solving, and maybe even a little bit of joy along the way.

Ready to learn how?

Get comfortable—or should we say uncomfortable—and let's dive into the steps of this final Power Move.

Power Move #5: Respect the Pivot

1. **Get used to admitting your mistakes.** Bad things happen to good businesses every day. Some are self-inflicted wounds. Others are just bad industry breaks. The "what" doesn't matter, but the "what do I do now?" does.
2. **Dive into the data driving the problem.** While intuition is a critical starting point, data needs to be the GPS of your decision-making journey. It helps you spot problems and their potential causes before they snowball into full-blown disasters.
3. **Know when to take a wrecking ball to your own business.** Do you have the guts to make the pivot? Sometimes, you have to knock down what's not working (even if you loved it once) and start building smarter. Dramatic? Maybe. Necessary? Absolutely.
4. **Master the art of the micro-move.** Sometimes a baby-step pivot after a horrible mistake is good enough to get you back on track. It might not solve all your business problems, but it will stop the exhausting cycle of spinning your wheels and getting nowhere.
5. **Feel the feels and then file them.** The only thing we think hurts more than a business failure is childbirth. Unlike childbirth, business failures tend to stick in your brain like white on rice.

Step 1: Get Used to Admitting Your Mistakes

Bad things happen to good businesses every day. The "what" doesn't matter, but the "what do I do now?" does. Your business mistakes might not always be catastrophic, but how quickly you address them will make a huge difference. Victoria's dad used to say, "The second you stop moving is the second you're dead in the water." It turns out, the same goes for a strategy you launched with high hopes but that quickly starts to fall apart. Clinging to it won't make it work any better. It just delays the inevitable pivot you need to make.

One strategy we charged into with our eyes so glued to the prize we missed all the warning signs was the sale process for Clermont. We nearly pulled off one of our biggest miscalculations—selling our company to the wrong suitor—all in the name of chasing the finish line. Thankfully, our ever-wise kitchen cabinet came to the rescue before we signed on the dotted line.

So how did we let this happen? Well, the COVID-driven pause in Clermont's momentum was quickly followed by several years of rapid growth, propelling us to a pivotal crossroads. We couldn't scale to eight figures without some serious growth capital. So, we—*gulp*—hired those same vest-wearing bros (a.k.a. investment bankers) we have talked about and launched a sale process. The problem was we drastically underestimated how draining that process would be—professionally and personally—while still juggling client work and trying to keep the revenue on an upswing. (Nothing scares off a buyer like a growth chart that flatlines mid-sale.) But we were convinced it would all pay off once we went to market. We imagined suitors lining up, term sheets flying.

Yeah, that's not what happened.

Ninety-seven percent of CEOs report taking steps to change how they've created, delivered, and captured value in the past five years.

After 20-plus meet and greets (kind of like corporate speed dating), we finally got an offer that seemed like a slap in the face. (And no, we're not being dramatic.) If you've ever listed your house and gotten an offer well below the listing price, you know the sting of seeing your blood, sweat, and tears priced like a clearance sale. If you remember our saga from Power Move #2, you know we didn't just walk away from that first offer—we sprinted. We took a beat, caught our breath, and did what any battle-tested founders would do: we pivoted, hard. Instead of rushing to sell, we regrouped, retooled, and got brutally honest about where we'd screwed up. We fired our banker (good riddance), waited out the out clause, and set about crafting a way better story for the next round of buyers.

Of course, we're not the only ones who've faceplanted and had to pivot. Everyone makes mistakes. Even those glossy, spreadsheet-loving CEOs and buttoned-up execs who look like they've never spilled coffee on their power suits. Spoiler—they all mess up, too. But the real difference isn't who avoids mistakes (no one does), it's who learns, pivots, and comes back swinging.

- Ninety-seven percent of CEOs report taking steps to change how they've created, delivered, and captured value in the past five years.[2]
- Sixty-one percent of executives acknowledged that their firms often struggle to bridge the gap between strategy formulation and execution.[3]

- Two-thirds to three-quarters of large organizations struggle to execute their strategies, highlighting the persistent gap between planning and implementation.[4]

If industry titans rarely get it right the first time, how can a start-up entrepreneur expect anything different? One of our favorite badass founders Whitney Wolfe Herd (the founder of Bumble) says, "When you accept that failure is a good thing, it can actually be a huge propeller toward success."[5] This principle applies equally to business: identify the problem. Devise a strategy to fix it. Then move forward.

Sadly, almost selling our business for a song wasn't even close to our worst mistake. We made a lot of product mistakes. We overpriced and underpriced. We introduced products well before the market was ready. We hired terrible senior people, including a so-called industry superstar who lasted exactly one month before hitting on a junior associate in the company kitchen. Eventually, we got exceptionally good at failing forward—like a chef in pursuit of a Michelin star, turning every burnt dish into a masterpiece. Some days, it felt like our mistakes made the Titanic look like a masterclass in safe navigation and Elon Musk seem like the world's most well-adjusted parent.

But through it all, we persisted. Because here's the truth: learning how to recognize, course correct, and move past your mistakes is one of the most essential skills on the path to real success. So how do you know if you're heading down the wrong road? Here are a few ways we recommend staying nimble:

- **Skip the guesswork.** Track everything. Financials, key performance indicators (KPIs), actual expenses versus budgeted expenses, and forecasted expenses—weekly, monthly, and quarterly. Keep your actuals versus budget and forecast under a constant microscope. One off-week might just be a little noise, but a few in a row? That's a signal. Small issues have a sneaky way of growing if you're not watching, like an expense category quietly ballooning as a percentage of sales, needing more staff hours to squeeze out the same amount of revenue, or rising interest costs because receivables are dragging and your credit line is being used more. Always look for trends and be ready to find their causes. (Hang tight; we are going to take a deep dive on exactly what data is most critical in the next section.)

- **Benchmark like a boss.** Don't assume the game changers are happening only inside your business; sometimes they're happening around it. Carve out 15 minutes a day to scan national, local, and industry news. Keep an eye out for anything that could shake up your world, including regulations that might drive up your input costs or industry acquisitions that either tighten the screws on your margins or swing open the doors to new market opportunities. We loved hearing that our biggest competitors had been scooped up by giant holding companies. Why? Because we knew their niche teams, the ones that competed with us, would get lost in the shuffle. Cue a few months of chaos—distracted leadership, nervous clients, and whispers of price hikes and layoffs. Meanwhile, we'd swoop in, ready to scoop up clients (and maybe even a few employees).

Revisit those holy grail reports from Power Move #1 when mapping your TAM. Above all, stay curious. Ask questions. Then ask a few more. Remember, every meeting, client, pitch, and networking, is an opportunity to learn something new.

- **Listen to your gut.** If something feels off, it probably is, even if your dashboard gives you a false sense of security. When your gut hesitates, it's time to zoom out, reassess, and ask better questions. Victoria's superpower is detecting client dissatisfaction from a mile away based solely on the kinds of questions they asked on calls she wasn't even on. (She uses this superpower on her kids too; she can sniff out something going on—with friends, with school, with life—from the next street over.) If a client suddenly wanted more data, uninvited our senior lead from a recurring meeting, or dragged their feet on something they'd deemed a five-alarm fire two weeks earlier, she knew the vibes were off. That's why she set up biweekly check-ins across all client teams: not to micromanage but to ask the kinds of pointed questions that made everyone stop and think, *Is this client drifting? How can we close the gap?* Without that system and her amazing gut instincts, the first sign we got would've been a termination notice, and a very unpleasant surprise on our financial dashboard.

Once you've identified an issue, act fast, but don't flail around. Be decisive. And for God's sake, remember that "respecting the pivot" doesn't mean "blowing up the whole business." (At least, not every time.) Sometimes, a few small tweaks are all it takes to test a new approach without torching what's working. Stay adaptable but intentional.

Now that you've recognized that you have a business problem, it's time to do some digging.

Step 2: Dive into the Data Driving the Problem

Gut instinct is great for picking out shoes or knowing when your kid is about to fake a stomachache, but when it comes to running a business, data is your real ride-or-die. Intuition might get you started, but data is the GPS that keeps you from driving straight into a ditch. It's your early-warning system, the thing that flashes *Danger Ahead!* before a tiny hiccup turns into a full-blown dumpster fire. When things start to go off the rails (and trust us, they will), you need to roll up your sleeves, dig into the numbers, and get cozy with those trendlines. Data tells you what's breaking, why it's breaking, and where to steer next, so you can pivot before your business ends up as a cautionary tale on someone else's podcast. Most of our ugliest business headaches at Clermont could be traced straight back to sales and marketing strategy. There was one stretch that nearly broke us. Our pipeline was in a sustained nosedive for nearly six months. For a company that was used to 50 percent top-line growth, it felt like watching a slow-motion car crash you couldn't stop.

Back in the day, our sales engine was our pride and joy, a scrappy mix of direct marketing and unapologetic cold calling. Sounds old school, but it worked. For every 10 calls, we'd land a couple of meetings, and from those, we'd usually snag a client worth $100,000 a year and a lifetime value close to a million. We called it *caveman marketing*, and for years, it was our secret weapon. But, slowly and almost invisibly, the magic started to fade. So why didn't we see the warning signs sooner? Maybe we were too busy putting out daily fires or too distracted by the chaos of work and family. Or maybe we just got a little cocky, coasting on past wins. Whatever the reason, we missed the slow leak. Victoria's original dashboard tracked the pipeline, but not the number of new business meetings. By the time we pieced together the ugly truth, our meeting-to-close rate was dropping 10 percent every month. We were headed for an iceberg, and the ship was already taking on water. Naturally, our first move was to turn up the heat on our sales team. We grilled them in meetings, demanded more calls and more reports, and even tried to eavesdrop on their pitches. When that didn't work, we blamed the economy, until we saw our competitors thriving. At our lowest point, our pipeline was a quarter of its usual size. That's when we finally stopped pointing fingers and started asking the right questions.

Once we dug into the numbers, the problem was glaringly obvious: it wasn't our close rate; it was the lack of new meetings. Fewer first-time meetings meant fewer leads, a shrinking pipeline, and a death spiral for growth. With the real issue in hand, we got to work on a smarter data strategy, one that would help us spot trouble early and pivot before things got this ugly again.

In business, flailing is optional; strategizing is survival. Here are our favorite tried-and-true data hacks to spotting the signs earlier:

- **Add an operating dashboard to your financial cheat sheet.** A financial dashboard was always our trusty compass for the long haul. It told us when to hit the accelerator or slam the brakes on major decisions, including new hires, big-ticket tools, and strategic bets. It was essential. But ours had one fatal flaw: it revealed problems only once they'd already started impacting our pocketbook. (Smooth-talking MBAs call these *lagging indicators*.) But not our operating dashboard. That bad boy drilled into the heartbeat of sales and marketing. Outbound email volume, open rates, click-throughs, meeting counts, close rates, service break-downs—you name it, we tracked it. It was chock-full of the color-coded charts and trend lines Victoria really loves (only second to her family calendar with all the basketball, soccer, and volleyball practices color coded by time and kid). With it, we tracked the core growth with the same obsessive energy moms bring to summer camp sign-ups.

  Thanks to that data, we could pivot on the fly, testing new ad strategies, mixing up sales team pairings to see who clicked better, and experimenting with virtual versus in-person intro meetings. Once we realized virtual intros were performing just as well as in-person ones, we promptly slashed the travel budget and rerouted those dollars to boost sponsorship opportunities. Our financial dashboard took about nine months to show an upswing, but our operating dashboard started lighting up almost immediately and led to more follow-up meetings, proposal requests, and opportunities in the pipeline. That operating dashboard quickly became a secret weapon, allowing us to stress-test real-time sales tweaks rather than wait weeks (and in one case, three years) for a final contract to be signed.

- **Ask your employees.** (And don't just nod along; listen to their answers!) Our team turned out to be a gold mine of insights, often spotting personnel issues, system inefficiencies, and customer frustrations long before they would catch us walking down the hall muttering, "What gives?" to ourselves. The real challenge? Getting them to spill the beans. To be brutally honest, we waited way too long to start listening. In the early years, we were moving too fast, always sprinting with our heads down. It took a couple of bold (and forever respected) team members cornering us with hard truths to snap us out of it. That moment kicked off a shift. We started building a culture where honesty wasn't just welcome; it was expected. And we invested real time and money to make it stick.

  We also rolled out an anonymous feedback loop: virtual and in-person "water cooler" chats, led by our brilliant HR consultant, plus our annual anonymous employee survey, which became our crystal ball. It flagged bad-fit hires, shaky client accounts, and even culture shifts we hadn't noticed yet. Sure, in the beginning, some alarms were a little premature—maybe the person vanishing into the bathroom for 15 minutes really did just have a questionable breakfast burrito. But after refining how we filtered and followed up on what came in, we realized this system was one of our most powerful early-warning tools. It gave us valuable data that helped course correct before things spiraled into full-on financial damage.

- **Go full supersleuth on your competitors who are absolutely crushing it.** The hard truth is that sometimes they're simply doing it better than you, and there's plenty to learn. We gleaned insights through casual social encounters, extensive research, chatting with competitors' customers, and even recruiting their employees. We quietly collected intel on how our competitors' sales teams went to market, which products were their cash cows, how often their senior execs actually worked on day-to-day clients, and even what kind of year-end bonuses they paid. Sure, this strategy was a bit biased and incomplete, so it's crucial not to overcorrect or place too much weight on this input. But ignoring it is a risk you can't afford.

  In our case, pricing was our biggest revelation. Channeling our inner Jessica Jones, we discovered that our prices on a few key products were about 30 percent lower than some competitors whose work we believed was inferior. So we made a bold move and adjusted our prices overnight. And guess what? Half of those changes stuck, and our profit margins improved.

Data can sometimes feel rigid and confining, like that overly cautious friend who insists on comparing the route with Google Maps and Waze every five minutes. But it's also a treasure trove of insights that can help you more quickly identify the best path to victory. Trusting your gut is important, but data provides the hard evidence to turn your gut instinct into a guaranteed win. For us, wins turned into the somewhat-uncomfortable victory hugs that remain today Victoria's favorite way to make Beth squirm.

Now that data is your friend, you might feel like you've just summited the business mountain and are ready to plant your flag! But getting to the top is only half the climb. Next, you have to figure out what to do with all that insight. Enter one of our all-time favorite (and highly scientific, of course) strategies: the

"Do the Opposite" method. It's simple, it's powerful, and it's practically a rite of passage for every future female founder.

Step 3: Know When to Take a Wrecking Ball to Your Own Business

When part of your business isn't working, it's gotta go. And excising it with a surgeon's scalpel doesn't always work. Sometimes, you have to go full Miley Cyrus mode and swing in like a wrecking ball. Knock down what's not working (even if you loved it once) and start building smarter. We creatively call our own version of this tactic the "Do the Opposite of What You Have Been Doing" approach. A member of our Kitchen Cabinet once tried to rename it the "Paradigm Shift Strategy." We threw our cocktail napkin at her—too fancy. While unconventional, our "Do the Opposite" method has proven to be one of our most effective hat tricks (and probably best-kept secrets to our success).

This radical approach was born during the most frustrating chapters of Clermont, when the sales strategy we just told you about—hustle hard, book meetings, close deals—suddenly stopped working. Not only were we getting fewer meetings and watching our pipeline shrink, but the few meetings we had were. . .not closing. . .and we were closers! Cue the panic.

We tried everything: more metrics, more meetings, more last-minute flights to pitch in person. Still nothing. And eventually, the stress started to seep into our usually solid "work wife" dynamic. Our team watched us stomp out of each other's offices more days than not, mad as hell and rehashing the same question: "Why weren't the leads converting?" Then in a moment of total exasperation, one of us threw out the old cliché, "You know the definition of insanity is doing the same thing over and over and expecting a different result." The other paused, looked up, and said, "Wait, why don't we actually *do the opposite*?"

We discovered that this wasn't a half-bad parenting strategy either. Beth and her oldest son clashed a lot in high school and into college. They were cut from the same cloth: stubborn, independent, with a shared streak of procrastination and a tendency to zig whenever someone suggested they zag. When he left for college, she was utterly spent—emotionally, mentally, and spiritually—and half convinced they were one heated phone call away from starring in a prime-time episode of *Estranged Mothers & Sons: The Jerry Springer Show*. She knew she couldn't make him study harder or go out less from that far away, and trying to control this would strain their relationship even further. So she made a quiet, intentional shift. She stopped asking about grades. She didn't lecture when he called to say he'd slept through a final or—yes, this actually happened—got caught using ChatGPT on a test. (That professor was not amused—and was also delusional about AI, but that story is for another book.) Instead, she listened. She stayed calm. She showed up with support, not scrutiny. (This was hard as hell for anyone thinking of trying it. Be warned.)

And something changed. The tension started to fade. The calls became less about managing disaster and more about connection. Slowly, phone calls turned into conversations. Fast-forward a few years? Weekly FaceTimes and slobbery goodbyes (at least from Beth) became the norm. It turns out doing the opposite can also be the ultimate relationship hack. With all five kids still at home, Victoria deploys the "Do the Opposite" strategy literally daily. Her favorite moments are when tempers flare, tears flow, or doors slam (usually the teenager, of course). It's a surefire way to break the cycle of whatever's happening. It's simple: when one (or many) of them are crying, seething, screaming—you name it—she quickly says, "Don't smile. No, seriously, it's not okay. Don't smile." And, almost without fail, the corners of the mouth twitch up, the tension eases, and the moment resets, making room for rational thought to slip back in. It sounds simple because it is. Now, some might call this reverse psychology, but sometimes, "Do the Opposite" isn't about a dramatic turnaround; sometimes it's just giving space for a clear head, a fresh perspective, or a breath of fresh air.

Abandoning a strategy that's worked in the past seems like an act of desperation. But in our minds, how the hell could it get worse? Turns out a lot of very smart women entrepreneurs demolished all or part of their business just like we did. A few of our favorite "Do the Opposite" pivots from other businesses include the following:

- **Drybar:** Ali Webb moved her mobile blowout service to permanent retail locations when she realized she couldn't get the experience right and wasn't getting enough repeat customers. Ultimately expanding to more than 100 locations, Drybar's revenue increased from $1.5 million in 2010 to $39 million in only three years.
- **The Honest Company:** Same for Jessica Alba's Honest Company. What if she had stayed focused on baby products only? Some brilliant exec (we prefer to think it was Jessica) realized the bulk of the company's margins were going to new customer acquisition costs as their babies aged out. So they pivoted and found new products to sell to the same customers at different stages of motherhood. Genius. In 2023 alone, the company pulled in $344 million in revenue—a solid 10 percent bump from the year before. But the real overachiever? The household and wellness segment (a.k.a. everything not baby), which outperformed the baby wipe category with 59 percent year-over-year growth.[6]
- **Glossier:** While Glossier had no trouble attracting customers, its supply chain was a total mess. As demand skyrocketed, the company's logistics buckled under the pressure,

leaving more than 60,000 customers stuck on backorder. With so many shoppers jumping ship for other brands, revenues took a nosedive. The root of Glossier's problem? Their entire brand was built around using high-quality, ethically sourced ingredients, and it turned out, finding reliable suppliers for those standards was a lot harder than expected. After a brutal 30 percent revenue drop, the team hit reset: they overhauled their sourcing strategy, rebuilt their supply chain, and came back stronger (and more sustainable), ultimately winning back customers like us.

Back to our caveman marketing problem. For years, we relied on a volume-based approach to sell our core business, sending broad outreach to everyone who had interacted with our thought leadership and hoping a few would agree to a first meeting. It was more intelligent guesswork than a fine-tuned strategy, but it worked. We developed a deep bench of buyers from our investor relations days at Clermont and Ashton Partners and thought, *Perfect, we'll just leverage the hell out of them to grow our shiny new ESG practice.*

Our contacts were happy to meet with us. People loved us. They hugged us when we walked into their offices. Then they promptly bought—nothing. Zero. Zilch. "No budget for ESG," they'd say. "Sustainability just isn't a priority right now." Our go-to buyers, the ones who knew and trusted us, weren't the right audience for ESG. We needed a new buyer. In some cases, a new target company altogether. Cue the collective groan.

So, we hit the research hard. We sliced our public company list by sector and dug into industry-specific ESG trends. We stalked—uh, researched—who was getting quoted in the press or speaking at ESG conferences. Then, we buckled down and wrote painfully tailored emails that pinpointed exactly what their ESG communications were missing and how to fix it. Different message, different buyer, entirely different outcome.

That pivot changed everything. Though we felt dense for not realizing it sooner, we finally saw the light. If we bundled ESG with our investor relations offering, it flopped, because our clients—the investor relations officers that we were pitching—weren't the ones who'd use it. Not yet anyway. It seems obvious in hindsight, but it forced a total rethink of how we showed up in the market. We had to create an entirely new set of buyers for our ESG product versus relying on our old clients to buy more services from us. We had to split the baby. We changed our messaging, website, team segmentation, and even how we positioned ourselves as thought leaders in the market. (Beth flexed into ESG while Victoria kept on as an investor relations talking head.)

Big corporations can throw money at consultants to diagnose what's broken. But for entrepreneurs like us, the path is scrappier—and more personal. We had to rely on each other, lean hard on our data, and be willing to do a complete 180-degree turn on strategy and tactics when the situation called for it. Do that a few times and you will gain the clarity, and the courage, to make the tough calls faster and get back on the path to growth. You'll be amazed at how much impact those tiny, strategic tweaks can have without sending you into the full-blown "I'm a total fraud and my dream business is headed for failure"–type meltdown that usually comes right before a major pivot.

Step 4: Master the Art of the Micro-Move

Sometimes a baby-step pivot after a horrible mistake is good enough to get you back on track. It might not solve all your business problems, but it will stop the exhausting cycle of spinning your wheels and getting nowhere. (Think of it as a brain detox without the vile green juice.) Taking any action is a win when you're stuck. Victoria is a creature of habit, and change doesn't come easy—especially since she's got a healthy dose of stubbornness in the mix. Embracing the pivot has been more art than science for her. But she's learned that even a tiny shift can snap you out of tunnel vision and spark new thinking. A pivot helps redirect focus from an old, stalled-out strategy toward something fresh and potentially game changing. Even a cautious step forward is still movement, and it sets you up for the next pivot when the time comes.

In some ways, this step is like washing your hair the minute you get home from a haircut that, despite the $200 price tag, still needs a little tweaking. To give your new strategy its best shot at turning heads (in a good way), follow these simple guidelines:

- **Set bite-sized goals and objectives so you don't have to course correct. Again. And again.** Set goals so small you can't help but win; think snack-sized, not supersized. Forget trying to yank your business back to those days of wild, double-digit growth when your revenue was tiny and every win felt like a rocket launch. And don't waste your energy trying to drag your entire customer base into your shiny new product overnight. That's a recipe for disappointment and a whole lot of stress.

  What you're really after? A few sparks of hope. Maybe it's just a sign that things are slowing their downward slide, or—dare we say it—starting to level out. You're not clawing your way back to the top in a single leap; you're looking for proof the freefall is finally slowing, even if it's just a little.

  We've learned that our gut instincts for "big, bold" pivots in sales and marketing weren't always the magic bullet. We used to go hard when a few strategic tweaks would have done the trick. To keep ourselves in check, we handed the reins to our head of sales, whose motto was basically "slow and steady wins the race." (Meanwhile, we were chanting, "Add seven figures to the pipeline, or bust!") The reality: neither approach was perfect.

The real win came when we stopped trying to outdo each other and found a middle ground. Instead of obsessing over pipeline numbers, we tracked the number of new meetings booked—old school and new school, side by side. Our goal? Just a tiny uptick by quarter's end. No fireworks, no viral moments, just a little less ugly when you squint. Swallow your pride and get comfortable with baby steps rather than giant leaps.

- **Make sure your team is on the bus with you, not forgotten *Home Alone*, Kevin McCallister style.** As usual, we learned this the hard way with an earlier product crisis. (And yes, like Kevin, we had *a lot* of crises of our own making.) During a late-night texting session, we unilaterally decided to water down our first ESG product and get rid of the parts clients told us they didn't want. The problem was that we didn't bring the head of the product into our crazy text exchange. Instead, we just told her to do it. Well, her team didn't do it. Or didn't do much of it. So, we ended up with a cheaper product with mostly the same features, and the sales team just learned to tell potential clients to ignore the features they didn't want to use. Guess how the margins turned out on that one?

  With the next crisis, we approached things differently, looping in the head of sales in those midnight text sessions and meeting face-to-face with the team that would be selling the product. We even let them set their own short-term bonus structure for added incentive. This collaborative approach not only worked but it also had unexpected upsides. The sales team had a greater sense of ownership in the process and felt more comfortable giving us real-time client feedback and ideas for improvement.

- **Tweak your strategy often.** Be prepared to tweak your strategies and try different methods, like Ina Garten in the kitchen, until it's right. (Did we hear "espresso martini with orange vodka"? *Chef's kiss.*)

  For our big ESG sales challenge at Clermont, after we segmented the offering away from the investor relations side of the house, we ultimately tested 10 different thought leadership approaches, explored more than 40 SEO keywords, launched countless new email campaigns, and even restructured the responsibilities of a key junior sales team member. We accepted that progress was going to follow a "two steps forward, one step back" pattern and that each day would bring highs and lows. At the end of every week, we doubled down on elements that showed promise and abandoned the losers.

  Pivoting is really about learning as you go and getting better all the time. You'll try lots of different things before it all comes together, kind of like an IKEA desk. (*Really, IKEA, 832 parts with just an Allen wrench?*) Inevitably, you'll have to make choices about what to prioritize. Some potentially valuable ideas may remain periodically unexplored due to time or resource constraints. (Much like those extra parts left in the IKEA box when you're done that you quietly tuck away, hoping they weren't essential.) But when your numbers start improving, just keep following your success, one little pivot at a time.

  You're not just building a business; you're mastering the art of the micro-pivot: dodging, weaving, and adjusting course with every piece of feedback and shift in the market. The secret is staying in motion. Static isn't in your playbook, and that's exactly what sets you apart.

Step 5: Feel the Feels, Then File Them

The only thing we think hurts more than a business failure is childbirth. (We have had plenty of both, trust us.) The labor is painful, and you can't breathe a sigh of relief until the very end when you have a brand-new baby (or strategy) and can watch it grow. In the thick of things, you will most certainly swear never to go through such a process again. While many moms forget the suffering the moment they're snuggling their new bundle of joy, with business moms, it's another story.

Unlike childbirth, business failures tend to stick in your brain. Once you navigate one problem, more likely than not, another one is going to pop up. Think of roadblocks as rites of passage that make you stronger. So, you must get good at learning your lesson and moving on to your next opportunity for success. If not, they will hold you back.

The best thing Beth ever told Victoria after a particularly gut-wrenching competitive pitch that didn't go her way was this: "Feel it. Feel it hard. Get pissed off; go have some wine; go to sleep. And tomorrow, let it go. We need to get back in the saddle." Now, the best part of this advice was that it was absolutely perfect in that moment, but it also became our mantra to each other every time we needed it. As well-adjusted as each of us may seem at any given moment (yeah, we have convinced ourselves of this; let us have it), our real secret sauce is being able to give each other a kick in the ass or a shoulder to cry on whenever it's needed. Pivoting doesn't just apply to business—it's a way of life, especially when you're building a company and a family at the same time. We've lost count of how many personal brick walls we hit while trying to keep the business moving forward. One of Victoria's toughest came the day she found out she was pregnant with her fifth firecracker, Evelyn.

Of course, Evelyn completed their family, and imagining life without her seems downright depressing. But the timing was not ideal. We had just bought out our original partners at Clermont, and as we started cleaning up the financial chaos left by data-blind decisions, we realized we'd need to take pay cuts even though the business was booming. It would take us a year to get past this, but we could see real, profitable growth in the future—being able to invest in our team, move out of the subleased corner of Victoria's brother's office, and launch what we called our ESG baby.

So when Victoria walked into the office and said to Beth, "We're going to be a family of seven," she braced for impact. Not because she wasn't thrilled, but because she knew what it meant: stepping back, even slightly, during a blink-and-you'll-miss-it maternity leave. She figured Beth might be supportive—eventually—but also understandably frustrated. After all, Beth was already running zone defense at home with four teens and pre-teens. Instead, Beth lit up. "Oh my God, I'm so excited for you!" No drama, just joy. We both knew we'd need a serious execution plan to stay on track. Beth took on more operational work, and Victoria, ever the client whisperer, stayed engaged, even taking a client call from her delivery room. It wasn't easy, but we did it. We didn't lose a single client, and we barely missed a beat. The truth is pivots like that take a toll.

When you come out the other side of a hard turn, don't immediately sprint to the next milestone. Give yourself a pause. Shut the laptop, play hooky with your kids, or binge-watch *Real Housewives*, Victoria style. Because if you don't, you risk spiraling into over-analysis or worst-case-scenario mode, as we've been known to do a time or two. And trust us, the business will still be there when you hit play again.

After plenty of living, learning, and the occasional meltdown, we landed on a three-part formula for some solid reflection. It's designed to help you process the chaos, learn the lesson, and move on, because there's always another challenge waiting around the corner. (Probably right after school pick-up.)

- **First, take a victory lap for the things you were right about.** Even if your self-doubt and negative thoughts are still running rampant, you have to course correct before your mood affects other parts of your business. Your employees will read you like a book and start updating their résumés if you wallow too long. Taking a victory lap, even if you are limping, will remind you (and them) why you have every right to act the part of the confident, optimistic ass-kicker you are.

  Beth was a pro at this. We could go from a tense conversation about sales, a major strategic shift, or even a call with the school principal, and she'd stand up and walk into our morning staff meeting, cracking a self-deprecating joke that had the whole team rolling on the floor. Victoria? Let's just say she's not winning the World Series of Poker anytime soon. But over time, she learned, for the sake of the team, the business, and her own sanity, how to put on a brave face. It became a rule in her house, too. Whether it's a sibling fight, a bad grade, or friendship drama, the kids have to shake it off and talk about something good that happened that day. And nine times out of ten, the tears stop, and after a few minutes, they might even start to laugh a little.

- **Second, don't just take it from us, have a few heart-to-heart talks with your Kitchen Cabinet about their own failures.** Everyone has experienced setbacks. Many have faced multiple career crises and live to tell the story. Women remember the details as if they happened yesterday. But here's the secret: listening to others' tales of woe can be surprisingly uplifting. It's like a support group but with fewer tissues and more wine. When you hear from those who've dusted themselves off and gone on to conquer the business world, it's a reminder that failure is just another stop on the road to success.

- **Third, if you can muster the courage, write down the experience.** Outline the three things you wish you had done differently and three things you absolutely nailed. Every business problem may come dressed in a different costume, but over time, entrepreneurs start to recognize the pattern. Getting the experience down on paper helps you spot it faster next time and shift into fix-it mode before the drama even starts. In our case, we know that Beth is the one to push the alarm signal first and loudest when she senses something isn't right. Victoria's special sauce is making tweak after tweak to get a strategy to work. We both know that if we have the same conversation, "Why isn't our current plan working?" for more than five consecutive weekly strategy meetings, it's time to deploy the "Do the Opposite" method. Sounds like a crazy formula, but for us, it works.

Power Move #5 is all about the plot twists because building a business (while managing real life and goldfish snack requests every five minutes) is basically a masterclass in handling the unexpected. As we wrote this chapter, replaying our wins, blunders, and those classic "what now?" moments—we felt it. Reflecting on the chaos and clarity wasn't just cathartic, it reminded us why we keep coming back for more. It's the constant reinvention, the scrappy brilliance, the never-a-dull-moment energy that only entrepreneurship delivers. And if you're anything like us, you're going to love that part too.

Just remember, moving on from a tough moment doesn't mean erasing it. (We still bring up the mean girls from high school more often than we'd like to admit, even as we convince ourselves that we have aged so much better.) If it shook you, shake it off. But take the lesson with you. That's how you get stronger, savvier, and way more unshakable next time.

You've made it through the power moves; high five for that. But we're not quite done. Next up: scaling the business. With your eyes wide open and your playbook in hand, you're ready to take on what's next.

■ ■ ■

Gut Check

Do I Know When to Pivot?

- ☐ Where in my business am I spending the most energy but seeing the least return? *(If your effort-to-impact ratio feels wildly off, that's the most obvious sign that it's time to take a fresh look at that part of the business. Strategic clarity rarely shows up in the same environment where the burnout began.)*
- ☐ Have I heard the same feedback (or silence) more than three times? *(At that point, it's not anecdotal; it's likely a pattern. And a pattern is a signal that smart founders listen before the market makes the pivot decision for them.)*
- ☐ What part of my offering feels hardest to explain, sell, or scale? *(If you can't explain it to customers, you won't sell it. You may be pouring resources into something that's out of sync with market demand or your core value proposition. Don't ignore the friction.)*
- ☐ What's changed in my industry, customer behavior, or life circumstances that my original plan no longer fits? *(Your strategy may have been built for a different market moment—a now-obsolete tech trend, or a life stage when you had more time and fewer responsibilities. A pivot isn't a panic move; it's how resilient businesses stay relevant and profitable.)*
- ☐ Have I asked my team (or my audience) what they think I should stop doing? *(Sometimes the best ideas for pivots are already floating in your Slack channel or casual customer check-in calls. Employees and loyal customers are usually the first to notice what's become clunky or irrelevant about your product. Ask them!)*

PART

III

Scaling with Purpose: Your Road Map Forward

CHAPTER 9

Stop Growing. Start Scaling. (Yes, There's a Difference.)

We ditched the cushy corporate consulting gig, steady paychecks, fancy titles, and a little prestige to build something that was actually ours. In the beginning, we were juggling six kids (with Victoria baking two more in the oven), all while chasing the dream: build something big enough to cash out and maybe, just maybe, hit that entrepreneurial jackpot. We knew the drill. Hire smart people, turn our secret sauce into a product, and build systems, so we weren't the ones grinding for every single dollar. We were under no illusions; it was going to be a slog. But every time we brought on a new consultant, we got one step closer to the real goal—a business that didn't mean missing bedtime stories, bath time, or helping with algebra homework. That was the vision, and we were all in.

Fast-forward to year two, we'd crossed seven figures in revenue (note, that was starting with a two), bought out two partners, made some solid hires, and had real momentum. From the outside, we looked like we were killing it. On the inside? We were taking pay cuts just to keep up with expenses. The cracks were showing. It was time to stop duct-taping things together and start building real infrastructure. Up until now, we've been priming you—mind, body, and business plan—to finally get your dream off the ground. But this is where the training wheels come off and the real hustle begins. The moment when you stop just looking successful and start actually making your business work for you (translation: profitable, not just popular).

So, let's set the scene. Maybe you're already living it. Revenue charts are up and to the right, new clients keep sliding into your inbox, and your product is flying off the shelves. Feels like you've made it, right? Not so fast. Here's the gut check: if your business is booming but your bank account still looks anemic—or worse, you're not even paying yourself a real salary for all those late nights and missed weekends—then trust us, something is broken under the hood. You might be stuck in the entrepreneur's hamster wheel. While revenue is up, so are your hours, your stress, and your expenses. You're running faster just to stay in place, trading time for money with zero leverage. Sure, your top-line numbers look sexy, but your margins are paper thin or totally MIA. That means no breathing room, no owner distributions, and definitely no spontaneous trips to the Caribbean. Instead, you're stuck with stay-cations and a nagging sense that something's got to give.

If you're nodding along, it's time to get brutally honest about what's working and what's just working you into the ground. Because real success isn't about looking busy; it's about building a business that pays you, sustains you, and gives you the freedom you set out to find in the first place. Let's fix that gap, once and for all.

Scaling is a whole different vibe.

> *If your business is booming but your bank account still looks anemic—or worse, you're not even paying yourself a real salary for all those late nights and missed weekends—then trust us, something is broken under the hood.*

Suddenly, your systems and team are pulling their weight, your business runs smoother, and you're finally free from being the engine behind every single win.

We started scaling the minute we hit our come-to-Jesus moment. We had bought out our other partners, one of which wasn't actively managing cash flow, and we were a few payrolls away from running out of money. To make matters worse, we'd just rescinded the offer to that fabulous junior hire we couldn't afford. To get us back on track, we had to slash our own salaries, overhaul our finances to put cash flow at the center of everything, and double down on sales. Oh yeah, and Victoria just found out she was pregnant with baby number five.

Well, the sales strategy worked—too well. We brought in too many clients at once, charged too little, and were slow to get signed contracts and issue invoices to our large corporates. That meant no money to hire the people we desperately needed. And even if we had the cash, we didn't have the time to post a job listing, interview candidates, or put together a benefits package—basically, anything that might convince a sane person to join us. While our revenue charts looked like a rocket launch, our bottom line was a bloodbath. To make it worse, both of us were still pulling in less than six figures—a far cry from those cushy corporate paychecks we'd left behind and nowhere near enough to keep our families afloat. Those of you who are fans of our "Do the Opposite" rule will love what we did next. We did what any type A, slightly unhinged, deeply driven female founders would do: we went hunting for office space. No more squatting in Victoria's brother's extra offices. We overhauled our systems, tightened up operations, and got ruthless (in the best way) about which clients deserved to work with us. We knew we were delivering a premium product, so we stopped apologizing for it and started charging what we were worth. And yes, after way too many late nights and caffeine-fueled strategy sessions, we started hiring again. That first scrappy little bank loan gave us just enough breathing room to get our feet under us. But if you've read Power Move #5, you know by now, we're not in the business of following the script. Doing the unexpected has been our not-so-secret weapon, and so far, it's never let us down.

Every entrepreneur's path to scale looks a little different, but if you're a mom building a business, you don't just need to be good at scaling; you need to be a damn expert. Think of a solo practitioner billing hourly. She can only earn more by working more. More hours, more late-night emails, more "blazer on top, jammies on the bottom" Zoom calls. But if she builds a small team of rock stars, launches a full product suite, or adds digital programs, she starts making money even when she's not glued to a screen or bribing her kids with fruit snacks to keep them quiet during meetings.

Let's revisit our favorite healthy snack maker, who recently went through a transformative scale-up. She raised a little money, stopped hand-mixing energy bites in her kitchen at midnight, hired a baker and a food scientist, and rented a commercial kitchen with machines that actually bag the snacks for her. Suddenly, she's not drowning in production. She's focused on selling, growing, and trying to figure out how to see her newborn more often than just middle-of-the-night feedings.

Scaling isn't just about chasing bigger numbers, it's about building a business that works for you, not the other way around. Real scaling is more profitable, more sustainable, and, yes, way more fun. But let's not sugarcoat it; it's also tougher than just grinding out growth. But it's worth every second—before, during, and after.

For moms especially, scaling is the ultimate Power Move. It's not about burning yourself out or sacrificing your sanity on the altar of "hustle." It's about getting strategic, using your smarts to multiply your impact, and fiercely protecting your time for the stuff only you can do. That means focusing on the moves that actually push your business forward, while leaving plenty of room for dance recitals, baseball games, and those lazy Sunday afternoons that make life sweet.

But before you embark on your scaling era, there's one non-negotiable mindset shift you'll need to make and a new golden rule you have to learn. Before we reveal those, though, a quick story.

Beth learned our new golden rule at a cringy mandatory executive summit she was forced—err, asked—to attend in her corporate gig. Oh, the irony. She still wakes up in night sweats, haunted by memories of the matching logo vests and an after-hours "casino night" where she spent most of the evening hiding behind a fake ficus, clutching a martini, alongside the only other woman brave enough not to fake a "client emergency." Most of it, thankfully, has been blocked out, except for one line a professor hammered into everyone's heads on repeat: "What got you here won't get you there." That's the new golden rule, friends. It's the only piece of corporate-speak we're allowing in this book, and it took us nine chapters to even say it out loud. But damn it's good.

What got you here was sweating every detail. Overthinking every move. Perfecting every project. Triple-checking every email. Leading every meeting personally. Those instincts are the very ones that will strangle your ability to scale. It's time to trade the to-do list for the big-girl chair at the head of the table and focus your considerable firepower on the business' most critical issues. If you don't, or you can't, prepare to stay small.

You're the CEO; Time to Act Like It

When it's time to scale, your first Power Move isn't rolling out a flashy new product or making headlines with a splashy partnership. Nope, scaling starts with something way less Instagrammable: learning to let go and delegate. Giving up control and handing off daily tasks is the make-or-break moment for even the savviest solopreneurs. Why? Because if you refuse to delegate, you're still clinging to every single tactic you used in year one: micromanaging, firefighting, and convincing yourself no one else could possibly do it as well as you. That's the fast lane to burnout, not breakthrough.

Delegation isn't just a "nice to have"; it's the secret sauce that separates the hustlers from the true builders. If you want your business to grow beyond what you can personally touch, you have to trust others to take the wheel on some of those day-to-day moves.

If you want your business to grow beyond what you can personally touch, you have to trust others to take the wheel on some of those day-to-day moves.

It's uncomfortable at first, but it's the only way to create the space (and sanity) you need to actually lead, innovate, and scale like a boss.

Trust us, we've heard every version of the same story from businesses that failed to scale: "But I'm the only one who can [insert magical unicorn task here]." Or "I just can't find anyone good enough to [insert sacred job function here]." And our personal favorite—mostly because we've said it too—"The client will leave if I'm not personally leading the account." (We are both sheepishly shrinking into our chairs as we write this.)

It's easy to spot these excuses in others, but living them is a whole different story. In our partnership, we landed on opposite ends of the delegation spectrum, and the results were just as messy (and enlightening) as you'd expect. Beth was almost too good at delegating; she'd hand something off and be on to the next big idea before the handoff was even halfway done. (At home she was still getting up at five o'clock in the morning to put a dinner in the slow cooker and sign the 50 pieces of homework that inexplicably showed up in her kids' backpacks every day.) Victoria was, to put it lightly, on the opposite end of the spectrum. Her control-freak tendencies actually served us well in the early days—invoices sent, bills paid, team intact, and financials always up to date. But as the pace picked up, she hit a wall. She was missing the few key times she got with her kids around the dinner table, caught in a constant scramble to catch up.

The breaking point came when we landed several high-stakes, high-billing crisis clients. Victoria kept managing her regular workload by day and pushed invoicing and collections until after the kids were in bed. You know, that sacred window when most moms are just looking to pass out on the couch and watch terrible (but oh-so-good) TV. But crisis work doesn't stick to that schedule. Press releases have to be put out before the markets open, with the most critical facts and figures only crossing your email after midnight. Emergency meetings pop up with only a few hours' notice. Client calls come at any time of the night. And suddenly, even her superwoman powers weren't enough.

That's when we learned that only a few tasks need you and your full, undistracted attention when you're a CEO in scaling mode. And yes, those things are usually difficult, inconvenient, and constantly changing. But here's the deal: if revenue and profits stall, that's on you. And if they grow? That's probably because of a seed you planted six months ago that's just now starting to bloom. That is the job. Full stop. Well, maybe it's also handing out bonuses and remembering everyone's birthday.

Here is how Victoria got herself out of the mess she was in. To force herself to delegate, she broke up tasks into three groups. We still categorize work into these buckets and so should you.

- **The first bucket is for the tasks that absolutely need your attention right now.** These are the lifeblood of your business—your vision, your brain, and your passion. Launching a new product line? That's you. Spotting a strategy—or a team member—that's not pulling enough weight? Also, you. Discovering the problem and the patch for a system that used to work but doesn't anymore? Sorry, still you. If it has the potential to swing your revenues or profits by 10 percent or more, it stays firmly on your plate. Think of these tasks as business CPR. You can't exactly outsource those to an intern. Or even a really well-meaning colleague.

  Your job, Ms. CEO, is to always keep one extremely paranoid eye on the horizon (and the other nervously twitching while side-eyeing the staff members who took over your old jobs). Never stop scanning the horizon for the next big opportunity or slick competitor gunning for your lunch. Beth could spot a new competitive threat faster than the sound of your toddler grabbing that second cookie just as you turned to start dinner. The moment Beth tipped her off, Victoria would go full detective mode, diving headfirst into social media rabbit holes, DMing everyone we knew in the industry and outright asking clients if anyone new was sliding into their inboxes. (This, no joke, included snapping a quick pic of the sign-in book at a prospect's reception desk and then hiding in a bathroom stall to look at said contraband pic to decipher who we were competing with for their business.) Depending on the threat level, we'd either end up shrugging it off and getting back to business or get to work plotting our pivot. (See Power Move #5.) Either way, this kind of paranoid super sleuthing should, and did, live squarely in our job descriptions.

- **The second bucket is for the tasks that can be kicked off for someone else to take over.** You can swoop in when they break, but otherwise these tasks should run without you. Think client onboarding, invoice generation, sales proposals, and tactical HR items like benefits and PTO tracking. These systems need to hum like a well-oiled machine. If you find yourself editing every single invoice—like Victoria did, mortifyingly far into Clermont's scaling—it's time to step away from QuickBooks. Seriously. Your job isn't to keep tinkering with templates. It's to fix the system or fix the people. Identify the real problem, architect the right solution, bring in the right team to build it, and then (this is the hard part) let them go do it. Check in. Be quality control. Be your team's greatest coach and mentor. But remember, your job isn't to make the donuts. A team of smart, focused people working 40 hours a week on a system is going to beat your half-distracted, half-hour stabs at fixing a complex problem every single time.
- **Finally, the last bucket is for the things that should have been let go of yesterday.** (Looking directly at you, Victoria.) These are the rote, repetitive tasks that don't need your daily dose of brilliance. Things like data entry, social media scheduling, and chasing down receipts. If it can be templated, trained, or tracked, it can be outsourced.

Our personal #3 was human resources. As we started to scale, our days got swallowed whole by recruiting, interviewing, and reference-checking. Suddenly, we were losing great candidates left and right because we couldn't get offers out fast enough. We made some truly cringe-worthy hiring mistakes, mostly because we were trying to squeeze vetting into the five-minute cracks between meetings and school pickups.

At first, we tried to delegate bits and pieces to our team, but that just meant we spent even more hours coaching them through tasks we barely understood ourselves. (The blind leading the blind, anyone?) I wish we could say we had a lightning-bolt moment and immediately hired a recruiting rockstar. We absolutely did not. Instead, we tiptoed in, bringing someone on as a contractor and then dragged our feet for way too long before finally making her permanent. When we did pull the trigger, it was like someone handed us back 20 hours a week (plus all the time we spent complaining about how bad we were at recruiting in the first place). Lesson learned. If you want your sanity back, don't wait to bring in the pros.

Delegating these tasks frees you up to focus on your most important job: shaping and sustaining the vision. As the founder, you'll spot trends, opportunities, and risks long before your team even knows what hit them. Why? Because you're the one who dreamed this business into existence in the first place. Your vision is your secret weapon, and no matter how talented your team is, they'll only ever catch glimpses of it. You're the one who sees the whole picture.

Of course, there is always a catch. To actually *see* it, you have to clear your field of vision. So delegate. Step back. Breathe. Think. Some of our best ideas showed up when we finally gave ourselves a little space. Our ESG segment came to Beth after a few days off and a long hike through the cliffs of Bodega Bay. Victoria, meanwhile, would roll in on Tuesdays after a long weekend in Northern Michigan armed with brilliant sales ideas and a new strategy for reeling in a hot-but-not-quite-there lead. A solid business vision can hit you anywhere, anytime, but it needs some space to get through the clutter in your head.

Scaling isn't just about outsourcing at work—it's about outsourcing at home, too. The same rules apply. First, there are the non-negotiables you absolutely have to own, especially when it comes to your kids' long-term comfort, mental health, and character building. No one else can define those for your family, and yes, just like your business priorities, they'll shift over time. But it's safe to say if your kid is in pain, physical or mental, you want to be the first one on the scene. For Victoria, this was, and still remains, making it to their big games, checking in with how they are doing at school, who they are playing with at recess, and making sure she is there for bedtime (at least most of the time).

Then there are the logistical grind tasks like scheduling tutoring, managing after-school chaos, and arranging rides. You can outsource a lot of this, but you still have to be the quarterback calling the plays. How that looks depends on your resources. When Victoria bought her first house, she insisted on a neighborhood packed with kids (read: carpool gold mine). Armed with her color-coded Outlook calendar, she'd run point on the quarterly schedule and, more crucially, the daily carpool circuit. Without that structure, her day would collapse. And when her kids were little, a full-time nanny wasn't a luxury, it was the only way we could build Clermont.

And then there's the stuff that stings, the things you have to let go. Who your kid sits with at lunch. The birthday party they didn't get invited to. The after-school hangouts you missed the memo on. When you're building a business, you're going to lose some of those battles.

Victoria felt like she'd failed as a mom countless times with her oldest daughter, Ali. The missed Valentine's Day party, the summer beach day with the other moms and daughters, you name it. But now, as a freshman in high school, Ali shows Victoria every day just how much she's grown—her confidence, her street smarts (which serve her well when she's negotiating curfew), and her unshakable sense of self.

At the end of the day, scaling your business—and your life—isn't about doing more. It's about doing less of the wrong stuff and more of the right stuff. Focus like your sanity depends on it (because it might). Outsource with intention. Accept, with a deep breath and maybe a glass or two of wine, that someone else might actually do it better than you. And get used to eating humble pie when faced with your own replaceability.

Build the Backend That Buys You Your Time Back

Now that you have learned the big D, *delegate*, you have some open time in your schedule. It's time to invest that time, and a little bit of money, in building. This is not the sexy stuff but the systems that will help save your sanity. Think of the backend as a company "chore chart." Done right, it will mean you can finally close the laptop without worrying that your entire operation will crumble the minute you start your first homecooked dinner of the week or show up for soccer practice like the mom you swore you'd be. Remember when we said there are things you set up once, then let someone else run until they (or the universe) inevitably mess it up and you have to step back in? These are those things.

Architecting a reliable backend means building simple, repeatable processes for all the must-do stuff, so you're not manually reinventing the wheel whenever something breaks (or panic-Googling "chart of accounts" at midnight). Systematizing shifts you out of bottleneck mode and into boss mode. Your business starts humming along. Well, maybe not humming, but at least it no longer feels like it's careening out of control.

There are four critical areas you must get a handle on: sales and marketing, finance, people, and your own calendar; the last one being the sneakiest saboteur of them all.

Sales and Marketing

When it comes to sales and marketing, you need two things: a smart team and a wildly responsive system to execute and report on progress. Let someone else worry about sales collateral, marketing decks, and event planning. Your job is to read the reports and figure out what they are trying to tell you. Our simple minds looked at each output as red, yellow, or green. It either needed an immediate fix, was something we had better start watching more closely, or something we could blissfully ignore.

Now, full transparency—we're control freaks. (Couldn't even manage a polite fake gasp, could you?) Even after hiring a stellar sales lead and bringing in a top-tier marketing firm, we never entirely stepped away. We tracked trends, joined the big meetings, chaired quarterly strategy sessions, and, yes, often shouted wild ideas from the sidelines (a few of which were actually quite good). We reinserted ourselves when we spotted troubling trends—or golden opportunities—that could actually move the revenue needle. Thanks to the systems we put in place, and the glorious reports it generated, problems found us, not the other way around. And that's the only time (well, almost) we stepped in. Here are a few greatest hits (and yes, we're only sharing the ones that make us look brilliant):

- **Email open rates were slipping.** The team's approach—just send more—wasn't solving the problem. Victoria dug deeper and found the root cause: our email platform had updated its settings, and our messages were getting flagged as spam. With a few behind-the-scenes adjustments and more calls to HubSpot's service team than we can count, she got things back on track.

- **Prospect calls were slowing down.** Our thought leadership content wasn't landing us initial prospect meetings the way it used to, and no one could pinpoint why. Our team tried coming up with better topics, different writing styles, more charts and graphs, you name it. We decided this was above our pay grade and hired an expert firm to help analyze SEO and search data and figure out why people weren't finding or reading our stuff. Turns out, timing and keyword choice mattered more than we thought. Once we optimized both, engagement started climbing again.
- **We started losing competitive pitches.** That wasn't typical for us. After some digging, we realized our same-sized competitors were sending CEOs and senior leaders to the pitch even if those leaders had no intention of working on the account. We started showing up, too, but with a clear message about the specific role we'd play. No bait-and-switch, just transparency and founder-level involvement where it counted.

In the end, we stayed close enough to catch the trends and step in when it mattered but far enough back that the sales team didn't revolt. We'll call that a win.

Finance

As hard as it may be to tear yourself away from sales and marketing, unless you're Victoria, you'll be downright giddy to hand off the financials. Enter your accountant. These women are serious—the kind who don't think your jokes are funny and are constantly sighing as they open your QuickBooks account. Let them handle the number crunching, invoice chasing, payroll running, and your repeated promises to "find that missing receipt at the bottom of my carry-on tonight" from now on. Pay them to deliver smart weekly dashboards and colorful monthly reports filled with graphs and charts and then brace themselves for your tears, a tantrum, or a slightly uncomfortable hug, depending on the direction of the trendlines.

Let them own the reporting and analyzing while you focus on the big-picture decision-making: pricing, investments, when to reinvest versus finally pay yourself, and whether that "game-changing" software upgrade is actually worth the splurge. Think of your accountant as your own personal Weather Channel reporter. She'll tell you if it's smooth sailing or stormy out there, but you're still the one flying the plane.

And yes, full-time accountants can be pretty expensive. We instead relied on outsourced bookkeepers and fractional CFOs for years, eventually discovering a secret weapon: part-time moms with previous careers in accounting. We gave them the flexibility to work the way they wanted, and in return we got value far beyond what we could pay—and a partner in crime to exchange "what happened at my kid's lunch table" stories with.

People

Human resources is one area that shouldn't sit entirely on your plate. But some parts? Those are squarely in founder territory. Hiring your senior leadership team, breaking tie votes on tricky personnel issues, or stepping in when a toxic dynamic starts brewing—that's your lane. The rest—benefits, onboarding, PTO tracking, performance reviews planning and execution, process docs—should be delegated. And honestly, your team would prefer to have someone else to go to rather than you for many of these things. You need to remember that you're the architect of the team, not the office manager.

Senior hires always came with a serious price tag, as they should. But whenever one of us wasn't 100 percent convinced the role was crucial or the timing was right, we'd sit down and write the job description ourselves. Putting it all on paper forced us to get brutally honest; sometimes it made a rock-solid case for hiring, and other times it exposed that we could (and should) wait.

We also made it a rule to interview every final candidate for mid-level roles and above, even if we weren't the ones managing them day-to-day. It wasn't about micromanaging or second-guessing our team's judgment. It was about protecting our culture and making sure no single opinion could tip the scales too far. Those final interviews didn't always uncover hidden red flags or reveal the next unicorn, but they gave us peace of mind and sent a clear message: hiring isn't just another box to check. It's a core part of our strategy, and we treat it like the high-stakes move it is.

Your Time

The last thing you need to backstop touches everything: your entire business *and* your personal life. Yep, it's your calendar. And don't tell us, "I've got this." Because you most likely don't. Just hear us out. Calendar tools have quite literally changed our lives. As our business scaled, so did the chaos. We were constantly on the road, keeping current clients happy while trying to market and sell our way into new business. When we finally made it back to the office, everyone wanted a piece of our time. And we wanted to give it. We were big on culture and worked hard to keep it strong, even when we weren't physically around.

But here's what happened. After a full day of spontaneous catch-ups and hallway strategy sessions, it was somehow 5:30 p.m. and we hadn't started our actual work. So, we went home, did the dinner-bedtime-dishes routine, and opened the laptop back up around 8:30 p.m. We weren't exactly firing on all cylinders by then, going to bed late and waking up to do it all over again. We desperately needed a way to get more work done during the day and get some rest and time with our kids at night.

Victoria took charge of both of our calendars at first, and then, we made one of our single most important hires—Rhonda—who started as our executive assistant but grew into office manager, recruiting manager, office mom, and everything in between. But before the universe sent us Rhonda, Victoria took the heavy hand, and her secret boiled down to these principles:

- **Build in buffer time.** Back-to-back meetings sound efficient until you realize you haven't peed since 8 a.m.
- **Batch your standing meetings.** We stacked ours on one day a week and accepted that no "real work" was happening that day. Survival was the win.
- **Time-block like a boss.** Not just for productivity but for sanity. Sometimes the block said, "Do actual work," and sometimes it said, "Breathe, please."
- **Leave space for client curveballs.** In a client-facing business, the only certainty is unpredictability. We reserved chunks of time for unscheduled but inevitable client calls. Clients were essentially paying for on-demand access to the most senior people at the firm—us. We never knew exactly when those calls would come, but they came often enough that we religiously blocked off an hour each day. That hour was either spent fielding client calls or catching up on the work we were supposed to be doing during the times they

> actually called. On the rare days the phone stayed quiet, we tackled longer-term projects—the kind that demand more focus than you can give while parked watching your kid's eighth soccer practice of the week.

Your personal schedule needs a refresh too. Don't underestimate the magic of an old-school, giant family calendar. Seriously—get one. You have heard about Victoria's Outlook family calendar she shares with Bill. It has everything from kids' activities, work launches, and deadlines to what's for dinner and the ever-important carpool plans. Forget the Pinterest dream of a cheerful "family calendar meeting" where you fill it out together as a group. Instead, block 30 quiet minutes every Sunday to update it solo while yelling questions to your kid or with your nanny on speed dial. It's not glamorous, but it will save your sanity.

Beth swore by hers. She'd snap a photo and carry it on her phone all week, fully aware she'd be the one getting the "who is supposed to pick up [fill in child's name]" call. But she always slept like a rock on Sunday nights because even if the week ahead looked totally bonkers, at least there was a plan to cover it.

Scale Your Single Offering into a Boxed Set

Once you're confident you can sell more and you've built solid systems so you can stop desperately searching for the mythical twenty-fifth hour in the day, you've hit a critical crossroads. Or a massive danger zone, depending on your perspective. The solopreneur just sticks with that one offering, riding it until the wheels fall off. The megalomaniac entrepreneur gets bored immediately and launches 12 new products, none of which has found product-market fit yet. You, the rational mompreneur, are going to do it smarter. You're going to build out from where you are, thoughtfully and strategically, like expanding in concentric circles. Your next moves should either productize to scale how you deliver what's in your brain to more than one client at a time or expand into a related product or service that your current buyer—or someone very close to them—already needs, even if they don't know it yet. Try not to bet the farm on any single idea. Growth is great but so is keeping your house, your sanity, and your monthly mystery reader spot in your kid's kindergarten class. Add new services one at a time, or in whatever manageable bundle lets you still be the mom you want to be, the friend who shows up, and maybe even someone who occasionally sleeps.

If you're ready to go big, skip ahead to the note at the end of the chapter on fundraising. If your cash flow's solid and you're self-funding for now, keep reading.

The secret to incremental growth is to productize. You have to figure out how to make your inputs more efficient—assigning standardized work to more affordable team members or outsourcing at cheaper rates while leaving a percentage of the project dollars for your pearls of wisdom. Yes, you might have to let go of a few bells and whistles, but you can still deliver a solid product with less input from your senior (and most expensive) staff. If you're in a product business, your focus should be on cutting input costs and balancing premium features that wow with cost-effective ones that customers will never miss.

At Clermont, we streamlined by having analysts handle research and foundational findings and brought in a data visualization specialist to transform that work into client-ready charts and reports quickly. The senior people only swooped in at the end to add insights and recommendations. We didn't turn custom work into fully standardized products, mostly because our offerings were high-ticket ones that had to include these smart senior-level insights to justify their price tag. But, by shifting some work around, we were able to boost our margins and delivery capacity by roughly 30 percent.

Next, try to package your services into clear, easy-to-understand tiers. Through experience, we learned that having a single tier across all clients rarely maximizes profitability. Instead, offer multiple tiers with incredibly clear differentiation between them. Differences could be based on hours, number of deliverables, or seniority of team members working on the account. Reserve your highest rates for urgent, crisis-level work when clients will happily sign off on the costs to get themselves out of the mess they are in.

In Clermont's ESG segment, we followed a similar playbook—auditing where clients fell short and providing them an example set of disclosures if they were in a DIY kind of mood. But we also tempted them with an easy upgrade if they wanted us to create customized disclosures. To make sure we could make money at each tier, we invested heavily in systematizing our delivery process behind the scenes. We documented every workflow, trained our team thoroughly, and made sure resources were easily accessible for new hires. The payoff? Our middle layer leveled up fast, which freed up senior staff to spend less time with each client but with greater efficiency—a critical driver of growth and profit as we scaled. To make these changes, you must have a team to work with. (Yes, that means you, Ms. Solopreneur, who wants to double her income.) Start small if you must—contractors or fractional hires—but the math must work. Meaning you need to bill more than you pay. Begin outsourcing admin, delivery, and tech tasks early and document the hell out of your processes so that you can train others as you scale.

If you're running a professional services firm like we did, recurring projects and retainer packages are your new best friends. They stabilize cash flow, cut down on constant client chasing, and build deeper, stickier relationships. In fact, keeping current clients happy might just be the most underrated growth strategy out there.

For product-based businesses, the same idea holds. Double down on your bestsellers, expand your sales channels, and bundle products to boost average order value. And remember, retention matters. Each sale should be the beginning of the relationship, not the grand finale.

Content and coaching businesses? You'll need to lean even harder into digital and social. Scalable revenue streams like courses, templates, workshops, and memberships are key. They not only diversify your income but also warm up future one-on-one clients while you sleep.

Remember, scaling your offer into a bundle or tier isn't about doing everything or chasing every shiny object. It's about strategy in building your product or service set, becoming a master at stacking smart offers, and concurrently stringing together a well-trained team of delivery agents or fully automated systems that run whether you're in the office, off at a soccer tournament, or waging war against the latest family-wide plague that your youngest brought home from a sleepover.

Hire Like a Boss, Not Their BFF

Speaking of building out a team, there is a real method to this madness when you are scaling. Unfortunately, it's no longer about whom you'd like to have a drink with or hang out with after work. Sometimes you need to hire the person who gives you a blank look every time you crack a joke but is the best in the biz at what they do. Victoria wrestled with this early on while we were building the team at Clermont. She thought "culture fit" meant everyone had to love each other, so we passed on a few rockstar candidates just because they didn't vibe with our personalities. Big miss. In a perfect world, you hire someone who's both a killer talent and the kind of person you'd add to your Mah Jong group. But those are rare. Don't confuse "culture fit" with "just like us."

So how do you find the perfect team? Detailed job descriptions, structured interview processes, and third, fourth, and sometimes fifth sets of eyes to help you make smart, unbiased decisions. Whether you're hiring junior support or senior leadership, the rules stay the same: know what you are looking for, skillset-wise, inside and out. And talk to people in the field who have held or hired for the role before. Make sure when you write a job description, every task ties directly to one of three things: making money, saving money, or freeing up your time so you can do either.

Standardizing your hiring process early protects you from emotional (and expensive) decisions later. And always, always go back to your financial projections. Know exactly how much revenue needs to be generated to justify the hire and make sure you have a plan (note: we said a plan, not always the revenues) to get there before you send the offer letter.

The smartest entrepreneurs learn to hire ahead of the curve, before revenue, staffing, or growth bottlenecks turn into real problems. Your first hires are going to make you uncomfortable. Your first senior hire might keep you up at night. (And let us tell you, that first big hire we made for the ESG segment literally gave Victoria the night sweats—even before menopause kicked in!) But, if you're passing on opportunities that would grow your business because you don't have time to onboard them, that's your flashing neon sign. You've got to hire in order to scale.

Unfortunately, you may have to temporarily give up your salary, bonuses, or other investments to afford the right hire at the right time. It's a strategic trade, not a permanent one. Yeah, we know, this last part is easier said than done. Especially when your income is what's keeping the lights on at home. It can feel impossible. But sometimes that short-term hit is exactly what clears the runway for something bigger. You're shifting gears. Betting on yourself. Because the real payoff? It's not today's paycheck. It's what you're building for tomorrow.

Remember when we said we were in this exact same spot? Well, it didn't feel good for either Beth or Victoria, but for Victoria, it hit differently. She was still building her financial foundation, while Beth already had one exit under her belt. For Victoria, it felt impossible. She was pulling in as much as her husband, so taking a pay cut meant real changes at home. There were tears the day we made the call to slash the salary. And in the months that followed, the bills at home piled up, and the credit card balances crept higher. But Victoria believed in the plan we had in place to get Clermont back to profitability. It was tough as hell, no doubt. But without that moment, we wouldn't have made it to our exit six years later.

Just as we said with delegation, building a team or support doesn't just apply to the business. The same rules apply at home and, in our experience, these hires often happen in tandem with business ones. In fact, personal hiring has unlocked just as much business growth for us as professional hiring.

To figure out whom to hire for your own family needs, ask yourself this: where's the daily pinch point? For Beth, it was hockey practice, which was originally manageable but then suddenly rescheduled to 5:10 p.m., 45 minutes away. Hiring someone to drive Sam to practice for the season? The best $80 she spent that week. Other things we've outsourced without shame (and highly recommend): grocery shopping (praise be, Instacart), meal prep (a few days a week makes all the difference), errands (kids *hate* them—let's stop calling dragging them along "quality time"), and even the random stuff like hanging pictures or wrapping holiday gifts. Yes, seriously. TaskRabbit and Facebook community groups exist for a reason.

In the early days, hiring is all about triage—solving the pain points that keep you up at night, whether they're personal or professional. Later, once you cross that million-dollar revenue mark, you'll finally have the breathing room (and budget) to make the investments needed to drive growth and efficiencies in the business. Those smart, targeted hires—the ones who give you back precious time, energy, or revenue—are what scaling the business is all about.

Evolve Your Kitchen Cabinet

As you scale your business, your Kitchen Cabinet—that trusted group of advisors, mentors, and sanity-savers—needs to evolve right along with you. The same early-stage advice that helped you launch may not be the advice that gets you to seven figures. You're going to need a few strategic additions. Start by adding mentors who have some experience scaling businesses, not just starting them. There's a big difference between launching something and building something sustainable, and you need people who've scoped out the terrain ahead of you. If possible, look for advisors who have navigated at least one or two rough patches: people who have seen a recession, a market downturn, or a major industry shake-up. Their war stories are gold when you're making tough calls.

Also consider joining a women's CEO group, especially if it's a real, in-person community where you can engage meaningfully. Virtual groups have their place, but nothing replaces the depth of relationships and real-world perspective that come from showing up consistently and investing time in a high-caliber circle. People always ask us about joining some of the more expensive groups out there touting the best networking. Our experience was that many times it was mostly service providers selling to each other and slowly building a group of intimates is a better use of your precious time. Naturally, we turned to our Kitchen Cabinet for ideas—because, you know, we always do. Beth tapped into her university alumni network, which turned out to be a goldmine of powerful female special interest groups (and a handy hookup for football tickets come game day). Meanwhile, Victoria discovered her town was secretly a hive of female entrepreneurial energy, with small groups and events she jumped at getting involved with. We both also tapped into virtual women's networks available online, and after a few false starts, Beth landed in a gem of a club (shoutout to her Australian posse) that acts as equal parts therapist on speed dial, focus group, and marketing guru.

And don't hesitate to reach out to women who are operating at a level you aspire to. Neither of us ever thought twice about asking someone at a much bigger firm or platform to grab lunch, dinner, or even just a quick coffee. Looking back, it's a bit mind blowing how many brilliant, accomplished women said yes. People love to help those who are serious, respectful of their time, and doing interesting things. Your next advisor—or future investor or board member—might just be one bold invitation away. (And when it's your turn, pay it forward. Always. Even if it's just twenty 20 minutes on the phone, show up and give it your best.) In addition to your advisors and mentors, you'll want to start building relationships with investors and bankers, even if funding isn't on your radar yet. (Go reread Power Move #3 if you need to be reminded why.) Understanding how they think, the metrics they obsess over, and how they size up businesses can be a serious game changer. And remember, you do *not* want your first conversation with an investor to happen when you're already stressed, desperate for cash, or racing against payroll. It's far smarter (and much more strategic) to connect early, when you have the headspace to learn, build trust, and position yourself thoughtfully.

Finally, it's time to get serious about collaboration over competition, especially with other women-led businesses. The myth that there's only room for one woman at the table is outdated and, frankly, harmful. The truth is that the right partnerships can open doors faster than years of solo hustle ever could. Strategic collaborations, including comarketing, bundled services, joint ventures, and simply sharing knowledge, can expand your reach, add credibility, and build resilience into your business model. Women who support women don't just build stronger companies—they build entire ecosystems where everyone wins.

We'll never forget meeting with the CEO of another firm in our industry. After agreeing to have drinks with us, she spent two painful hours stonewalling every question we asked and looking disinterested as we shared stories about our firm. She wouldn't share a single detail about her business and instead tried (not so subtly) to mine us for competitive intel. Beth still laughs at (and stands by) her grand vision at the time of merging our firms into the biggest woman-led powerhouse in the industry. Needless to say, that didn't happen. And yes, running into her at every industry event after that was as awkward as you'd imagine. But here's the flip side: when collaboration does work, it works beautifully. We've swapped overflow business, passed along conflicted clients, and even recommended other women-led firms to investment bankers when acquisition opportunities arose. There's almost always a payoff when you show up with generosity and play the long game. (And no, we never referred business to our painful drinks partner!)

Final Thought

At some point in your business, you'll hit a wall—and that wall usually looks a lot like you. Some of you brilliant mompreneurs already avoided this problem by building a business brand from day one (gold star for you). We weren't that smart. We started with personal brands and eventually realized that if we wanted to truly scale, we needed something bigger than our own names and faces.

You'll know it's time to make the shift when a few things start happening: (1) you become the bottleneck for everything, (2) client expectations start to exceed what any one person (even a supermom) can deliver, and (3) you want to be more present with your family. That last one is the most important. When you start missing more things than you actually make, it's time to look in the mirror and have a tough conversation. Because that was not your goal when you started this business; your goal was to create financial freedom for yourself so you could be with your family.

Before you dive into scaling, take a big step back and ask yourself one question. What's your personal vision for the business? Are you building a laid-back lifestyle business, or are you aiming for a full-scale, all-gas-no-brakes empire? Sketch out a three- to five-year plan anchored to your magic number: your revenue target and dream size. Then get practical. What will it really take to get there? How many employees? How much overhead? Will you need outside capital? Once you map out the rough picture, circle back to the Triple M (the Mom's Mayhem Matrix) and make sure your new business model still gets you to your intended destination. Or, if you're switching quadrants entirely, be crystal clear on what you're doing and the impact it will have. The more honest you are here, the better prepared you'll be for the ripple effects that scaling can have on your family life and on how long it will take to hit your financial freedom number.

Building a brand bigger than yourself doesn't mean stepping back—it means stepping up. You become the visionary, the voice, and the driving force but no longer the one shouldering the weight alone.

Chapter Endnote: A Word on Fundraising

If you're thinking about raising capital as part of scaling your business, here's the first thing you need to know: raise money when you can, not when you need it. There will never be a perfect moment when the market conditions are ideal, your projections are flawless, and your kids are all magically sleeping through the night. Opportunities in business—especially around funding—move fast. Position yourself early and be ready when the window opens.

Second, we have to talk about the "mom penalty." It's real. Women founders already face obstacles in fundraising, and moms often get an extra layer of doubt and second-guessing thrown at them. There are ways to navigate this:

- Show up with a real, proven business model—not just a big idea but actual traction, customers, and revenue.
- Whenever possible, make sure there's another woman, ideally another mom, in the room when you pitch. Allies matter.
- Be flawless in your preparation and delivery. It's unfair, but in many rooms, you'll be held to a higher standard.
- If you can, bring your mentors to the table. Having well-respected advisors backing you gives you an edge.
- Lean into the growing pool of resources built specifically for women founders. There are more funds, accelerators, and networks out there now than ever before, and they exist for a reason: because women like you are building companies worth betting on.

Finally, if you're serious about raising money, make it your mission to set up at least 10 informational interviews before you ever actively raise. Talk to angel investors to understand what early-stage capital expects. Talk to lenders to see if smart debt might fit your growth better than equity dilution. And talk to venture fund investors and the CEOs of the companies they invest in to get a realistic view of what this life really looks like—and whether you want that for *your* business.

Each conversation will make you sharper, more strategic, and far more confident, whether you ultimately decide to fundraise now, later, or never. Some business models can be bootstrapped, but many can't. Either way, it's smart to understand what a fundraiser can offer *and* what it will cost you. Only then can you decide if outside capital truly aligns with your personal goals and is the right move for you, your business, and your family's future.

■ ■ ■

Gut Check

Am I Still Doing or Am I Finally Leading?

- ☐ If I stepped away from my business for 10 full days with no laptop or clear line of communication, would it continue operating smoothly, or would the wheels start to come off by day three? *(What function would fail first: client delivery, back-end operations, internal decision-making. . . or your own sense of control?)*
- ☐ What tasks am I still holding onto that someone else could handle 80 percent as well—for a fraction of my hourly rate—and with the right training, maybe even better? *(If you cleared those off your plate, what would you finally have time for? Closing bigger deals, building new revenue streams, refining your vision, or simply creating the white space that sparks your next big idea?)*
- ☐ What's one process in my business that I've been patching with duct tape, late nights, and good intentions? *(Is this the quarter you finally invest the time and resources to fix it right—streamline, automate, delegate—or will you wait until it breaks under pressure at the worst possible moment?)*
- ☐ Is my calendar a reflection of my values and strategic priorities—or a graveyard of obligations I agreed to months ago? *(Audit your schedule with the same rigor you bring to a client engagement or your product road map. Can you time-block space for high-leverage thinking, team development, relationship-building, or even recharging?)*
- ☐ Do I trust my team—or am I double-checking everything behind them? *(Trust isn't just a feeling—it's earned through smart hiring, strong onboarding, and clear goal setting. Have you built the foundation that allows others to succeed without you?)*

CHAPTER 10

The Path to Sustainable Success: Choose Your Own Adventure

You've made it to the end of *Entrepreneur Like a Mother*! According to every stat on book reading, you probably skipped a few chapters to land here. But let's pretend you savored every word along the way. Either way, thank you. But this is *far from* the end of the road. It's the beginning of something bigger. You didn't pick up this book just to read about scaling a business while managing carpools, client calls, and the 47 mental tabs open in your head. You picked it up because you're building something, something that matters to you and your family. And something that will give you the financial and personal freedom that corporate America could never give you.

Now that you've seen what's possible, the next step is doing the work, but not all at once, and not alone. Depending on where you are in your journey, we've created three focused tracks to meet you right where you are. You can go through each one in order, or you may be somewhere in between.

We know many of you aren't just building businesses. You're stepping into the CEO role for the first time. That shift means expanding your focus beyond today's deadlines to the levers that change everything: scale, funding, exits, and legacy. The moves that drive long-term value. And income. We're here for all of it. More content on leadership, strategy, and capital is coming your way, because once you start playing the game at that level, we know you're going to win it.

But even the biggest businesses start with a first move. So start here.

What follows is your quick-start matrix.

Choose Your Starting Point

CONCEPT TO CASH.
This track is for the mom who's ready to take the leap from "someday" to "let's go." You've got the spark, the concept, and maybe even a few sticky notes full of plans. Now it's time to pressure-test that idea, validate the market, and turn your vision into something that earns.

LAUNCH TO PROFIT.
This is aimed at the mom who's turning a side hustle into a real business. You've got the idea and early traction with actual sales. Now you need structure, pricing, and, more than likely, your first hires (or your first boundaries).

SCRAPPY TO SCALABLE.
We are looking at you, mama founder! You are generating real revenue and are now ready to take it to the next level. You'll dive into systems, delegation, profit levers, and smarter growth that doesn't require 80-hour weeks.

And just in case no one said it today, you don't have to choose between being a powerhouse entrepreneur and a present, imperfect mother. We didn't have it all figured out either at the beginning (or even now). But we're here to tell you: the kids will be just fine, you're going to be even better, and your bank account is going to have numbers in it you couldn't have imagined.

Now let's build the business that will get you there. Pick the track that works for your goals, your schedule, and your actual life. When you make it through and are ready for another one, come on back and keep it going!

Time to get moving. Your way. Your rules. Let's go.

Track 1: Concept to Cash

You've got the brilliant idea, and now it's time to prove it, pressure-test it, and turn it into real revenue. Know your buyer. Understand the market. Size up its growth potential—not just in theory but in cold, hard dollars—and test it. *Power Move #1: Prioritize the Right Idea over Your Passion Project*, in Chapter 4, is your go-to resource for this track. It's packed with practical tools—buyer personas, TAM calculations, and ways to pressure-test your idea—all designed to make sure your business can truly fatten your wallet.

	30-day BUILD THE BUYER BLUEPRINT	90-day GREENLIGHT THE MARKET	180-day TESTING WITH YOUR TRIBE
GOAL	Identify one or two ideal buyer personas	Make sure your market is worth the hustle	Pressure-test your idea with a friendly firing squad
ACTION	Build quick-hit profiles that uncover motivations, pain points, and buying triggers	Use AI + smart search queries to uncover market size, growth trends, and tailwinds	Pitch your concept to three to five prospects who fit your buying persona(s)
RESULT	Cute names; killer clarity (think "Blow it Up Beth" or "Voice of Reason Victoria")	TAM tops $100 million *and* has staying power	Red light (back to the drawing board), yellow light (refine and rework), green light (move fast, but stay sharp)
GUT CHECK	Do I know where to find them and could I test with a focus group if needed?	Is it big enough, growing, and can I reach my slice of it?	Do I have proof of genuine interest and a clear product path to market it?

Your idea may be a million-dollar sleeper, but if no one's willing to buy it, it's worthless.

Month 1 in this track is all about identifying two clear, compelling buyer personas. Go beyond age and income and dig into the real stuff. What are your buyer's stress points, spending habits, and exact triggers that make them say, "Take my money!"?

Once you know your buyer, it's time to pull out the calculator and size up your market. Look at its current size, growth trajectory, and your potential differentiation within it. Estimate the market by calculating the top-down and bottom-up TAM based on the buyer personas you created. Your goal is to make sure the market is worth the hustle.

You'll round out this track by pitching your product or service idea to a friendly "firing squad" while it's still in beta. It's a small but mighty action. You will pitch your idea to three people who exemplify your buying persona. These may be people you call "friends," but you aren't looking for "yes" women or men. You are looking for brutally honest, high-quality feedback before wasting time, money, or momentum scaling something flawed. Think of it as your early-stage BS detector, served with a side of tough love.

Track 2: Launch to Profit

If you've got the idea and some early traction, this is the track for you. It's time to lock in structure, set smart pricing, and make your first big moves. But before you dive in, you must define what you will and won't sacrifice to turn your business into a profitable engine that truly changes your earning power. In this track, you'll loop back to three of the Power Moves from the book. Pay close attention because we'll point exactly where you need to focus.

	30-day	*90-day*	*180-day*
	SET FINANCIAL GUARDRAILS	NAIL PRODUCT FEATURES	ASSEMBLE THE A-TEAM ADVISORS
GOAL	Know your business inflows and outflows cold; no surprises, no guesswork	Pinpoint the optimal features that solve your customers' actual problems, not the ones you think they have	Surround yourself with trusted advisors who challenge your thinking, fill your blind spots, and keep you focused
ACTION	Define your Freedom Number and financial non-negotiables	Identify your buyer's biggest pain points; pressure-test your features to solve them	Build relationships with trusted contacts who bring expertise, strong networks, and/or sharp instincts to support your launch
RESULT	Playbook of personal/business financial guardrails	Prioritized MVP feature set that has the best chance of resonating with your customers' needs	Your go-to crew that provides insight, challenge, and clarity
GUT CHECK	How many months/years do I have to get my business off the ground?	Am I confident my buying persona(s) will pay for the product with these features?	Do I have at least three people I can call for advice before making my next big move?

This track starts with the math. You're defining two things:

- Your Freedom Number
- Your financial non-negotiables

Chapter 6 dives deep into this, including the mistakes we made so you don't have to.

Start with your Freedom Number. This isn't some fantasy "someday I'll be rich and famous" goal. It's your right-now, what-I-need-to-breathe number. The figure that lets you quit the job, fire the boss, ditch the commute, or walk away from anything that no longer lights you up. Here's how to find it:

- Take stock of all investable capital. Add up checking, savings, emergency funds, brokerage accounts, and even that dusty savings account you forgot about. If you have a partner, factor in what they can realistically contribute to the household if your earnings dip.
- Refresh your monthly personal budget. What's coming in? What's going out?
- Calculate business start-up costs. Think: tech, freelancers, marketing, and everything in between.

Then it's time to put everything together. Add your business start-up costs to your monthly budget requirements. This is the number you need to live. Compare those costs with your investable capital. Does your funding cover your Freedom Number? Ideally, yes. Even better if it gives you a cushion. If it does, you're ready to go. If not, something has to shift. Once you can cover this number, you are on the path to freedom.

Now, it's time to commit to your non-negotiables. This is a *you* exercise—no cheating, no faking it. Look yourself in the mirror and get real about what you're willing to do to build a profitable business.

Start by asking the tough financial questions:

- What expenses do I refuse to cut, even in tight months/years?
- What amount of debt am I willing to take on to fund the business?

Then set the boundaries you need in place to stay sane and solvent:

- Will you take on unprofitable clients or products?
- How long will you tolerate negative cash flow?
- What milestones does the business need to reach before your first hire?

These questions—and the hard lines you draw—define your "hard nos." Nail these down now, and you can be confident you are starting a business that won't break you, your budget, or your sanity.

With your financial guardrails in place, it's time to nail product-market fit. The objective: pinpoint the optimal feature set that solves your customer's real problems, not the ones you think they have. Start by identifying your buyer's biggest pain points, and then pressure-test the features designed to solve them. The result? A clear, prioritized MVP that has the best chance of resonating. Need a refresher on MVPs? Flip back to Chapter 7.

The big hairy goal in this track: assemble your A-team of advisors.

Surround yourself with trusted advisors who challenge your thinking, fill your blind spots, and keep you focused. We know what you're thinking: "Easier said than done!" That's where Beth's advice comes in—start with small concentric circles and build out.

Make a list of 10 people to reach out to:

- Five for immediate feedback
- Five to get to know and see if they're interested and the right fit

Then start planting the seeds. Connect with people who've scaled a business and can help you turn your idea into sustainable revenue while avoiding rookie mistakes. Coffee if local; 15-minute Zoom or phone call if not. Or start small—a DM or intro from a mutual friend works too. The key is simple: start, however you're comfortable. Need some ideas on building your Kitchen Cabinet? Head back to Chapter 5.

Track 3: Scrappy to Scalable

This is where we get serious about systems, delegation, and profit levers, because growth shouldn't mean you are careening toward burnout. A big part of this track is shifting your mindset from *doer* to *strategist*. If you want to scale, you can't think like an associate anymore; you need to think like a CEO. Chapter 9 (you did finish it, right? *wink*) is your home base for executing everything in the Scrappy to Scalable track.

	30-day	*90-day*	*180-day*
	FLEX YOUR FOUNDER FOCUS	BUTTON UP YOUR BACK END	SCALE A SINGLE OFFERING INTO A BOXED SET
GOAL	Drop the busy work that's choking your growth to make room to scale like a seven- (or eight-) figure boss	Stop being the entire OS of your business; start builiding the systems, people, and calendar boundaries to scale	Turn what's working into a business that runs, grows, and delivers financial freedom
ACTION	Reimagine your to-do list; identify what falls apart without you and what could thrive with training or a better process	Identify the chaos, delegate for max impact, find the tipping point, make the handoff stick	Outline what you are scaling, choose a scale strategy to match, and productize
RESULT	Prioritize the to-do list **Bucket A** High Stakes, High Impact; **Bucket B** Build It, Back Off; **Bucket C** Let. It. Go.	Visibility into the areas of the business for key hire(s), outsourcing opportunities, or systemization will support the business as you scale it	A road map to expanding a business, profitably, to support your financial freedom
GUT CHECK	Does my to-do list have less entries on it than a month ago?	Do I have a path to a seven-, eight-, or nine-figure business, with a pitchdeck for any additional funding needs?	Can I scale to the next level, growing both revenue and margins, by sticking to this road map?

The first 30 days are about flexing your founder focus. Start with one ruthless question: What breaks if I stop hovering? List the things you do every day that would fall apart if you disappeared for 48 hours. Then audit each item: Could I (1) hire and train someone, (2) outsource it, or (3) document an SOP to streamline and speed it up?

Next, zoom out to your weekly to-dos and sort them into three buckets based on this prioritization matrix.

BUCKET A: HIGH STAKES, HIGH IMPACT MOVES	These belong to only you. They include high-leverage decisions, like new product development, strategy pivots, vision work, and big client conversations.
BUCKET B: BUILD IT, THEN BACK OFF	You architect it; someone else runs it. This is invoicing, recruiting, proposal templates, social media strategy, etc.
BUCKET C: LET IT GO, FOR REAL	These are tasks someone else can, and should, own, i.e., payables/receivables, calendar blocking, social scheduling, and website updates.

Your aim for this month: protect A, systemize B, and delegate C. Each week, pick one task from Bucket C and hand it off. Fully. No shadow delegating. No, "just one more check." Let them do it their way, even if it's not as perfectly magical as yours. Then rinse and repeat until every last one is gone. You now should have a good handle on your personal to-do list and what you can (and should) take off it. Your 90-day goal in this track is making it happen by buttoning up your back end through hire(s), outsourcing, and smart systemization. Start with four core areas: sales and marketing, finance, people, and your time. For each, answer these:

- What's currently duct-taped together?
- What breaks when you're not around?
- What are you still doing that someone else could do as well, or better?

Once you have your lists, assign each item to one of three paths: hire it, outsource it, or systemize it. These sound similar, and they should. Building out the back end is all about where your attention should be focused to scale. Next, identify the hurdle or trigger point to make it happen: Do you need a job description, an RFP, or a solution sourcing request? Write it down. Then do it.

Here's the kicker: follow-up is everything. Build hiring and systemizing into your actual goals—weekly, monthly, and yearly. Not just the big flashy stuff like "grow 50 percent this year" but the practical wins like "hire a bookkeeper so Victoria stops doing invoices at three o'clock in the morning."

Finally, add two things:

- **A carrot (or a stick).** Reward progress and/or hold yourself accountable.
- **Public commitment.** Share it with your team, post it on your site, or announce it on social media for accountability.

The holy grail of scaling is turning what's working into a business that runs, grows, and delivers financial freedom. Your 180-day goal is about scaling your core offering, but remember, you can scale only what works. So start by answering three questions:

- What's your core offering?
- Why is it working?
- What are people asking for next?

Next, pick your scale strategy (yes, three options again!):

- **Productize:** Turn your one-to-one product or service into something scalable.

- **Add-on:** Layer on related products or services your current buyers need.
- **Tier up:** Create pricing tiers for different levels of support, urgency, or deliverables.

Whatever strategy you choose, the math has to work. Do a quick margin check: Can the cost of delivering your expanded offering support your long-term margin goals? If not, it doesn't stay. Back to the drawing board. When you can scale to the next level while growing revenue and margins, congratulations, you have your road map.

A Final Word

By 2050, more than half of the wealth in the United States will be in the hands of women.[1] That means more access to capital for women for the first time—well, ever. When that shift happens, the vest-wearing-bro era will (finally) start to fade. Maybe it won't disappear completely, but at least there'll be a miniskirt equivalent.

Whether or not you choose to raise capital or go it alone, this change still means something big: women will be doing more business with women, buying more from women, and sitting at the table leading more of the deals. And as a woman business owner, you're going to feel more confident, more supported, and more in control.

Take this journey one page at a time, one thought at a time. There's no race. Your pace is the right pace. What matters is that you keep going. This framework has worked for us and for countless women we've coached, and we know it can work for you too.

We can't wait to see what you build—and to cheer you on every step of the way.

Notes

Chapter 1

1. Block Advisors, "2024 State of Women's Small Business Report by Block Advisors Reveals Resilience Despite Persistent Support Barriers," *Block Advisors*, October 8, 2024. https://investors.hrblock.com/news-releases/news-release-details/2024-state-womens-small-business-report-block-advisors-reveals.
2. Amanda Elam, PhD, Babson College, GEM Global (Lead Author), "GEM 2024/2025 Women's Entrepreneurship Report: Navigating Challenges, Driving Change," *Global Enterpreneurship Monitor*, November 2025. https://gemconsortium.org/report/gem-20242025-womens-entre preneurship-report-navigating-challenges-driving-change-2.
3. Citi GPS: Global Perspectives & Solutions, "Women Entrepreneurs: Catalyzing Growth, Innovation, and Equality," *Citi*, March 2022. https://ir.citi.com/gps/4tvkohSoc%2Bv614IZGyo19dc5yiov31GLehre8 t4YkGPkZycemOaPeOM9l5RWRhQN5o5udyLrgyc%3D.
4. Kim Fedyk, "Every Day I Am Plagued with Mom Guilt," *Medium*, April 20, 2024. https://medium.com/bitchy/every-day-i-am-plagued-with-mom-guilt-390b099c8d69.
5. Coni Longden-Jefferson, "The Mom Guilt Matrix," *elvie*, November 28, 2024.https://global.elvie.com/en-us/guides/mental-health-self-care/the-mom-guilt-matrix.
6. Cathryn Streifel, "Why Better Care Policies Matter for Gender Equality and the Economy," *PRB*, March 7, 2024. https://www.prb.org/articles/why-better-care-policies-matter-for-gender-equality-and-the-economy/.
7. Gretchen Livingston, "For Most Highly Educated Women, Motherhood Doesn't Start Until the 30s," *Pew Research Center*, January 15, 2025. https://www.pewresearch.org/short-reads/2015/01/15/for-most-highly-educated-women-motherhood-doesnt-start-until-the-30s/.

8. Jamie Cattanach and Dan Shepard, "Average Age of Entrepreneurs in Largest US Metros Drops to 36 From 40," *lendingtree*, September 18, 2023. https://www.lendingtree.com/business/small/youngest-entrepreneurs-study/.

Chapter 2

1. Public Relay, "Exploring the Gender Gap in CEO Media Representation," *Public Relay*, February 27, 2024. https://publicrelay.com/blog/the-ceo-gender-gap/.
2. Emily Tomasik and Jeffrey Gottfried, "U.S. Journalists' Beats Vary Widely by Gender and Other Factors," *Pew Research Center*, April 4, 2023. https://www.pewresearch.org/short-reads/2023/04/04/us-journalists-beats-vary-widely-by-gender-and-other-factors/.
3. Pitchbook, "US VC Female Founders Dashboard," *Pitchbook*, December 5, 2025. https://pitchbook.com/news/articles/the-vc-female-founders-dashboard.
4. Wikipedia, "Time Person of the Year," Wikipedia. https://en.wikipedia.org/wiki/Time_Person_of_the_Year.
5. EY, "Stina Ehrensvärd from Sweden Named EY World Entrepreneur of the Year™ 2025," *EY*, June 6, 2025. https://www.prnewswire.com/news-releases/stina-ehrensvard-from-sweden-named-ey-world-entrepreneur-of-the-year-2025-302475042.html.
6. Inc., "Inc. 5000 2023: Meet the Fastest Growing Private Companies in America," *Inc.* https://www.inc.com/inc5000/2023.
7. Liz Long, "Four Ways to Maximize Family Time as an Entrepreneur," *Forbes. com*, February 6, 2018. https://www.forbes.com/sites/lizlong/2018/02/06/four-ways-to-maximize-family-time-as-an-entrepreneur/.
8. Pratiksha Rastogi, "From Deals to Diapers - Mompreneurs Can Handle It All," *SME10X*, May 12, 2024. https://www.sme10x.com/people/from-deals-to-diapers-mompreneurs-can-handle-it-all.
9. Trevor Clawson, "Founders and Motherhood: Advice on Balancing Leadership and Childcare," *Forbes.com*, July 13, 2025. https://www.forbes.com/sites/trevorclawson/2025/07/13/founders-and-motherhood-advice-on-balancing-leadership-and-childcare/.
10. Editorial Team, "The Rise of the Modern Entrepreneur: How Men Are Redefining Success in 2025," *Formidable Men US*, February 2025. https://formidablemenus.com/the-rise-of-the-modern-entrepreneur-how-men-are-redefining-success-in-2025/.
11. Arielle Pardes, "Who Do Young Entrepreneurs Look Up To? Elon Musk," *Wired*, January 13, 2022. https://www.wired.com/story/young-entrepreneurs-elon-musk/.

12. Hannah Sparks, "I'm a Billionaire Entrepreneur at 34—This Is My Easy Secret to Success," *New York Post*, November 24, 2024. https://nypost.com/2024/11/24/personal-finance/tech-billionaire-ankur-jains-secret-to-success-start-with-a-problem/.
13. Sini Maria Heikkila, "Our Report Reveals that Gender Stereotypes Undermine Women's Entrepreneurship," *Cherie Blair Foundation for Women*, January 26, 2022. https://cherieblairfoundation.org/news-list/gender-stereotypes-undermine-womens-entrepreneurship/.
14. National Women's Business Council, "Women and Entrepreneurship," *National Women's Business Council.* https://www.nwbc.gov/wp-content/uploads/2023/11/NWBC-A-Media-Resource-on-Women-and-Entrepreneurship.pdf.
15. Pitchbook, "US VC Female Founders Dashboard," *Pitchbook*, December 5, 2025. https://pitchbook.com/news/articles/the-vc-female-founders-dashboard.
16. Katie Goff, "SBA Loan Statistics: Race and Gender," *Bankrate*, November 22, 2023. https://www.bankrate.com/loans/small-business/sba-loan-race-and-gender-statistics/.
17. Noah Brandt, "Women in Business Statistics in 2025 (Latest U.S. Data)," *ecommerce tips*, March 11, 2025. https://ecommercetips.org/women-in-business/.
18. Founders Forum Group, "All Posts Resources Women in VC & Startup Funding: Statistics & Trends (2025 Report)," *Founders Forum Group*, May 23, 2025. https://ff.co/women-funding-statistics-2025/.
19. Lendio, "2024 Woman-Owned Business Statistics," www.lendio.com, March 22, 2024. https://www.lendio.com/blog/women-business-statistics.
20. Katie Goff, "SBA Loan Statistics: Race and Gender," *Bankrate*, November 22, 2023. https://www.bankrate.com/loans/small-business/sba-loan-race-and-gender-statistics/.
21. Chairman Ben Cardin, "Women's Small Business Ownership and Entrepreneurship Report," *U.S. Senate Committee on Small Business & Entrepreneurship*, July 2023. https://www.sbc.senate.gov/public/_cache/files/7/5/75d60b31-44fe-45ec-89ed-965dd86d91c7/096878CDBA99D58F614B497D27D1EAB4.women-entrepreneurship-report-final-sr.pdf.

Chapter 3

1. McKinsey Global Institute, "How Hybrid Work Has Changed the Way People Work, Live, and Shop," *McKinsey Global Institute*, July 13, 2023. https://www.mckinsey.com/mgi/our-research/empty-spaces-and-hybrid-places-chapter-1.

2. David McCann, "Companies' Employee Turnover Rate Eased to 18% in 2024," cfo.com, March 24, 2025. https://www.cfo.com/news/companies-employee-turnover-rate-eased-to-18-in-2024/743093/.
3. Institute for Women's Policy Research, "Gender and Racial Wage Gaps Worsened in 2023 and Pay Equity Still Decades Away," *Institute for Women's Policy Research*, September 2024. https://iwpr.org/wp-content/uploads/2024/09/IWPR-National-Wage-Gap-Fact-Sheet-2024.pdf.
4. Lean In., "Women Are Paid Less than Men—and the Gap Is Closing Too Slowly," *Lean In*. https://leanin.org/equal-pay-data-about-the-gender-pay-gap.
5. Institute for Women's Policy Research, "Gender and Racial Wage Gaps Worsened in 2023 and Pay Equity Still Decades Away."
6. "Women Are Paid Less than Men—and the Gap Is Closing Too Slowly," *Lean In*.
7. Spencer Stuart, "Fortune 500 C-Suite Snapshot 2024: Profiles in Functional Leadership," *SpencerStuart*, February 2025. https://www.spencerstuart.com/research-and-insight/fortune-500-c-suite-snapshot-2024-profiles-in-functional-leadership.
8. Lean, "Women in the Workplace," *Lean In; McKinsey & Company*, 2024 (Page 11). https://cdn-static.leanin.org/women-in-the-workplace/2024-pdf.
9. Lean, "Women in the Workplace," *Lean In; McKinsey & Company*, 2024 (Page 42). https://cdn-static.leanin.org/women-in-the-workplace/2024-pdf.

Chapter 4

1. Sandy Carter, "Who Runs the World? Women Control 85% of Purchases, 29% of STEM Roles," *Forbes.com*, March 7, 2024. https://www.forbes.com/sites/digital-assets/2024/03/07/who-runs-the-world-women-control-85-of-purchases-29-of-stem-roles/.

Chapter 5

1. Chief, "Chief's Study Finds 80% of Women Leaders Use Networking to Drive CareerSuccess," *Chief Survey*, July 19, 2023. https://www.businesswire.com/news/home/20230719423838/en/Chiefs-Study-finds-80-of-Women-Leaders-Use-Net-working-to-Drive-Career-Success.

2. Edward Asiedu, Monica Lambon-Quayefio, Francesca Truffa, and Ashley Wong, "Female Entrepreneurship and Professional Networks," *The World Bank*, February 23, 2023. https://thedocs.worldbank.org/en/doc/b29bda5a71a736d4cfb2e-dad7676389b-0050022023/original/women-entrepreneurs02272023.pdf.
3. Pitchbook, "US VC Female Founders Dashboard," *Pitchbook*, December 5, 2025.

Chapter 7

1. Marc Emmer, "95 Percent of New Products Fail. Here Are 6 Steps to Make Sure Yours Don't," *Inc.*, July 6, 2018. https://www.inc.com/marc-emmer/95-percent-of-new-products-fail-here-are-6-steps-to-make-sure-yours-dont.html.
2. Alessandro Buffoni, Alice de Angelis, Volker Grüntges, and Alex Krieg, "How to Make Sure Your Next Product or Service Launch Drives Growth," *McKinsey & Company*, October 13, 2017. https://www.mckinsey.com/capabilities/growth-marketing-and-sales/our-insights/how-to-make-sure-your-next-product-or-service-launch-drives-growth.
3. Maria D. Musumeci, Caitlin M. Cunningham, and Theresa L. White, "Disgustingly Perfect: An Examination of Disgust, Perfectionism, and Gender," *National Library of Medicine*, February 8, 2022. https://pmc.ncbi.nlm.nih.gov/articles/PMC9136022/.

Chapter 8

1. CB Insights, "The Top 12 Reasons Startups Fail," *CB Insights*, 2021. https://www.cbinsights.com/reports/CB-Insights_Top-Reasons-Startups-Fail.pdf.
2. PwC, "Thriving in an Age of Continuous Reinvention," *PwC's 27th Annual Global CEO Survey*, 2024. https://www.pwc.com/gx/en/ceo-survey/2024/download/27th-ceo-survey.pdf.
3. The Economist, Sponsored by PMI, "Why Good Strategies Fail Lessons for the C-Suite," *The Economist Intelligence Unit Limited*, March 2013. https://www.pmi.org/-/media/pmi/documents/public/pdf/learning/thought-leadership/why-good-strategies-fail-report.pdf.

4. Donald Sull, Rebecca Homkes and Charles Sull, "Why Strategy Execution Unravels—and What to Do About It," *Harvard Business Review*, March 2015. https://hbr.org/2015/03/why-strategy-execution-unravelsand-what-to-do-about-it.
5. Megan Bruneau, "The Failure Factor. Meet the Woman Who Revolutionized Dating—Twice," *Forbes*, July 12, 2016. https://www.forbes.com/sites/meganbruneau/2016/07/12/meet-the-woman-who-revolutionized-dating-twice/.
6. "The Honest Company Reports Fourth Quarter and Full Year 2023 Financial Results and Provides Full Year 2024 Financial Outlook," *The Honest Company*, March 6, 2024. https://www.globenewswire.com/news-release/2024/03/06/2841758/0/en/The-Honest-Company-Reports-Fourth-Quarter-and-Full-Year-2023-Financial-Results-and-Provides-Full-Year-2024-Financial-Outlook.html.

Chapter 10

1. Bank of America Institute, "Women and Wealth: Growing the Pie, Creating Opportunities," *Bank of America Institute*, March 5, 2025. https://institute.bankofamerica.com/content/dam/economic-insights/women-and-wealth-creating-opportunities.pdf.

Acknowledgments

To our moms—who taught us the job. We hope we are 1 percent as impactful as you both have been.

To our kids—who never once asked us to be smaller. You accepted our failings, averted your eyes at our mistakes, and gave us unwavering love. You're the reason we started. You're the reason we kept going. And you're living proof that kids don't need perfect mothers—they need mothers who love them to death.

To Victoria's husband, Bill—who has exemplified the true meaning of partnership in every form: cheerleader, confidant, IT extraordinaire, and the ever-reliable "Can you please go pick up [fill in the blank]?" This success stands on his unwavering support.

To the other men in our lives—our fathers and brothers and Beth's amazing boyfriend—thanks for always having our backs, always having a Band-Aid (literal or otherwise), and never letting us lose hope. You're the antidote to the patriarchy, and we are forever grateful to you.

To our besties—the ones who constantly showed up in the moments that mattered most. You know who you are. You talked us off ledges. You celebrated our wins and made us look past our losses. Every woman needs someone like you: a listening ear, nonstop wine nights, and an unwavering belief in us.

To our clients—who trusted two (youngish) women with super important issues and listened to our blunt advice even if a kid was crying in the background. You gave us the pattern recognition that became our superpower. You proved that small teams with the right strategy can compete with anyone. Thank you for taking a leap of faith on us.

To the mom entrepreneurs in our community—the women building businesses between school pickups, the ones questioning whether they can have both, the ones who've been told to wait for "someday." You inspired every chapter. Your questions shaped our frameworks. Your success proves our point. This book is for you, but it's also because of you. To each other—thank God for our amazing relationship. We are each other's Kitchen Cabinet, co-conspirators, and best friends. Our relationship made it all worth it.

And, to the patriarchy: suck it.

Beth Mazza and Victoria Sivrais

About the Authors

Beth Mazza is a two-time entrepreneur and mom of four flawless, adult "kids," who beg her weekly to stop sharing her "inside thoughts." She is also part of a crazy Italian family that makes *My Big Fat Greek Wedding* look like the *Gilded Age*. She's launched and sold two strategic advisory firms, held her own in the boardrooms of Fortune 1,000 giants you'd recognize instantly, and once lived through a client saga juicy enough to inspire two episodes of an HBO miniseries.

Victoria Sivrais is an entrepreneur, mom of five, and master of chaos. Her fearlessness was forged by a serial-entrepreneur dad, a lionhearted mom, and four steadfast brothers. She leapt early from corporate to consulting, setting her on the path to build and sell Clermont Partners, while earning acclaim for guiding S&P 500 leaders through messy, make-or-break decisions—often with a kid on the hip. Her rule is simple: stay teachable, stay hungry, and, above all, marry someone who always says, "You got this!"

Index

T

W